Psychosocial Wellbeing of Divorced Women

A Liberative Pastoral Care and Counselling Paradigm

Psychosocial Wellbeing of Divorced Women

A Liberative Pastoral Care and Counselling Paradigm

P. Zubeno Kithan

Christian World Imprints

First Published in 2021 by

Christian World Imprints
Christian Publishing & Books from India
C-3, Wazirpur Industrial Area
Delhi-110052
cwidelhi2017@gmail.com
www.ChristianWorldImprints.com
Phone: +91 11 41526079

ISBN: 978-93-5148-525-4 (HB)
ISBN: 978-93-5148-526-1 (PB)

Printed in India.

Contents

The book in its original form is the dissertation submitted to the Senate of Serampore College, towards the Doctor of Theology degree and is published with written permission. The candidate is responsible for the title, contents, and opinions expressed in it.

The Original Title of the dissertation is "Psychosocial Wellbeing of Divorced Women in Select Districts of Nagaland: Challenges for Pastoral Care and Counselling."

Foreword

I am delighted to write this foreword for the book *Psychosocial Wellbeing of Divorced Women: A Liberative Pastoral Care and Counselling Paradigm,* not only because I have known and taught Zubeno Kithan for more than 6 years but also the contextual relevance of the book for the ministry and mission of the church in India. The issue is quite relevant in today's context as divorce is becoming increasingly a reality for many people. *Psychosocial Wellbeing of Divorced Women* takes very seriously the multifaceted nature of divorce experience. This book explores the centrality of theology and pastoral care and counselling as a way of understanding and responding to the profound human tragic experience. Having found the plight of divorced women through empirical research in the Naga context, the author expanded the traditional approaches to pastoral care and counselling to the broader approach to deal with the issue face by divorced women. The author takes us on an expedition that will undoubtedly change how many of us especially pastoral counsellors understand and respond to many issues including the issue of divorce.

Readers of this book will not only find meticulous, fresh, and profound perspectives on divorce but will also learn the theological and pastoral responses needed to respond to the complexities divorced women go through and to help guide and nurture them back to wholeness and healing. Much has been written on the plight of divorced women within the pastoral care and counselling literature, but in terms of its theological emphasis, this book offers a new perspective. Readers with an interest in divorced women's wellbeing and women studies will not be disappointed by what they encounter in this book. Divorced women go through multidimensional experiences that hold on to the crucial realization that acknowledging the complex experience is vital for authentic understanding and intervention through the ministry of pastoral care and counselling.

Dr. Zubeno argues that divorce is a pervasive problem across communities in India, she provides pastors and pastoral caregivers with crucial help in understanding the psychosocial and spiritual needs of divorced women. One of the things that emerged from the book is the liberating approach in pastoral care and counselling where the author sought to challenge the narrow understanding of pastoral care and counselling and its practices. Divorce presents a unique set of challenges for pastoral care and counselling. Therefore, it has to be innovative in dealing with the many issues facing divorced women today. Since many of the issues divorced women face are societal rather than individual, the ministry of pastoral care and counselling need to address issues beyond the intrapersonal and interpersonal level and start addressing issues in the larger socio-cultural, economic, and political structures and systems where individuals are embedded. Failing to effectively deal with the interconnection between the individual and her/his wider world will not produce functional intervention and care. To have a meaningful and long-lasting impact, pastoral care and counselling need to address the wider web of human society without negating the personal aspects. The structural changes such as systemic oppression and discrimination both in domestic as well as societal front must be addressed through the ministry of pastoral care and counselling. This comes through very strong in this book which will go a long way in helping divorced women.

The author spells out the importance of a holistic approach to pastoral care and counselling for healing and wholeness to take place. Drawing from the communitarian value within the Naga community where every individual was given equal respect and dignity in the community characterized by sharing and mutual love and care, where justice and equality were the norms with a strong sense of communal responsibility and obligations where the widows, the sick and the persons with disabilities are taken care of by the community. Rediscovering the Naga traditional ethos based on the communitarian relationship can be a viable starting point for liberating divorced women from their struggles. The ministry of pastoral care and counselling need to exhibit this communitarian care for everyone.

In this book, the author weaves together the stories of divorced women and theological reflection to offer helpful tools for ministers, counsellors, academicians and anyone else called to care pastorally for those struggling with divorce. She reflects pastoral reflections on oppression. The final chapter focused on practical skill cares that address the challenges of divorced women especially based on the liberative model proposed by the author.

This book provides valuable information and covers the necessary components of pastoral care and counselling particularly in dealing with the psychosocial wellbeing of divorced women. It is my hope and expectation that this book will provide an effective learning experience and referenced resource not only for divorced women who experience multifaceted problems but also for the pastoral counsellors and Christian educators to understand the plight of divorced women and work towards their wellbeing, wholeness, and liberation.

Prof. Dr. Joseph George
Dean, Division of Doctoral Studies
United Theological College, Bangalore

Acknowledgements

Many people had been instrumental in helping me reach this feat. I would like to acknowledge my indebtedness to Professor Dr. Joseph George who made this work possible. His tireless mentorship, guidance and unwavering support and encouragement in the process of my research are praiseworthy. His wealth of knowledge and expertise is particularly commendable.

My thanks also go to the United Theological College, Bangalore, the former principal Rev. Dr. John Samuel Raj and the current principal Rev. Dr. Chilkuri Vasantha Rao and the dean(s) of doctoral division Dr. Nalini Arles, Rev. Dr. Santhosh Kumar and Dr. Joseph George and members of the faculty and staff for their kind support and encouragement. My profound gratitude also goes to Rev. Dr. Dexter Maben my tutor who had been a source of strength and encouragement all throughout my studies.

I extend my sincere gratitude also to Rev. Dr. P. G. George, the former dean and Rev. Dr. Limatula Longkumer, the present dean, Department of Research/SATHRI of the Senate of Serampore College/University for granting me scholarship for three years and for their support and encouragement.

My sincere thanks go to the women who so willingly participated in my research and gave their time generously in filling the questionnaire. They trusted and shared their sacred stories of their life journey with me in the hope that I might learn and others might be helped. Special thanks go to the church leaders in Nagaland who diligently gave their services in reaching the participants of the study. Without their active and timely help and service, my work would not have come to this stage.

I wish to also express my profound gratitude to my parents and members of my family for their constant motivation, support, and encouragement all throughout my studies. I am grateful for their unconditional love and support, optimism and patience. I am also grateful to my colleagues and friends for being with me along the way and for their comments and suggestions that greatly improved the manuscript.

Special thanks are due to Dr. Mariamma Philip, Assistant Professor, Department of Biostatistics, and her team in NIMHANS, Bangalore for checking the tool for its reliability and validity. Without their passionate participation and input, the research would not have been successfully conducted.

I place on record my sincere thanks to the Academy of Mission (Missionsakademie), Hamburg, Germany for giving me the opportunity to be part of the program as a short-term scholarship holder. I am especially indebted to Rev. Dr. Uta Andree, Prof. Dr. Werner Kahl and Rev. Dr. Sonke Lorberg-Fehring for providing excellent atmosphere for research and their invaluable inputs. My earnest thanks also go to Rev. Hanna Stahl who has been a source of encouragement in the process of my research and helped me in many ways than one. I hope this piece of work will contribute to psychosocial wellbeing of divorced women who are struggling for wholeness of life in the church and society.

I am also indebted to Rev. Dr. A. Israel David for helping me strengthen the manuscript. Words are inadequate to express my thanks to Rev. Jeremiah Swamidason for tirelessly helping me in many ways. I wish to thank all my unnamed friends, teachers and leaders who have assisted in sharpening my thoughts and ideas in completing this humble work.

Above all, I thank God for granting me good health and wellbeing to carry out this research.

P. Zubeno Kithan

List of Tables

List of Abbreviation

D.Th.	Doctor of Theology
NGO	Non-Governmental Organization
NIMHANS	National Institute of Mental Health and Neurosciences
NT	New Testament
OT	Old Testament
PCOD	Polycystic Ovarian Disease
Ph.D.	Doctor of Philosophy
PWI-(A)	Personal Wellbeing Index - Adult
REBT	Rational Emotive Behaviour Therapy
S D	Standard Deviation
SATHRI	South Asia Theological Research Institute
SPSS	Statistical Package for the Social Sciences
SWBI	Subjective Well-Being Inventory
WHO	World Health Organization
QOL	Quality of Life

Introduction

Divorce is a devastating life event that requires a significant redefinition of life. It involves the disruption of one of the most affectional bonds between spouses that has far-reaching implications not only for the divorcing couples but also for the children, the extended family, and the community as a whole. Divorce presents psychosocial ramifications particularly for women as they experience significantly reduced standard of living, emotional pain and in many cases the loss of important parental relationship that affects their wellbeing. Despite advances in quality of life, the condition of divorced women remains to be deplorable in the society.

Substantial evidence has accumulated over the past decades indicating the adverse effects on wellbeing following divorce especially for women. When a marriage fails, relational crisis occurs and has real consequences that invariably assault a person's sense of wholeness and wellbeing and impair his/her functioning. Divorce has been rated as number one stressor by many writers and researchers. The situation is even worst in a patriarchal setting with the social, cultural, and economic milieu, which at times ignores the basic human rights of this vulnerable section. This coupled with higher remarriages rate with men; the number of divorced women continues to exceed that of men. Moreover, with women becoming more educated, economically independent, and aware of their rights, divorce rates are on the rise along with psychosocial ramifications. Such stressors are harbingers of psychiatric illness such as depression, anxiety, and substance abuse. However, the problems face by divorced women is often ignored. With more and more women experiencing divorce which require them not only to take decision that affect their immediate future but also impact their overall wellbeing in the long run, it is imperative to find ways to address the problems face by divorced women.

Comprehensive Understanding of Divorce

Divorce is a complex phenomenon that must be viewed in its multidimensional context as these factors are intertwined. Divorce is not caused by one single factor but it involves multiple levels and is a complex phenomenon. While divorce is always a unique, personal, and subjective experience, there are common denominators within the process of most divorce. It is linked to a wide spectrum of psychosocial distress such as anxiety, depression, low self-esteem, shame, guilt, hurt, anger, fear, frustration, embarrassment, and social isolation etc. Divorce also has been linked to economic distress particularly for women. All these factors are interwoven that leads to increased tension and diminished sense of wellbeing for divorced women.

Howard Clinebell opines, "Marital conflict is fundamentally the conflict of two need systems—the needs of one person collide head on with the needs of the other."[1] With divorce, women experience a loss of dreams and if children are involved, there can be a great sense of guilt for letting the children go or may also fear of becoming a single parent or of raising children single handedly.[2] Thus, divorce is a painful experience.

Divorce is a "legal dissolution of a socially recognized marital relationship that alters the obligations and privileges of the two persons involved. It is also a major life transition that has far-reaching social, pathological, legal, economic, and personal consequences."[3] In many cases, divorce is the end of family and brings about personal, familial and social disorganization. According to S. Pothen, "Divorce is a failure of marital life and has serious repercussion on the individual, family as well as the community."[4] The transition from being married to being divorced is a stressful one. It may leave deep psychic scars which lead to depression, anxiety, low self-esteem, anger, guilt or self-doubt. The emotional suffering and pain involved in divorce may be intense and severe. If not resolved, these feelings may produce infected grief wounds that heal slowly or not at all.[5] Similarly, Joseph George contends that "Every divorce situation cause relational friction, emotional strain and personal pain."[6] Divorce is not just a single event but involves a complex process that requires extensive reorganization and adjustments. Paul Bohannon underscores six overlapping divorce stages known as "six stations." The first stage is emotional divorce involving decrease in emotional investment in the marriage when it becomes clear that the marriage has reached an impasse. The couple experience withdrawal and decrease conflict as one of the spouses focuses on exiting the marriage rather than solving problem together. The second

1 Howard J. Clinebell, *Basic Types of Pastoral Counseling* (Nashville: Abingdon Press, 1984), 98.

2 Michele R. Davidson, *A Nurse Guide to Women's Mental Health* (New York: Springer Publishing Company, 2012), 255.

3 Bharti Sharma, "Mental and Emotional Impact of Divorce on Women," in Journal of the Indian Academy of Applied Psychology 37/1 (January 2011): 125.

4 S. Pothen, Divorce: *Its Causes and Consequences in Hindu Society* (New Delhi: Shakti Books, 1986), 182.

5 P. L. Koteskey, "Divorce," in *Baker Encyclopedia of Psychology,* edited by David G. Benner (Michigan: Baker Book House, 1985), 320.

6 Joseph George, "Marriage & Family Counselling," in *A Study Book on Counselling*, edited by George Varghese (Tiruvilla: Christian Sahithy Samithy, 2012), 91.

stage is legal divorce that involves the process of dissolving the legal connection as married couple. The third stage is economic divorce where the couple split the existing property and relocate and re-establish separate household. The fourth stage is the co-parental divorce where the parents draw a detail plan for child custody, pattern of childcare and negotiate living arrangements. The fifth stage is the community divorce that involves change in friends and communities resulting in experiencing loneliness, which he called "community divorce." The sixth station is psychic divorce, which involves redefinition of oneself and regaining psychological autonomy through emotional separation from the ex-spouse.[7] Even if women opt for divorce because they need to be freed from destructive relationships, pain and grief are usually mingled with their sense of relief, release, and liberation.[8]

Sociologists see divorce as a major social problem and that divorced women are more likely to experience alienation, stigma and discrimination because of patriarchy; once a woman is divorced, she loses privileges in the society and because of the social attitudes/stigma toward divorce, it makes post-divorce adjustment complicated especially for women. C. Wright in his book, *The Sociological Imagination* says, "When people divorce, the consequences for the individual concerned can be traumatic."[9] The divorced couples may face emotional distress and may ultimately change their attitudes towards marriage and the family. Bohannon opines that divorce also affects the social relationships and social status of the couple outside the family. The stresses of the divorce experience may place higher demands on their social network. Friends may withdraw because they feel awkward taking sides, disapprove of the change, or feel threatened by their newly single friend.[10] Divorce, thereby results not only in the loss of a spouse but also status and privileges. It involves letting go of the emotional security and safety provided by the spouse and the social network associated with marriage. This loss makes many people "anxious and fearful and gives them a very real sense of having lost the essential segment of their identity."[11]

The loss of a spouse through divorce may affect the self-image in ways similar to bereavement. Clinical investigators of marital disruption have acknowledged

---

7 Paul Bohannon, *Divorce and After: An Analysis of the Emotional and Social Problems of Divorce* (New York: Anchor, 1970), 3-6.

8 Howard J. Clinebell, *Basic Types of Pastoral Care & Counseling: Resources for the Ministry of Healing and Growth*, revised by Bridget Clare McKeever, 3rd edition (Nashville: Abingdon Press, 2011), 331.

9 C. Wright, *The Sociological Imagination*, revised edition (New York: Oxford University Press, 1999), 74.

10 Cited by Alison Clark-Steward and Cornelia Berntano, *Divorce Causes and Consequences* (London: Yale University Press, 2006), 22.

11 Joseph Guttmann, *Divorce in Psychosocial Perspective: Theory and Research* (New Jersey: Lawrence Erlbaum Associates, Inc. Publishers, 2009), 98.

the potentially devastating impact of divorce on self-esteem.[12] William Goode has pointed out the similarities of divorce and bereavement in the process of adjustment. In both, a set of role relations has been disrupted and adjustments are required throughout the family network. Economic problems are likely to be pressing; the problem of finding emotional solace, friendship, and love also becomes difficult. In both divorce and bereavement, the spouse remaining with the children feels that it is much harder than before the breakup.[13] In contrast to these many emotional similarities, perhaps all societies are better adjusted to dealing with death than with divorce. The reason being, rituals, ceremonies, surround bereavement and obligations because it is viewed as an unwanted tragedy whereas divorce is viewed as a state that one or both parties intended. Moreover, the death of a spouse creates an obligation for families and friends to help the bereaved but in the case of divorce, even when one spouse is unhappy about the divorce only a very close friends or members of the family may feel obligated to offer emotional comfort.[14]

India being a patriarchal society, it is very likely that divorced women would experience more social exclusion and loneliness and suffer from feelings of rootlessness and lack of identity because her identity was formerly associated with that of her husband's.[15] Although empirical evidence on the consequences of divorce in Indian context is limited, studies of divorce effects based on data from western countries are suggestive. There has not been a major research on divorce in Indian context and the lack of appropriate data means that marital dissolution has not received appropriate attention.

In the past, most of the marriages lasted a lifetime in India but in recent times, there has been a massive increase in divorce rate.[16] The statistics from the family court in India records affirm that there is a steady increase in the rate of divorce cases. Hindustan Times reports that the divorce rate in India is increasing among young married couples:

> This is an unusual trend in a country where the divorce rate was just 1 in 1,000 ten years ago, and is still a relatively low 13 per 1,000- as compared to the US average of 500 per 1,000. While India has no central or state wise registry of divorce data, family court officials say that the number of divorce applicants have doubled and even tripled

---

12 David A. Chiriboga and Linda S. Catron, *Divorce: Crisis, Challenge or Relief* (New York: New York University Press, 1991), 165.

13 William J. Goode, *The Family* (New Delhi: Prentice-Hall of India Private Limited, 1982), 162.

14 Goode, *The Family*..., 163.

15 Elizabeth B. Hurlock, *Developmental Psychology: A Life-Span Approach* (New Delhi: Tata McGraw-Hill Publishing Company Limited, 1981), 326.

16 Dinesh Angolkar, "Family in the Post-Modern Era," in *Marriage Tradition, Changes, Challenges Ahead*, edited by Bendangmenla Longkumer (Delhi: ISPCK, 2018), 42.

in cities such as Mumbai, Delhi, Bengaluru, Kolkata and Lucknow over the past five years.[17]

Naga Scenario

Divorce is an emerging issue in Nagaland. It had been observed that divorce rate in Nagaland has been steadily increasing over the past few decades and is seen as one of the main social issues. BBC reports that divorce rate is comparatively higher in the Northeast India.[18] According to *The Shillong Times*, March 10, 2015, 2011 census, divorce cases among Northeast women are on the rise. Meghalaya, Mizoram, and Nagaland are three states, which have the dubious distinction of having more divorced or separated women in proportion to men. There are three times as many women who are currently single after having been in wedlock. According to the census, Mizoram has the highest number of divorced and separated women with 6.9 percent as compared to 4.8 percent men; Meghalaya has 5.1 percent as compared to 2.3 percent men and Nagaland 2.3 percent as compared to 0.9 percent men.[19] The reason is not because women are in majority but it is much easier for men to remarry in a patriarchal structure of the society.

In the absence of government statistics and church records on divorce in Nagaland, an enquiry from different churches show that divorce is a prevalent and disturbing phenomenon and this finding was validated in the research. Some of the divorce cases may go unreported since some couples also part ways informally without obtaining legal separation.

Status of Women in Naga Society

Naga society is often applauded for its progressive outlook towards women. Many people allege that Naga women enjoy higher social status compared to the other parts of the country. However, research shows that this assumption is often deceptive and hence contradicted by many. Limatula Longkumer asserts, "The theory of the high status and role of women in the Naga society is absolutely wrong."[20] In contrast to the popular image of the status of Naga women, equality at best is seen only in theory but in actual fact, it has not been experienced

---

17 http://www.hindustantimes.com/sexandrelationships/why-number-of-young-indian-couples-getting-divorced-has-risen-sharply/article1-1303204.aspx (Accessed on 04/01/2020).

18 Soutik Biwas, "What divorce and separation tells us about modern India." BBC https://www.bbc.com/news/world-asia-india-37481054 (Accessed on 04/01/2020).

19 The census recorded only those who were divorced and not separated and there will be many unofficial/unrecorded cases. The Shillong Times (Tuesday, 10 March 2015), Accessed on 24 July 2015.

20 N. Limatula Longkumer, "Christianity and Naga Women," in *Transforming Theology from Empowering Women: A Theological and Hermeneutical Reflection in the Context of North East India*, edited by R. L. Hnuni (Jorhat: Women's Studies Eastern Theological College, 1999), 55.

by women in terms of equal rights, access, treatment and opportunity mainly because of the oppressive customary laws and cultural practices. Naga society is a patriarchal and patrilineal one. The relatively subordinate position of women thrives because of the customs, norms and traditions of the society. Nagas are governed by customary law,[21] which is intrinsically related to their identity and culture.[22] The customary law which is believed to help maintain law and order in the society and with one another is bias. Instead of safeguarding the interest of all members, women in Naga society suffer immensely in varied ways. The societal and familial norms and values are patriarchal in nature.

There is a clear-cut gender disparity between males and females. At the very young age, Naga boys and girls are being socialized differently. While boys are socialized to be masculine, strong, aggressive, dominant, protective, and outgoing, girls are taught to be submissive, fragile, emotional etc. In a patriarchal society, women are always seen as inferior and are socialized into being silent about their experience. In other words, women are being silenced from asserting their rights.

Even if women are educated, that does not automatically push them into taking up employment because men are perceived as the breadwinners and women to domestic chores. In many cases, even if women are better educated and highly qualified, they are denied employment opportunities. There is a hidden discrimination against women in employment because of the perception that men are breadwinners[23] and women as household and childcare providers.

Denial of equality to women is pronounced in political arena. One classic example of the status of Naga women is well reflected in the agitation against the TR Zeliang government who announced the election of urban municipal bodies with the 33 percent reservation for women. Many tribal bodies condemned the government that resulted in violent protest leading to social unrest and strikes where two young men were killed. Hokiye Sema, the president of the Central Naga Tribal Council, commented, "In Naga society, a woman is not equal to a man. We give women all respect but they cannot make decisions. Even in our village councils, women speak only if they are invited to give their opinion to the men. Giving women equality will destabilize our society and our ancient customs."[24] Naga tribal tradition is one of male control and dominance over community and

21 Rajesh Kumar, *A Universal's Guide to Constitution of India* (New Delhi: Universal law Publishing Co., 2011), 174.

22 Walter Fernandes and Gita Bharali, "Customary Law-Formal Law Interface: Impact on Tribal Culture," in *Christianity and Change in North East India*, edited by T. B. Subba et.al (New Delhi: Concept Publishing Company, 2009), 95.

23 Fernandes, Melville Pereira and Vizalenu Khatso, *Tribal Customary Laws in Northeast India: Gender and Class Implications* (Guwahati: North Eastern Social Research Centre, 2008), 23.

24 Amrit Dhillon, "In India's Nagaland, Men are on Strike Until Women Return to the Kitchen," in Stuff http://www.stuff.co.nz/world/asia/89574768/In-Indias-Nagaland-men-are-on-strike-until-women-return-to-the kitchen (Accessed on 29 November 2017).

society. As a consequence, those who exercise their dominance are not willing to reform in favour of gender equity. This is a typical example of the firm grip, which the customary law has, in the Naga political life. The authenticity of the much-applauded higher status of women in Naga society surfaced the harsh reality when many vehemently agitated in the name of protecting the culture and tradition of the Nagas. Men consider politics as their prerogative and deny women active participation because they see it as a threat to their power. Although, there is an increased recognition and a global commitment to redress gender imbalance in politics, Naga society is still lagging far behind. The continued discrimination and exclusion of Naga women from decision-making is nothing short of denial of basic human rights.

Another important domain that gives a vivid picture of the subordinate status of Naga women is their access to resources reflected in the inheritance laws. Women cannot inherit immovable property thereby affecting women's control over their livelihood. Inheritance and ownership are not merely issues of power and legitimacy, but are primarily rules allocating resources and life chances.[25] Customary laws deny equal rights to women particularly the rights to property and inheritance, which is one of the significant factors affecting women in their economic and social standing. Rosemary Dzuvichu who is a divorcee herself and the advisor of the Naga Mother's Association[26] posits that "Nagaland's special status has allowed unfettered discrimination in the name of "culture." Naga women have no power: Village councils are dominated by men. Naga women have no resources; Naga women cannot own land. "With no access to resources, how can women function as full citizens?"[27] She further asserts that,

> Women in Nagaland do not enjoy equal social and political status with men. They do not enjoy land, property or inheritance rights as per the customary laws. In sharp contrast with the Hindu Succession Act and the Muslim Personal Law, the Naga customary laws do not recognize inheritance or property rights even if you are the only child or daughter. So, when a man, who does not have a son, dies, the property and land will be inherited by a male relative who may be five or six cousins away in family line.[28]

25 M. Mann, "War and Social Theory: Into Battle with Classes, Nations and States," in *The Sociology of War and Peace*, edited by M. Shaw and C. Creighton (London: MacMillan, 1987), 307.

26 Leading Women's Rights Group in Nagaland.

27 Dhillon, "In India's Nagaland, Men are on Strike Until Women Return to the Kitchen..., (Accessed on 29 November 2017).

28 Quoted in Prasanta Mazumdar, "Standing Her Ground in Patriarchal Naga Society," in DNA. http://www.dnaindia.com/india/report-standing-her-ground-in-patriarchal-naga-society-1808598 (Accessed on 6 December 2017).

For the Nagas, "land is an important asset because the Naga economy largely depends on land-based resources for survival and all tribal identities are established on the land or territory people occupy. Land even had spiritual significance as connoted in the forms of dreams and visions where some places are regarded as sacred land."[29] Land being intrinsic to the identity of the Nagas, women who are not entitled to land inheritance suffer identity crisis as Toshimenla Jamir rightly observed, "Land remained intrinsic not only to their survival but was crucial for their very identity as well."[30] Land is understood as an identity and since women are not entitled to inherit land, they do not have identity.

In religious domain, women have lesser control. Women remain inferior with regard to church administration and leadership roles. Men head almost all the churches. Theologically trained women are denied of pastoral ministry and decision-making bodies. Thus, the religious domain is no different from other social and political domains.

Women in Naga society do not share equal rights and privileges in all spheres of life. Regardless of their contributions, they still remain inferior to men. Education has brought some changes in the lives of women, yet they are not given direct access and voice to participate in the church and society including the political domain. To this day, traditional customs and values thrive and women are relegated to subordinate status. The fact that women are denied of land inheritance is a denial of ownership of productive resources, women are also discriminated in socio-political, legal, and religious institutions. With no access to property and land, Naga women in general and divorced women in particular suffer, as they have to fend for themselves after the dissolution of marriage with no land to cultivate and survive. The lack of space to participate in decision-making bodies leads to neglect of various issues women face in the policymaking. There is no political empowerment of women as there is no representation of women in the top decision-making bodies. The plight of divorced women is related in their inequitable socio-economic status within the family as well as in the society. This resultant subordination and sense of powerlessness often thwarts their ability to voice out their rights or to seek help. What makes the situation of divorced women even more difficult is because of the fact that there is a gendered face of assumed reason for marital dissolution. Most often women are blamed for the cause of failed marriage because they are regarded as the custodian of the family.

For the Nagas, being married is an important social status and it is a sign of adulthood and respect. Therefore, most families put pressure on their children never to consider divorce. Divorced women may inevitably experience pain, shame, and embarrassment. Besides, most of the marriages take place after

29 North East Network Nagaland, Enquiry into the Status of Women in Nagaland (Guwahati: Labanya Press, 2016), 109.

30 Toshimenla Jamir, "Gender Land relations in Nagaland: Dilemma of Balancing Tradition and Modernity," in *International Journal of Gender and Women Studies* 2/1 (March, 2014): 122.

courtship, therefore, when divorce happens the persons involved are blamed and, in most cases, women are being blamed. Hence, women often receive little or no support from family; friends or the community, this lack of support may become an additional stressor in and of itself. In some cases, family may dissociate from a divorced daughter because she has tarnished the family honour and brought shame and disgrace upon the family. Other members of the extended family and the community may also ostracize divorced women. Often such disapproval turns into verbal and physical abuse as well as other kinds of violence such as harassment, disparagement, social ostracism, emotional withdrawal, and financial deprivation.[31] They may also suffer social exclusion. Consequently, it becomes difficult to start a new life after divorce by finding another husband or by living alone. Most divorced women end up living with their parents or married brothers or sisters and live a restricted life. Even if a woman finds shelter and support following divorce, her family feels the burden. The status of divorced women in Naga society is often considered as lower than that of married or unmarried women and they are socially devalued, stigmatized, marginalized and are more vulnerable to all social evils. Women are denied the rights and opportunities that are available to men, thereby making them victims of discrimination and injustice.[32]

Social and family stigma attached to divorce leads women to experience extreme stress. Moreover, women who are not employed face economic hardship and in turn lower their wellbeing. Yet many people consider divorce as a social embarrassment only and rarely pay attention to the negative impacts involving divorce. People do not realize the deep negative impact of divorce and shy away from it. Although there are few theologians and writers even among the Nagas, and others from the North East who have highlighted the existing discrimination of women, there is a lack of in-depth study on the problems pertaining to divorced women from a pastoral care and counselling perspective especially focusing on their psychosocial wellbeing. Moreover, the church's concern towards this issue is extremely limited in the Naga context.[33] Married couples do not have access to marriage counselling and many churches do not cater to this subject. Despite the increasing divorce rate in Nagaland little is known about the experience patterns divorced women go through in terms of social and psychological adjustment and its impact on their wellbeing.

---

31 Kamei Pamei Roselima, "Customary Law and Women in North East India," in *International Research Journal of Social Sciences* 3 (September, 2014): 59. Also refer Banerjee, Exploring integration of Gender Dimension into NEPED..., 3.

32 Sangita Dhal, "Mapping Women's Economic Empowerment: Imperative for Inclusive Growth and Gender Justice," in *Women's Link*, edited by Rakesh K. Singh 20/4 (October-December, 2003), 23.

33 Many of the churches do not have official record of divorce. Several pastors expressed the need for the churches to maintain record on divorce.

The role of the church in dealing with divorce is solely based on moralistic grounds negating the personal choices. The lack of agencies available to divorced women points to the need to explore strategies that enable existing institutional structures to be strengthened in order to combat the vulnerabilities of divorced women in Naga context. The theological understanding not to put asunder what God has joined together compounds the plight of divorced women in Naga context. The Church despises divorce and alienates divorced women since marriage is regarded as sacred and should not be broken based on the biblical injunction "Therefore, what God has joined together, let no one separate" and the Christian notion of "till death do us apart." Divorcees are made to feel guilty for breaking the marital covenant sanctified by God. Randall Nicholas opines, "For many women, marriage is not just a vow with spouse, but also a covenant with God. When these marriages dissolve, feelings of spiritual failure, guilt, and a broken relationship with God sometimes arise. Divorced women therefore, feel cut off and not worthy to participate in worship services."[34] In some Christian circles, divorcees are being excommunicated from the church and are also excluded from various forms of ministries. Divorcees yearn for comfort, inclusion and security, but the church as the body of Christ where people should experience love, care and acceptance often turns its face away.

This invisible group of people needs to be integrated into the society and the church and their problems and concerns need to be addressed by the church instead of being stigmatized and dissocialized. Divorced women needs and concerns should be addressed theologically and validate their experience in order to be more holistic in the approach of Christian ministry. Instead of focusing on how these women accept what social convention or the society dictates, the greater question is how Christian ministry especially in its care and counselling can address the issues faced by divorced women and work on changing the society and to be more inclusive. The church should increasingly give importance to social engagement and should consider such action as working towards healing and wholeness of all people including divorced women. Taking a cue from feminist therapy the church should strive towards social and political change. Christian ministry engaged in care and counselling needs to make strides in the direction of holistic ministry integrating social change in its theory and practice. Although many of the issues that emerge apply to women in general, there are still needs that remain unique to divorced women. With care and counselling intervention, divorced women who are experiencing internalized oppression may learn to embrace their own selves and develop their full potentials and live with dignity and authenticity. They may also be helped to work towards their own liberation.

34 J. Randall Nicholas, *Ending Marriage, Keeping Faith: A New Guide through the Spiritual Journey of Divorce* (Oregon: Wipf and Stock Publishers, 2002), 91.

The fact that divorce is becoming increasingly common in Nagaland necessitated the study of wellbeing of divorced women a worthwhile academic pursuit. Divorce as a stressful life event that brings about unprecedented changes has been written extensively. However, it could be argued that there has been comparatively little research on the application of these findings to the Naga context. Recognizing and responding to this research deficit is important for a number of reasons. First, with the rise in divorce cases comes a need for culturally specific research on the psychosocial impacts of marital dissolution. This is especially important given the diverse and unique cultural demography of Nagaland. Second, studies from a number of countries indicate that the direct application of research findings on post-divorce adjustment conducted in other parts of the country or world might be limited and as such requires additional local evidence to better inform initiatives such as counselling, support groups, and therapeutic intervention.

Psychosocial research literature is rich in theoretical discussions, but there is no agreed definition regarding how the term is defined and used reflecting varied research traditions and areas from which researchers have come to take an interest in the field. While some define psychosocial to include the interlinkages between psychological and social experience emphasizing the value of interaction and social and emotional consonance and the individual experience,[35] in this research psychosocial is defined as encompassing physical, mental, emotional/psychological, social, economic, and spiritual/religious domains.

The study was undertaken with an assumption that divorce leads to decline of physical, mental, emotional/psychological, social, economic, and religious/spiritual wellbeing of women. The hypothesis is studied under six sub-hypotheses.

Sub-hypothesis 1: It appears that divorced women experience decline in physical wellbeing compared with married women. *Sub-hypothesis 2*: It appears that divorced women experience decline in mental wellbeing compared with married women. *Sub-hypothesis 3*: It appears that divorced women experience decline in emotional/psychological wellbeing compared with married women. *Sub-hypothesis 4*: It appears that divorced women experience decline in social wellbeing compared with married women. *Sub hypothesis 5*: It appears that divorced women experience decline in economic wellbeing compared with married women. *Sub-hypothesis 6*: It appears that divorced women experience decline in spiritual/religious wellbeing compared with married women.

35 Zana Vathi, "The Interface between Return Migration and Psychosocial Wellbeing," in *Return Migration and Psychosocial Wellbeing: Discourses, Policy-Making and Outcomes for Migrants and Their Families*, edited by ZanaVathi and Russel King (London: Routledge, 2017), 5.

Chapter 1

Divorce and Its Remifications on Psychosocial Wellbeing

Introduction

The concept of divorce is one that has become increasingly pertinent to contemporary society. Families have undergone massive changes, transforming the structures and functions of marriage and family over the years. Even the term family is becoming increasingly ambiguous. Hence, taking the changes into consideration in the understanding of marriage and family is imperative to understand divorce. The current trends in marriage and divorce are the result of decades of social change. Numerous historical and social factors have contributed to the way marriage and divorce is viewed today. Divorce as a significant life-changing event presents psychosocial ramifications particularly for women.

Quality of life (QOL) and wellbeing are a global issue that has attracted the attention of many researchers and practitioners from different disciplines including social work, psychology, sociology, medicine, and health sciences. Substantial evidence has accumulated over the past several decades indicating the adverse effects on wellbeing following divorce especially for women. When a marriage fails, relational crisis occurs and has very real consequences. These consequences almost invariably assault the person's sense of wholeness and impair his/her functioning. Divorce has been rated as number one stressor by many researchers and writers. E. W. Burgess and H. J. Locke, pioneers in the study of Family and Sociology, opine that, "the most practical index of family disintegration for research purpose is divorce."[36]

According to J. Derrett, divorce cases reflect a sick society, not a healthy one.[37] This chapter deals with the theoretical appraisal of divorce and psychosocial wellbeing. The chapter is divided into three sections. The first section presents different theories of divorce, the second section consists of the causes of divorce and the third one deals with the psychosocial wellbeing.

Theories on Divorce

Researchers have used several theories to understand divorce and its impact on the individuals and members of the family and the society at large. A brief overview of some of the most commonly used theoretical perspectives is presented in this section.

Social Learning Theory

Social learning theory was founded by psychologist Albert Bandura who posits that learning is influenced by both psychological and behavioural factors. He believes that humans learn attitudes and behaviours by observing or modelling the behaviours, attitudes, and emotional reactions of others.[38] One of the main concepts of this theory is modelling and a child's main model is his/her parents. Children observe their parents and then subsequently model both their behaviour and attitudes. Parents are the initial and primary reinforcers of child behaviour because they generally have the primary responsibility for raising children and hence the opportunity to influence them. Parents have fundamental influence because of the powerful affective bonds they share with their children, which may make children particularly receptive to parental influence. Internalization of parental values and expectations occur through interactions with caregivers during early childhood.[39]

Children's observations of parents' marital behaviour may mediate the transmission of marital quality from parents to children as they learn a variety of interpersonal behaviours through observation. Consistent with these assumptions, studies show that parents and children tend to use similar conflict-resolution strategies, express similar effective styles in conflict situations, and exhibit similar levels of interpersonal anger.[40] With regard to parental divorce, "the observational

36 E. W. Burgess and H. J. Locke, *The Family* (New York: American Book Co., 1950), 627.

37 J. Derrett and M. Duncun, *The Death of Marriage Law* (New Delhi: Vikas Publishing House, 1971), 187.

38 Albert Bandura, *Social Leaning Theory* (New York: General Learning Press, 1971), 5.

39 Michale E. Lamb and Richard M. Lerner, *Handbook of Child Psychology and Developmental Science*, vol. 3 (New Jersey: John Wiley & Sons, Inc., 2015), 728.

40 Paul R. Amato and Alan Booth, "The Legacy of Parents' Marital Discord: Consequences for Children's Marital Quality," in *Journal of Personality and Social Psychology* 18/4 (2001): 628-629.

learning theory perspective assumes that children observe parents' interpersonal behaviour, process and store information, and later replicate the same behaviour in their own marriage."[41] Paul Amato posits that an increasing number of children from divorced family of origin experienced divorce in their own romantic relationships. He concludes that divorce had become a learned behaviour modelled from parents to their offspring.[42] Children of divorced parents also develop poor models of conflict resolutions. "As children observe extensive conflict between parents, they may develop conflict-prone and dysfunctional relationship behaviours through modelling."[43] Elizabeth Mullett and Arnold L. Stolberg found that children who experience parental divorce are twice more likely to experience divorce than compared to children from intact marriages.[44] Social learning theory can be used as a lens to understand how parental divorce effect children. Many works on intergenerational transmission of divorce have been based on social learning theory. Numerous researchers have used social learning theory to study the effects of divorce on children.

Nevertheless, social learning theory has its own weaknesses. One of the weaknesses is that it takes little account of the inherited behaviours. In fact, critics contend that non-social resources are stronger than social reinforcers. Many see the theory as a reflection of incorporating contemporary behaviour into sociological approaches to deviance and criminality as well as being influential in the development of such criminological theories as social control and deterrence theories.[45] Another critique is that social learning theory fails to take the gender differences into consideration. For instance, there are several gender differences that appear to be universal such as preferences for particular characteristics between male and female and differences in the thought pattern. Besides, male and female are socialized differently; while females are conditioned to engage in caring/close interpersonal relationship, the male role has an inherent rough/aggressive nature that must be enacted in order to retain machismo.[46] Another major criticism is its emphasis on cognitive side of human nature at the expense of the emotional

---

41 Amato and Allan Booth, "The Legacy of Parents Marital Discord.., 630.

42 Paul R. Amato, "Life-Span Adjustment of children to their Parent's Divorce," in Children and Divorce 4/1 (1994), 146.

43 H. Riggio, "Parental Marital Conflict and Divorce, Parent-child Relationships, Social Support, and Relationship Anxiety in Young Adulthood," in Personal Relationship 11 (2004): 102.

44 Elizabeth Mullet and Arnold L. Stolberg, "Divorce and its Impact on the Intimate Relationships of Young Adults," in Journal of Divorce and Remarriage 38-1/2 (2002): 42.

45 Barri R. Flower, *Male Crime and Deviance: Exploring Its Causes, Dynamics and Nature* (Illinois: Charles C. Thomas Publisher, Ltd., 2003), 28.

46 Karen E. Hart and William Allen Kritsonis, "Critical Analysis of an Original Writing on Social Learning Theory: Imitation of Film-Mediated Aggressive Models by: Albert Bandura, Doeothy Ross and Sheila A. Ross," in National Forum of Applied Educational Research Journal 20/3 (2006): 6.

side.[47] Nonetheless, social learning theory has made significant contributions to the understanding of the process of observational learning, the impact of media violence on the behaviour of children and psychotherapy.

The Social Exchange Theory

Social exchange theory is based on the premise that people view relationships in economic terms by considering the cost and rewards and the comparison of alternatives. During the 1900s, a German sociologist, George Simmel emphasized reciprocity in everyday life and that all human interactions involve some form of exchange.[48] Later, George Homans, an American sociologist, also argued, "Although values and norms govern behaviour, people attempt to maximize benefits, and minimize costs when interacting with others."[49] In the 20th century, exchange theory was applied to personal and interpersonal factors that mediate the formation, maintenance, and dissolution of relationship.[50] Consequently, if the costs of the relationship outweigh the benefits that can be obtained in alternate relationships, they are more likely to terminate their current relationship.[51]

John Thibaut and Harold Kelley, in their Interdependence Theory, argue that the attractiveness of a relationship is determined by two comparison levels between what one puts into a relationship and what one expects to get from it.[52] First, a spouse compares profits relative to other marriages. If she/he feels deprived, then the marital satisfaction of that spouse would be low, creating a motive for choosing divorce. However, many unhappy spouses remain married because of other constraints such as the costs associated with divorce. In the second comparison level, the spouse calculates the rewards and costs associated with possibilities other than marriage such as being single and divorced. Among the possible costs includes child support, alimony, peer disapproval, the church's disapproval, kinship group disapproval, sexual deprivation, loss of interaction with one's children, role loss etc. Some of the possible rewards include finding a more compatible partner, freeing members of the family from a confrontational

---

47 Bernardo J. Carducci, *The Psychology of Personality: Viewpoints, Research, and Applications* (West Sussex: John Wiley & Sons, 2007), 424.

48 George Simmel, *The Philosophy of Money* (London: Routledge, 1978), 92.

49 Cited in Maureen Baker, Families, *Labour and Love: Family Diversity in a Changing World* (Vancouver: UBC Press, 2001), 78.

50 Patricia L Munhall and Virginia Mackhen Fitzsimons, *The Emergence of Family into the 21st Century* (Boston: Jones and Bartlett Publishers, 2001), 45-46.

51 Kortet Mensah and Mark Fine, "Divorce and Children," in *Family Influences on Childhood Behaviour and Development: Evidence Based Prevention and Treatment Approaches*, edited by Thomas P. Gullotta and Gary M. Blau (New York: Routledge, Taylor and Francis Group, 2010), 145.

52 Cited by Florian Frensch, *The Social Side of Mergers and Acquisition: Cooperation Relationships after Mergers and Acquisitions* (Berlin: Springer Science & Business Media, 2007), 133.

and conflict-ridden home environment and freeing oneself from family responsibilities.[53]

This theory was used to explain why some relationships break up and why others last. When a partner feels that he/she contributes more time or emotional energy to a relationship, the person may develop feelings of resentment and start looking for gratification elsewhere.[54] Since people evaluate their relationships based on a comparison level, i.e., the standard they feel they should be receiving in terms of costs and rewards as well as a comparison level for alternatives, i.e., the reward they think are available in other relationships.[55] The desire for divorce can be seen as a situation when the cost of marriage exceeds the rewards. Divorce may seem attractive when the alternatives to marriage seem good. Hence, the possibility for financial and emotional independence, self-actualization, and other sources of affection proved to be important factors.[56] Most exchange theorists support the idea that profitable exchanges are valued and maintained.

Social exchange theory offers a useful framework for understanding the cognitive processes persons utilize to appraise satisfaction with marriage and to determine whether or not to remain in marital relationship. Most human interactions involve the exchange of commodities such as material, symbolic or affectional that creates interdependence between spouses and attraction to a rewarding relationship. Rewards may include companionship, sexual enjoyment, love, statuses, or money.[57] Costs, on the other hand, may be operationalized in terms of physical or emotional abuse, infidelity, or conflicting lifestyles that may lead to abhorrence, distrust, rejection, embarrassment, anxiety and powerlessness.[58] One of the widely used theories to explain divorce is social exchange theory.

While this theory has been credited as one powerful perspective to view the formation of relationships, it is not without limitations. One major criticism is that it is too simplistic and individualistic. For instance, the basic premise of social exchange theory is that persons make rational choices about whether or not to exchange with another person. Such narrow focus leaves no room for structural

53 James M. White, David M. Klein and Todd F. Martin, *Family Theories: An Introduction* (Los Angeles: SAGE Publications, Inc., 2015), 60.

54 Cited in Baker, *Families, Labour and Love: Family Diversity in a Changing World*..., 78.

55 Chris Segrin and Jeanne Flore, *Family Communication*, second edition (New York: Routledge Taylor and Francis, 2011), 70.

56 Cited in Douglas H. Sprenkle and Pilar Gonzalez-Doupe, "Divorce Therapy," in *Family Therapy Sourcebook*, second edition, edited by Fred P. Piercy, Douglas H. Sprenkle and Joseph L. Wetchler (New York: The Guilford Press, 1996), 188.

57 F.I. Nye, "Choice, Exchange and the Family," in *Contemporary Theories about the Family*, vol. 2, edited by W. R. Burr, R. Hill, F. I. Nye and I. L. Reiss (New York: Free Press, 1979), 2.

58 Nye, "Choice, Exchange and the Family"..., 3.

constraints such as economic conditions or social conventions.[59] Another downside is the conceptual confusion which is delineated as rewards and cost because what is rewarding to one spouse may be punishing to the other and what is punishing at a specific juncture in a marital relationship may be rewarding at another, so also spouses in a marital relationship can redefine a situation previously perceived as rewarding or punishing to its opposite. Besides, costs and rewards are difficult to define operationally as they differ from one individual to another.[60] It also fails to address the relational and cognitive processes by which rewards and costs are defined. Put it differently, this theory focuses on how partners weigh rewards relative to costs and thus becomes individualistic in context, and hence underplay emotions and fail to explain attitudes of altruism trivializing the importance of moral principles that dictate values such as kindness, forgiveness, and self-sacrifice.[61] Besides, relationships do not necessarily progress in a linear mode as the theory suggested which assumes that as benefits increase, satisfaction, intimacy, and maintenance also increase.[62] Though people make calculations at the interpersonal relationships level, they often make significant sacrifices within the relationships.[63] The theory negates romantic relationship and the value of marriage and family.

One crude difference between social and economic exchange is that the latter embodies specific obligations whereas the former embodies unspecified obligations.[64] The theory is limited, as it does not provide standards on which individuals may base decisions. What constitutes a cost or a benefit is subjective and based solely on an individual's experience. Critics note that much of the theory is predicated on economic assumptions such as perfect market, which

59 Timothy D. Pippert, *Road Dogs and Loners: Family Relationship Among Homeless Men* (New York: Lexington Books, 2007), 10.

60 For example, financial benefits could be very rewarding for one individual but only minimally for another. Hence, reducing all outcomes to a common standard is illogical. Paul A. Nakonezyn and Wayne H. Denton, "Marital Relationships: A Social Exchange Theory Perspective," in The American Journal of Family Therapy 36 (2008): 410.

61 Nakonezyn and Wayne H. Denton, "Marital Relationships: A Social Exchange Theory Perspective"..., 410.

62 Angela M. Sabates, *Social Psychology in Christian Perspective: Exploring the Human Condition* (Madison: Intervarsity Press, 2012), 454.

63 Katherine R. Allen and Angela C. Henderson, *Family Theories: Foundations and Applications* (Sussex: John Wiley & Sons Ltd., 2017), 135.

64 In economic exchange, the specific obligations of the actors are simultaneously agreed upon such as a product or service is sold for a specific price but in social exchange, one partner supplies benefits to another and although there is a general expectation of reciprocation, the exact nature of the return is not specified and not bargained unlike in economic exchange. Nakonezyn and W.H. Denton, "Marital Relationships: A Social Exchange Theory Perspective ...," 407.

may or may not apply to group behaviour.[65] Nonetheless social exchange theory continues to provide insight into the ways individuals and organizations create and evaluate relationships. It is evident that humans assess, to varying degrees, how much effort relationships entail relative to how much one benefits from it.

The Systems Theory

Family systems theory premises on the basic assumption that individuals within families are intrinsically connected to one another, hence attention is paid to the larger family unit. It focuses on what goes on at the family level rather than examining family members as individuals. One of the basic tenets of systems theory is that all members of the family are interdependent. What happens to one member effects all other members of the family and the actions of every member of the family influence the actions of other members. Systems theory contends that families are constantly in the process of influencing each other and this process never ends. Moreover, families as systems influence their environments and in turn are influenced by the circumstances and contexts around them.[66]

Murray Bowen developed the idea of family rather than individual as the primary unit for understanding human functioning. He argues that trying to understand problems only from the individual point of view gives limited information because individual's problems are strongly connected to their interactions with other members of the family. Individuals contain only a part of the problem, but they are not "the problem." Therefore, a good understanding of any individual is accomplished only by seeing that person as part of a larger whole and not as an isolated individual. Yet this concept is not the same as seeing the family as a group.[67] Bowen's theory expands the view of marriage beyond the individuals and the marital dyad to the interlocking relationships in the family. Bowen's family theory and factors influencing marital functioning is helpful in understanding the dynamics of family relationships.

According to his theory of differentiation of self, there are variations of adaptiveness among individuals predicted by varying levels of differentiation. People with higher levels of differentiation are responsible for themselves and to

---

65 Maura Jean Murphy, *Contingent Faculty: What Impacts Their Organizational Commitment?* (Dissertation, Doctor of Education, North Carolina State University, 2009), 52.

66 Mark A. Fine, Lawrence H. Ganong and David H. Demo, "A Risk and Resilience Perspective," in *Families and Change: Coping with Stressful Events and Transitions*, edited by Sharon J. Price, Christine A. Price and Patrick C. McKenry, fourth edition (California: Sage Publications, 2010), 112.

67 The group concept is still about a collection of individuals who have "group interactions." His approach conceives of the family a single emotional organism, not simply as a group of individuals who have somewhat closer emotional ties. Even though the forces may be invisible, the governing power of the emotional system over the individual can totally affect the trajectory of a person's life. Ronald W. Richardson, *Couples in Conflict: A Family System Approach to Marriage Counseling* (Minneapolis: Fortress Press, 2010), 7.

others, capable of clear thinking during emotional situations and are guided by a well-defined set of principles and goals and tend to have few physical, emotional and social symptoms and are more stable in marriage. On the contrary, people with lower levels of differentiation of self are under-responsible for themselves and over-responsible for others and are primarily guided by relationships with little or no resilience on thought and have little energy for self-direction and tend to have major physical, emotional and social symptoms and more marital disruption.[68] Bowen's argument was that fusion reaches its peak in the togetherness of marriage. Marriages vary in their level of fusion or differentiation.[69] "Marital conflict occurs when neither spouse will "give in" to the other to the fusion, or when the one who has been given in or adopting refuses to continue."[70]

The level of anxiety influence marital functioning as each individual has a basic or chronic level of anxiety that is rooted in one's family relationship. If the family of origin is unstable or emotionally reactive and the more dependent one is on the family, the more chronic anxiety an individual has to manage over a lifetime. One's position in the family also affects how much of anxiety one absorbs. Couples with higher levels of chronic anxiety experience more reactivity in their marriage and have more difficulty distinguishing between real and imagined threats.[71] In his multi-generational theory, Bowen opines that a husband and wife replicate the degree of fusion each had with one's family or origin.[72] Another way multi-generational fusion may manifest itself is overt dependency on the family of origin. This togetherness between a spouse and his/her family of origin may stabilize a marriage so long as the other spouse assumes an outside

68 Phil Klever, "Marital Fusion and Differentiation," in *Clinical Applications of Bowen Family Systems Theory*, edited by Peter Titelman (New York: Routledge, 2013), 121.

69 Sometimes the fusion expresses itself through one spouse regularly accommodating the other so much so that they operate more as one individual than two. Positively fused couples may report being very content but their bond is more vulnerable and unstable as stressors increase or as the oneness is threatened. In contrast, couples that are least fused have the most individuality which allows for a more steady, stable togetherness. Klever, "Marital Fusion and Differentiation..., 122.

70 Murray Bowen, *Family Therapy in Clinical Practice* (New York: Rowan & Littlefield Publishers Inc., 1978), 476.

71 Klever, "Marital Fusion and Differentiation…, 121.

72 The greater the fusion between the spouse and his/her family of origin, the more unstable and vulnerable the marriage is. Marriages are sometimes formed to escape the intensity of emotions with one's parents. The illusion is created that one has found a way to break free of the unresolved issues with one's family, only to find that the same emotional intensity reappears in the marriage. The more one manages parent-child intensity through distance, the greater the marital dependency, and the more the marital expectations go beyond what the partner can realistically provide because of weight of dependency and expectations marriage inevitable breaks down. Titelman, *Clinical Applications of Bowen Family System Theory…*, 123-124. Bowen, *Family Therapy in Clinical Practice…*, 476.

position, which Bowen terms it as pseudo-self.[73] The other spouse may even be adopted into the family as though he/she has no family of his/her own. However, when the other spouse expects to have an inside position with his/her partner or when his/her partner's fusion with the family is not comfortable, marital turmoil usually erupts.[74] In multi-generational transmission, Bowen describes the pattern that develops over multiple generations as children emerge from a paternal family with higher, equal, or lower basic levels of differentiation than the parents. When a child emerges with a lower level of self than the parents and marries a spouse with equal differentiation of self and this process is handed down from generation to generation to lower and the lower levels of differentiation the most severe emotional problems erupt.[75]

Family system theory had been the foundation of many important developments and has made a significant impact on the study of families and different traumatic events affecting individuals and families and has provided a useful lens through which a greater understanding of families has emerged. However, critics particularly feminist therapists have challenged the issue of gender inequality as not being fully addressed within family system theory including the power dynamics within families. The thrust of the critique was that family theorists and therapists have paid attention to issues of power and the effect on relatedness between the generations, i.e., the politics of growing up but had systematically failed to address the issue of power within same generational relationships such as couple relationships. Power inequalities between men and women are ignored. Family system theory ignores the larger socio-cultural and political context of family life. Feminist scholars argue that the roles of men and women in the family can be understood only within a broader social context because in many cases women lack equal access to economic survival in the larger social environment.[76] For instance, in a patriarchal setting where power is male exclusive, equality of influence between women and men cannot be assumed, but such inequalities are often overlooked in the systems theory. Family therapists assume that both men and women are equally responsible for maintaining dysfunctional behaviour. Family system theory is also critiqued for taking into consideration only male exclusive values such as autonomy, independence, and control, but do not take into consideration the feminine values such as relationships, connecting and nurturing.[77]

---

73 Bowen, *Family Therapy in Clinical Practice...*, 477.

74 Klever, "Marital Fusion and Differentiation..., 124.

75 Bowen, *Family Therapy in Clinical Practice ...*, 477.

76 William J. Doherty and David A. Baptiste, "Theories Emerging from Family Therapy," in *Sourcebook of Family Theory and Methods: A Contextual Approach*, edited by Pauline Boss et al., (New York: Springer Science + Business Media, 2009), 518.

77 Janet Yerby, "Family Systems Theory Reconsidered: Integrating Social Construction Theory and Dialectical Process," in Communication Theory 5/4 (November, 1995): 344.

Structural-Functional Theory

Structural-functional theory is a sociological theory focusing on the organizational structure of societies that consist of interrelation social units. It is based on the assumption that both individual and group behaviour serves as function for a larger society.[78] Talcott E. F. Parsons founded the theory on the works of anthropologists who investigated the organization as a system of primitive culture. This theory defines and explains society as a system with checks and balances. According to this view, individuals interact in a social system within a specific frame of time and place. The interaction is characterized by the use of symbols known to the actors.[79]

According to Parsons, the individual's personality system depends on the surrounding social structure meaning human's actions and motives can be explained in social terms. This applies even to intimate relationships. The cultural system offers a set of beliefs such as love is essential; everyone should love somebody etc., which is related to a series of symbols and standards for the expression of one's emotions and behaviour. One's emotions are developed in an atmosphere of free socialization. In fact, "socialization agents", such as parents, priests, teachers who transmits concepts and beliefs, socially mandate one's emotion.[80]

Society also provides a model on the organization of life. For instance, the state offers education and formation to its citizens and in turn contributes to the socialization of children. On the political front, decisions are taken on issues such as education, economy, law etc. If an individual complies with the norms of the society, he/she contributes to the functioning of society as a whole. As an institution, the family represents a model of partner selection and procreation. Therefore, according to this theory, divorce should not be seen only as a single phenomenon or personal failure of the individuals concerned, but should be seen in its larger social context. In addition, it may also be true that certain social ills are to be blamed for family breakdown. The spouses have to organize their lives according to internal family responsibilities, the requirement of job organization, social limitations, and gender roles etc. Furthermore, the influence of mass media on the family has increased considerably whereby unrealistic images of family functioning are often projected and transmitted.[81]

This theory posits that divorce has to be viewed in its social context rather than as a single individual phenomenon. It also explicates the function of human behaviour and social interaction in the context of the larger society. From the structural functional perspective, individuals and family members are viewed in

78 Margit Gaffal, *Psychosocial and Legal Perspectives of Marital Breakdown: With Special Emphasis on Spain* (London: Springer Science + Business Media, 2010), 40.

79 Talcott E. Parsons, *The Social System* (London: The Free Press of Glencoe, 1951), 5.

80 Gaffal, *Psychosocial and Legal Perspectives and Marital Breakdown…*, 42.

81 Gaffal, *Psychosocial and Legal Perspectives and Marital Breakdown…*, 42.

terms of the functions that must be performed to ensure the survival of society. Survival means that member of the individual in a particular society or group must persist, endure, and work diligently to attain and maintain the best interest of society negating what is best for individuals. This theory has been criticized as it fails to deal with social change and social dynamics only as disruptions to social equilibrium and peaceful maintenance leaving no room for such change as an important function in the long-term development and evolution of a social system.[82]

The Attachment Theory

Attachment theory is another psychological theory that has been applied to divorce. It was originally formulated by John Bowlby based on his observational studies of children who experienced separation from their parents during World War II. He was also influenced by ethological theories that explore similarities and differences in behaviour across species. Ultimately, he argues that attachment processes are evident in nonhuman as well as human primates and serves as an adaptive function for the survival of the species.[83] One of the most important tenets of attachment theory was that a young child needs to develop a relationship with at least one primary caregiver for normal social and emotional development. It describes the importance of parent-child bonds formed through patterns of interaction and internal working models of attachment during infancy.[84] According to him, there are different types of attachments: a secure attachment is the most positive type, which results from the needs of the infant being consistently met by caregivers while an avoidant attachment is formed when the infant's needs are not consistently met. If the infant's needs are inconsistently met, an anxious/ambivalent attachment style is formed.[85]

Based on the infants' responses to separation from and reunion with caretakers in a structured laboratory procedure, psychologist Mary Ainsworth identifies three distinct patterns of infant attachment: secure, anxious resistant and avoidant. Children who welcomed their caretaker's return after a brief separation, seek proximity, and are comforted are classified as securely attached and those who show ambivalence towards caregivers and showed inability to be comforted upon reunion are classified as anxious-resistant. Infants who avoid proximity or interaction with the caregivers on reunion were classified as avoidant.[86] Both

82 White and David M. Klein, *Family Theories...*, 61.

83 John Bowlby, *A Secure Base: Parent-child Attachment and Healthy Human Development* (London: Routledge, 1988), 4.

84 John Bowlby, *Loss, Sadness and Depression* (New York: Basic Books, Inc., Publishers, 1980), 39.

85 Bowlby, *A Secure Base: Parent-child Attachment and Healthy Human Development...*, 4.

86 Mary Ainsworth and S. M. Bells, "Attachment, Exploration and Separation: Individual Differences in Strange-Situation Behavior of One-year-olds," in Child Development 41 (1970): 53.

Bowlby and Ainsworth have speculated that these different attachment styles with caretakers form a prototype for later relationship outside the family.[87] This theory postulates that divorce and remarriage indicates an insecure attachment style in childhood.

Kim Bartholomew and Leonard M. Horowitz have applied this framework to adult relationships with four attachments styles such as secure, preoccupied, fearful avoidant and dismissive avoidant. Children establish negative or positive relationships in life depending on the attachment style formed with the caregivers.[88] Hence, in dealing with divorce it is important to look at the early attachment style that affects adults in their attempt to form romantic relationships.

Attachment theory has been used to explain coping and adjustment process in separating couples. The theory helps to understand the emotional processes divorcing couples go through. It also provides an important perspective on divorce because it involves the disruption and termination of a powerful attachment bond developed by the spouses. The theory has a great deal to say about separation from an attachment figure and the breaking of an attachment bond, both of which are core aspects of divorce. It is also used to explain the process of divorce. Existing research shows that individuals with insecure attachment styles are particularly vulnerable to divorce. It is also used to explain how parents and children adjust to divorce.[89]

Attachment theory has provided a solid foundation on which a number of researchers have built remarkable theoretical and practical applications relating to close relationships. The theory highlights the psychological loss associated with both separation and rejection. It offers a compelling explanation for the feelings associated with the trauma of separation and loss, fear, anxiety, anger, sadness and despair and their disruptive effects on personality development. Yet, attachment theory has its own critics. One of the main critiques of attachment theory is Judith Rice Harries who opines that too much emphasis on how a child become should not be placed on the parents alone. She disagrees with the idea that attachment behaviours formed in infancy help shape the attachment relationships people have as adults. Her contention was that people assume that kind and honest and respectable parents will beget kind, honest and respectable children and parents that are disrespectable and rude will have children that are the same way but this may not be true. According to her, parents do not shape their child's personality or character; rather a child's peers have more influence on

87 Mary Ainsworth, "Attachment Beyond Infancy," in American Psychologist 44 (1989): 711.

88 Kim Bartholomew and Leonard M. Horowitz, "Attachment Styles Among Young Adults: A Test of Four Category Model," in Journal of Personality and Social Psychology 61/2 (1991): 227.

89 Keran Kayser and Jessica K. J. Johnson, "Divorce," in *The Encyclopaedia of Social Work*: 4 Volume Set, edited by Terry Mizrahi and Larry Davis (Oxford: Oxford University Press, 2008), 81.

them than their parents do. For instance, immigrant children continue to speak their parent's native language at home, but can also learn their new language and speak without an accent while the parent's accent still remains the same. Children learn these things from their peers because they want to fit into the social group.[90]

The Contagion Theory

Contagion theory posits that divorce is contagious meaning the probability of divorce is influenced by divorces of other people. Social scientists speak of "social effects," "social network effects" or "neighbourhood effects" to describe the way in which social practices have wider, sometimes unintended, and unanticipated effects on surrounding communities and the wider society. Anthropologists, social psychologists, and neuroscientists have articulated "contagion" theories to describe the very visceral way people might seek to protect themselves from thoughts and behaviours they feel threaten their bodies, relationships, communities or worldviews.[91]

Gustav le Bon, a sociologist, has sparked an interest in the "group mind" and the "madness of crowds" by exploring the process of hysterical contagion in a variety of societies and natural settings. However, in the 1970s social psychologists proposed a theory of emotional contagion, focusing on individual rather than crowds. They have attempted to pin down the process by which an individual transmits his/her emotions to another person or small group. Clinicians, psychologists, physicians, and epidemiologists have begun to apply emotional contagion theory to collective emotions and the social contagion of various mental and physical diseases. This theory proposed that under certain conditions, partners and even entire communities may catch their fellows' moods and emotions.[92] In an article titled, "Breaking Up is Hard to Do, Unless Everyone Else Is Doing it Too," three social scientists have examined longitudinal data from Framingham Heart Study and found that attitudes toward divorce flow across social ties, spreading between and among siblings and even across friends and co-workers, to an extent that "divorce should be understood as a collective phenomenon that extends far beyond those directly affected."[93] In their study, they found significant relationships in divorce status between individuals extending up to two degrees of separation. Their contention was that, "a person's tendency to

90 Judith Rice Harries, *The Nurture Assumption: Why Children Turn Out the Way They Do* (New York: Free Press, 1998), 8.

91 M. Christian Green, "'There but for the Grace': The Ethics of Bystanders to Divorce," in Propositions, edited by W. Bradford Wilcod (New York: Institute of American Values, 2012), 5.

92 Elaine Hatfield, Megan Carpenter and Richard L. Rapson, "Emotional Contagion as a Precursor to Collective Emotions," in *Collective Emotions: Perspectives from Psychology, Philosophy and Sociology*, edited by Christian von Scheve and Mikko Salmela (Oxford: Oxford University Press, 2014), 119.

93 Green, "'There but for the Grace': The Ethics of Bystanders to Divorce…, 4.

divorce depends not just on his friend's divorce status, but also to his friend's friend."[94] Further, "a divorced friend or family member who lives hundreds of miles away have as much influence on [a person's]... risk of divorce as one who lives next door."[95]

Contagion theory seems to be opening many doors to better understand human behaviour. Scholars from varied disciplines such as neuroscience, biology, social psychology, sociology, and life span psychology recognized primitive emotional contagion as critically important in understanding human contagion, emotion, and behaviour.[96] Many researchers have investigated the contagion of emotion and behaviour of people in different communities.[97] There is considerable evidence that a variety of emotions are capable of affecting whole group of people especially when they are under stress, regardless of how such contagion operates is evident and how powerful the collective process of contagion is. Happiness, loneliness, obesity, and suicide have been similarly explained by social contagion theory. However, on the downside, as contagion theory is based on the premise that the behaviour of self-elected leaders in crowds leads to homogenous action as members of the crowd copy each other. This theory fails to explain why some crowds become violent while others remain passive.

The Crisis Theory

Crisis theory was first developed by Reuben Hill in 1947 and has been used by family stress researchers to describe, predict, and explain when a stressor event causes a crisis or disorganization in a family and also to predict the extent of the crisis. Hill developed this model based on the experience gained as a psychologist when working with traumatized families during the worldwide economic downturn of the Great Depression in the 1930s. In his work, he has analyzed the factors that had influence on family stability by comparing dysfunctional families to those who remained intact during the time of economic hardship.[98]

94 Green, "'There but for the Grace': The Ethics of Bystanders to Divorce..., 4.

95 Green, "'There but for the Grace': The Ethics of Bystanders to Divorce..., 4-5.

96 Hatfield, Megan Carpenter and Richard L. Rapson, "Emotional Contagion as a Precursor ..., 108.

97 For instance, in the Middle Ages, in the wake of the Black Death, dancing manias swept throughout Europe. Klawas describes the "sorrow and anxiety" which drove people "to the point of hysteria": The bubonic plague, the infamous Black Death appeared in the 21st century...it broke over Europe in a great wave. Entire villages were exterminated. Fields became neglected. Soon famine complicated the pestilence. And just as the plague receded and the population and economy began to recover, another wave struck... Hatfield, Megan Carpenter and Richard L. Rapson, "Emotional Contagion as a Precursor..., 114.

98 Reuben Hill, "Genetic Features of Families under Stress," in Social Casework, 49/2 (1948): 143.

Hill has described a set of variables and their interactions to explain the events leading to a family crisis. He posits that "A (the event) interacting with B (the family's crisis meeting resources) interacting with C (the definition the family makes of the event) produces X (the crisis)."[99] Hill's theoretical framework was further developed by Hamilton McCubbin and Joan Patterson in 1983 as "Double ABCX" model complimenting and expanding Hill's theory yet distinguished by its emphasis on the additional life stressors influencing the family's resilience and adaptation ability. They have expanded and added four factors that are believed to influence the family's adaptation over time. Their double ABCX model added post-crisis behaviours and explains how a family adapts to crisis over time. It also describes the psychological and social factors families use in managing crisis, the process families engage in to attain satisfactory resolution and the eventual outcome of these efforts.[100] Emphasis was made on family stress as a dynamic process of adjustment.[101] The crisis theory explains how a stressor event would result in family crisis and subsequent marital dissolution.[102] The resources of the family and the definition of crisis mediate the stressor event. For instance, parenting a new-born infant can be a major stressor, and the way a family reacts to such an event can predict the relative level of stress necessary for a person in that family to abruptly abandon his/her spouse. Crisis theory relies on the notion that marital satisfaction and stability stem from a couple's ability to handle crisis.

The ABCX model is a flexible framework that can be adapted to fit the family and focus on wellbeing among individuals within the family. Stress theory explains why some families fall into crisis when dealing with stress while others cope with the crisis. This theory is also useful to examine the interaction of the elements, resources, and perceptions of stressors when examining factors that predicts crisis. By using this model, one can explain how individuals' resources and perceptions impact their quality of life thereby possibly alleviating or preventing from having the harsh impact that can have on the day-to-day experiences. While this theory is well developed, it has its own limitations. For one thing, the model assumes that

99 Hill, "Genetic Features of Families under Stress ..., 143.

100 Yaov Lavee, Hamilton I. McCubbin and Joan M. Patterson, "The Double ABCX Model of Family Stress and Adaptation: An Empirical Test by Analysis of Structural Equations with Latent Variables," in Journal of Marriage and Family 47/4 (November, 1985): 816-817.

101 A postcrisis stage has been added to the original precrisis model, representing the ongoing adjustment following a crisis, which occurs when a family is unable to prevent change. They proposed four factors representing the "Double" in the ABCX model and variability in the family's ability to recover: (a) pile up of stressors; (b) family efforts to acquire new resources; (c) modifications of definition of the situation and (d) results of coping strategies. Hamilton I McCubbin and Joan M. Patterson, "The Family Stress Process: The Double ABCX Model of Adjustment and Adaptation," in *Social Stress and the Family: Advance and Developments in Family Stress Theory and Research*, edited by Hamilton I. McCubbin, Marvin B. Sussman and Jaon M.Petterson (New York: Routledge, 2013), 8.

102 Hill, "Genetic Features of Families under Stress ..., 143.

the outcome always involves crisis. The focus of ABCX model is on crisis, but according to Pauline G. Boss, stress and crisis are not the same and should not be used in the same manner. Boss argues that, on the one hand, stress is understood as a state of disturbed equilibrium and on the other hand, she defines crisis as a point of acute disequilibrium.[103] The double ABCX model has been criticized for its presentation of a crisis as an event-specific stressor, with opponents recognizing that most stressors in family life are not related to one single event.[104]

Boss further feels that crisis does not have to occur when a family is experiencing stress. Stress is viewed as a continuum. For her, family can experience low levels to high levels of stress without going into a crisis. Crisis occurs when the family can no longer deal with its stress and falls into a period of disorganization and unable to function at the same level it did prior to the crisis. At this point, the family must make readjustment to re-establish its previous level of functioning or create a new level of functioning. Coping and adaptation are interchangeable thereby an indication that when a family is in coping or adapting state, it is not necessarily in crisis, rather the family attempts to manage its stress. Either the manner by which the family responds to the stress can keep it from entering into a crisis situation or it can lead to crisis situation.[105] Yet, there are some families that ignore the stress thereby allowing it to function as if these situations were not present. They are conditioned to be resistant to stress and are unmoved by crisis. For instance, some individuals who live in racist environment and experience constant form of discrimination continue to maintain their wellbeing and function without falling apart or change their perceptions of happiness or alter their overall satisfaction with life.[106]

Sex Ratio Theory

Marcia Guttentag, former director of the Families and Stress Research Project at Harvard University, originally conceptualized the sex ratio theory. The theory was developed out of her concern about the rising mental health illness of young women including depression and attempted suicide. She conjectures how the apparent decline in mental health of young women may be related to the current cultural imagery of women and male-female relationships, which overtly characterized women as disposable and sexual relationships as short-term what

103 Pauline E. Boss, Chalandra M. Bryant and Jay A. Mancini, *Family Stress Management: A Contextual Approach*, third edition (Singapore: SAGE Publications, 2017), 56.

104 Vicky R. Bowden and Cindy Smith Greenberg, *Children and their Families: The Continuum of Care* (Philadelphia: Lippincott Williams & Wilkins, 2010), 17.

105 Pauline E. Boss, "Normative Family Stress: Family Boundary Changes Across the Life Span," in Family Relations 29 (1980): 446.

106 Vera A. White, "Race, Sex, Social Class: The Influence of Stress Responsiveness on Well-Being Among American Families" (Doctorate of Philosophy Dissertation, Kansas State University, 2007), 8.

she characterized as "Love'em leave 'em."[107] After her demise, Paul F. Secord completed her book. This theory tries to address the question of how social relations influence when sex ratios are substantially imbalanced at ages when men and women most commonly collaborate.[108]

Guttentag and Secord posited that the relative proportion of the population that is male or female is a significant factor in shaping male-female relationships and on gender differentiated social statuses.[109] The sex ratio thesis posits that male-female power relations operate on two distinct yet reflective levels: dyadic and structural. Dyadic power refers to the relative male-female power in two-person relationships, while structural power is defined as the relative amount of control that males and females generally have over social, political, and economic resources. Guttentag and Secord opined that the sex ratio directly influences whether males or females will have dyadic power such that the sex in oversupply will have less power and be more dependent on the sex in undersupply.[110] Imbalance sex ratio influence dyadic in interpersonal male-female relationship since males and females are fundamentally distinct yet complementary categories. Much like social exchange theory, they argued that each individual enters into relationships with different degrees of power and "(in)dependence", which is determined by whether or not the individual is a member of a numerical majority. In short, number and quality of alternative relationships influence dependency in a relationship.[111] They argued that the sex category that holds structural power is important since that group has the ability to influence resource access, accumulation, and dependency as well as to shape moral values and that male exclusively held structural power among all societies. This explains why even in high sex ratio areas where dyadic power is in women's favour, female dyadic control has been substantially limited by males structural control employed to define sex-specific norms. This historical structural power imbalance possess by men explains why women have been subjected to male definitions of morality and social convention even in sex ratio context. They spelled out the value system that rewards behaviours associated

107 Marcie Guttentag and Paul F. Secord, *Too Many Women? The Sex Ratio Question* (California: Sage Publication, 1983), 11-12.

108 Guttentag and Secord, *Too Many Women? The Sex Ratio Question...*, 7.

109 Guttentag and Secord, *Too Many Women? The Sex Ratio Question...*, 28.

110 Guttentag and Secord, *Too Many Women? The Sex Ratio Question...*, 30.

111 Dyadic power is fundamentally determined by the resources that each partner brings to the relationship, they part with more resources whether material (i.e. financial) or psychological (i.e. satisfaction) is expected to have greater dyadic power. Thus those who have less empowered will rely more heavily or be more dependent on the other and are consequently in a weaker position. The partner with fewer options or alternative relationships, i.e., heterosexual males in high sex ratio societies and heterosexual females in low sex ration societies will have less interpersonal power and be inclined to enter or remain in relationships that are materially and psychologically costly. Guttentag and Secord, *Too Many Women? The Sex Ratio Question...*, 152.

with masculinity such as aggression, competition and stoicism which functions to support male dominance. However, this male historical structural dominance can be challenged if the sex ratio remains low for a substantial and consistent period of time.[112] Under this condition, the gender lacking dyadic power may form coalitions or become politically organized to confront their disempowered position. Thus, in areas where sex ratio is considerably low for a long period of time women are predicted to become unhappy with the actual and possible social exchanges available to them and challenge male structural power through the formation of organizations to help correct their inferior social position initially and largely through economic independence. Such organizations could incite change that moves toward equalization of historical structural disparity favouring males.[113]

Research consistently supports the sex ratio theory delineated by Guttentag and Secord that sex ratios are significant predictor of female status and relational outcomes. Katherine Trend and Scott J. South have reported that in their study of 66 societies, divorce rate was found to be higher in societies with a low gender ratio.[114] In their analysis of the US population during the 1960-1975, David M. Heer and Amyra Grossbard-Shechtman have found that gender ratio was highly correlated with the divorce rate.[115] Yet, despite vast support for this theory there are also many critics owing to its lack of empirical analysis their hypothesis has gone largely unexamined. Some suggest that quantity alone may not be enough to predict marriage and family trend. Instead, the quality of available mates is also an important consideration.

Causes of Divorce

Although there are many reasons that cause divorce, only a few important ones are highlighted in this section.

Marrying at Young Age

According to research, the age of marriage is a highly significant predictor of marital stability or disruption. The age at which people marry is "the most consistent predictor of marital stability identified in social science research."[116]

---

112 Guttentag and Secord, *Too Many Women? The Sex-Ratio Question* ..., 154, 174.

113 Guttentag and Secord, *Too Many Women? The Sex Ratio Question* ..., 175.

114 Katherine Trend and Scott J. South, "Structural Determinants of the Divorce Rates: A Cross-Societal Analysis," in Journal of Marriage and the Family 51/2 (1989): 394-395. Also, refer Scott J. South and Katherine Trend, "Sex Ratios and Women's Roles: A Cross-National Analysis," in American Journal of Sociology, 93 (1988).

115 David M. Heer and Amyra Grossbard-Shechtman, "The Impact of the Female Marriage Squeeze and the Contraceptive Revolution on Sex ratio and the Women's Liberation Movement in the United States, 1960 to 1975," in Journal of Marriage and Family 43/1 (February, 1981): 55.

116 Strong and Theodore Cohen, *The Marriage and Family Experience:* ..., 483.

Young, especially teenage marriages are more likely to end in divorce than people who get married in their 20s or older. Nearly 50 percent of those who marry before age 18 and 40 percent of those who marry before turning 20 years old end in divorce, the reason being younger partners are less likely to be emotionally mature and are more likely to involve in premarital pregnancy. Only 25 percent of those who marry after 25 years end up divorced.[117] It has been shown quite consistently that marriages are more vulnerable to divorce when the bride is under the age of 20 at the time of marriage.[118] The much higher risk of divorce increased still further if the groom is also under 20.[119] The references quoted are from 1970s but recent research confirms this finding. One of the obvious reasons is that as men and women mature, their original reasons for marrying no longer apply.[120]

Cohabitation

Cohabitation has been associated with higher risk of divorce, though this may vary depending on the nature of cohabiting relationship.[121] According to some theoretical arguments, premarital cohabitation help stabilize subsequent marital relationships, because those who cohabit will gain more information about their partners than those who do not. Cohabiting partners who find that they are well suited might consider marriage while those who do not find themselves compatible will end their cohabitation. However, many empirical studies have found that premarital cohabitation is associated with higher risk of subsequent marital dissolution compared to couples who married without prior cohabitation.[122] While some researchers opine that the duration of the union has an effect on the relationship, others suggest that premarital cohabitation raises the risk of marriage dissolution because of selection effects.[123] For many couples, cohabitation represents a lesser commitment than marriage and this is true even in Sweden and Norway where cohabitation is widespread. Some individuals who opt for cohabitation opine that it requires less sexual faithfulness than in marriage or because cohabitation is viewed as an alternative to the lifelong commitment assumed by marriage. Moreover, it is easier to get into as well as exit. Therefore,

---

117 Strong and Theodore Cohen, *The Marriage and Family Experience: ...*, 483.

118 P.C. Glick and A. J. Norton, "Divorce and Age at Marriage," in Journal of Marriage and Family 33/6 (1971): 307.

119 R. Leete, *Population Trends* (London: HMSO, 1976), 33.

120 Jack Dominian, "Factors which Contribute to Marital Difficulties," in *Celebrating Christian Marriage*, edited by Adrian Thatcher (Edinburgh: T&T Clark Ltd., 2001), 165.

121 Strong and Cohen, *The Marriage and Family Experience ...*, 484.

122 Hill Kulu, "Premarital Cohabitation and Divorce: Support for the "Trial Marriage" Theory?" in Demographic Research 23 (Nov. 2010): 881.

123 Cohabiters may have unobserved characteristics that make them more prone to separation, such as less conventional attitudes about marriage and higher expectations about the quality of unions or poorer relationship skills. Cited in Kulu, "Premarital Cohabitation and Divorce: Support for the "Trial Marriage" Theory?..., 883.

there is less reason to work at maintaining a relationship that may never have been viewed as a lifelong commitment.[124]

Remarriages

Remarriages are a risk factor for divorce to a great extent because of the complexities of reconstituted families.[125] Remarriages include persons who have already proven that they can divorce; they may be more open to divorce as a solution and more ready to have recourse to it a second time. Moreover, spouses in remarriages may be less willing to compromise and may become disillusioned in the long run. Besides, there may be fewer norms that guide these relationships, making it more difficult for the spouses to feel secure within their respective roles. Furthermore, the structure of remarriage itself is more complex when children are brought in along with ex-spouse and ex-in-laws.[126]

Low Incomes and Poverty

Low income and poverty is another risk factor for divorce because financial stressors often have negative impact on a marital relationship. Economic hardships and problems affect family life adversely since the two are interdependent.[127] Overall, socio-economic status is inversely related to the likelihood of divorce. People in low status occupation with less education and less income are more likely to divorce than compared to people with high status occupations, more educated and more income. Earlier, it was assumed that higher status occupational groups had higher divorce rates. Nevertheless, William Goode in his survey found the opposite.[128] A plausible explanation on the high rate of divorce among the lower socio-economic population is the amount of chronic stress from economic pressure the couples face.

Growing Secularization

Writers such as Goode and C. Gibson argue that the growing secularization has resulted in marriage becoming less of a sacred, spiritual union and more of personal and practical commitment, which can be abandoned if it fails. Evidence

---

124 For instance, Homann-Morriott (2006) reports that couples who cohabit have somewhat less positive problem solving behaviours and are less supportive of each other on average than those who have not cohabited before marriage. Therefore, it cannot be said that cohabitation necessarily constitutes a "trial" marriage because of the lower levels of commitment. However, many such less committed couples move on to marriage, and may not be ready for the required commitment. As a result divorce may follow. Cited Ane-Marie Ambert, *Divorce: Facts, Causes & Consequences*, 3rd edn (Ontario: York University, 2009), 15.

125 Ambert, *Divorce: Facts, Causes & Consequences...*, 14.

126 Ambert, *Divorce: Facts, Causes & Consequences...*, 12.

127 Pothen, Divorce: Its Causes and Consequence..., 136.

128 Helen J. Raschke, "Divorce," in *Handbook of Marriage and the Family*, edited by Suzanne K. Steimetz and Marvin B. Sussman (New York: Plenum Press, 1987), 603.

for this lies in the fact that more than 60 percent of marriages no longer involve a religious ceremony. Many people opt for marriages outside the church and do not attach much religious significance to their marriages.[129]

Rapid Social Mobility

A very rapid upward social mobility where the acquisition of money and status is a prime mover is also a risk factor for marital stability. One of the reasons may be because such a pursuit of materialism takes time away from relationships or reflects individualistic values that are incompatible for a good conjugal life. Migration as a major life event can have a divorce-inducing effect, especially since one of the spouses can benefit from the move than the other.[130] Couples with strong social ties have a network of family and friends who provide support during difficult times and who express disapproval for behaviour that threatens the stability of the marriage. Andrew J. Cherlin explains, "Moving from one community to another could affect marriages because it disrupts social ties. Migration can separate people from friends and relatives who could help them through family crisis."[131]

Dowry

Dowry becomes a hindrance in marital happiness and in many cases, it leads to divorce. Mabel Fonseca who had studied marital disruption in Mumbai found that dowry was also a cause of marital disorganization, discord, and desertion.[132] Rama Mehta also found that dowry is an important issue in marital discord where women go through a lot of cruelty in the hands of their husbands and laws. In some cases, women are even forced to leave if they fail to meet the demands of their husbands and in-laws.[133]

Child Marriage

During the Vedic period, it was obligatory to have a girl child married before she attains puberty. The age of marriage was still lowered further in the Brahminical period. In spite of the Child Marriage Restraint Act, 1929 child marriage persists even in postmodern times.[134] It is still common in many communities especially in the lower strata of the Indian society. Children are married even before they

---

129 Ken Brown, *Introducing Sociology for AS Level*, second edition (Cambridge: Polity Press, 2006), 76.

130 Juho Harkonen, *Divorce: Trends, Patterns, Causes, Consequences* (Stockholm: Wiley-Blackwell, 2013), 15.

131 Andrew J. Cherlin, *The Marriage-go-round* (New York: Knopf Doubleday Publishing Group, 2009), 148, 149. Also cited by Linda A. Mooney, David Knox and Carline Schacht, *Understanding Social Problems*, ninth edition (Stamford: Cengage Learning, 2015), 152.

132 Mabel Fonseca, *Counselling for Marital Happiness* (Bombay: Manaktalas, 1966), 82.

133 Mehta, *Divorced Hindu Women...*, 40.

134 K. D. Gangrade, *Social Legislation in India*, vol. 1 (New Delhi: Concept Publishing Company (p) Ltd. 2011), 29.

understand the meaning of marriage. Since a young child has no definite sense, ideal, values, purpose, or interest in marriage when he/she grows, these things become clear to them and they develop a personality and identity of their own. Therefore, one spouse chosen in childhood may be unsuitable and irrelevant, if the other spouse has much disparity in education, training, enlightenment, and employment. Moreover, in child marriage the boy and the girl do not stay together until gauna is performed. In this long gap of separation, one spouse may develop interest and attachment to someone else.[135]

Rising Expectations of Marriage

A greater emphasis is now placed on mutual feeling of love and fulfilment than on obligations to marriage vows, family life, and children. More and more people are becoming individualistic and there is a tendency to focus on one's self-interests and personal happiness rather than on the interest of one's family and community. "Marital commitment lasts only as long as people are happy and feel that their own needs are being met."[136] Belief in the right to be happy, even if it means getting divorced is reflected in the attitudes towards divorce.[137] Before 1970, the law required a couple who wanted a divorce to prove that one of the spouses was at fault and had committed an act defined by the state as grounds for divorce such as adultery, cruelty or desertion.[138]

Functionalists argue that the divorce rate has risen because couples particularly women expect and demand more in their relationships today than their parents or grandparents might have settled for. The higher expectations mean couples are more likely to end a relationship when such expectations are not met.[139] The growing privatization and isolation of the nuclear family from extended kin and the community takes a toll on marital relationships. Psychologist Eli Finkel points out that people's expectations and ideals for marriage have been raised higher, so high in fact that they require a greater investment of time and energy to reach and realize. When a person is unable to invest the needed attention and energy, he/she may be unable to achieve the kind of idealized marriage giving a sense of failure to the marriage. Finkel refers to "the all-or-nothing" marriage, tracing its emergence to the transition from institutional marriage to companionate marriage and ultimately individualized marriage.[140]

135 Pothen, *Divorce: Its Causes and Consequences...*, 141.

136 Paul Amato, "Divorce in Social and Historical Context: Scientific Views," in Journal of Marriage and the Family 66/4 (November 2004): 960.

137 Mooney, David Knox and Caroline Schacht, *Understanding Social Problems...*, 152.

138 Mooney, David Knox and Caroline Schacht, *Understanding Social Problems...*, 152.

139 *Cited in Brown, Introducing Sociology for AS Level...*, 76.

140 *Cited in Strong and Cohen, The Marriage and Family Experience ...*, 302.

Increase in Work and Family Demands/Unequal Division of Labour

Traditionally, the role of women has been tied to bearing and raising children. However, women's education and employment opportunities are increasing in absolute term as well as relative to men. The flip side of women's increased involvement in work and earning results in women being burdened by increased demands from both work and family and are caught in the middle. This is another possible contributing factor to divorce. A research done by Robert Schoen, Stacy Rogers and Amato to investigate whether or not changes in work and family demands have affected marital quality, they compared two generations of married couples and found that the younger generation reported more marital discord compared to the older couples and this was explained by greater conflict related to balancing increased demands from work and family.[141]

Another cause of divorce is perceived inequities in the division of labour at home. Relationship strain arises because of the inequalities and power differential inherent in traditional gender roles. One particular source of stress for women is the unequal division of labour. The increased demands of work and family that accompanied the rise in women's participation in the workforce contributed to a higher divorce rate. The result of a study indicates that, among dual earner couples, perceived unfairness in the division of household labour is associated with more marital unhappiness for both husbands and wives, with a higher risk of divorce. The research suggests that perceptions of an unfair division of household labour not only decrease women's marital quality but also leads to role strain that makes them more likely to end unsatisfying marriages.[142] This perception of unfairness can lead to marital tension, resentment, and divorce.[143]

Intergenerational Transmission

One of the effects of parental divorce on children is an increased risk for marital distress and divorce termed as the intergenerational transmission of divorce because the risk for divorce is said to transmit to their offspring. Children of divorced parents have a divorce rate between 1.5 to 2 times higher compared to children from intact marriages. Social and behavioural scientists have identified a number of reasons for the intergenerational transmission of divorce including the

141 Robert Schoen, Stacy J Rogers and Paul Amato, "Wives' Employment and Spouses' Marital Happiness: Assessing the Direction of Influence Using Longitudinal Couple Data," in Journal of Family Issues 27/4 (April, 2006): 514.

142 Clarke-Steward and Cornelia Brentano, *Divorce: Causes and Consequences…*, 45.

143 Many parents particularly employed mothers come home to work a second shift, in caring for children and household chores. Wives are more likely then husbands to perceive the marital division of labor as unfair. Women want to be equal partners in their marriages, not just in earning income but also in sharing the work of household chores, child rearing, and marital communication and in making decisions for the family. Mooney, David Knox and Caroline Schacht, *Understanding Social Problems…*, 151.

genetic transmission of traits associated with marital instability, socio-economic factors, the social learning of poor communication skills and negative marital attitudes and imprudent mate selection by offspring of divorced parents.[144] Divorce in the first generation results in lower education and poorer relationships including divorce in the second generation. Moreover, the children of first generation divorce also manifested poorer parent-child relationships.[145] In fact, Amato and Alan Booth found that adult children's recollections of their parent's turbulent marriage mediated about half of the second generation's accounts of their own marital problems.[146]

The risk of divorce increases dramatically, if both the husband and wife's parents have been divorced. Sociologist Nicholas Wolfinger rightly states that when both spouses are children of divorces, their risk of divorce is three times greater than if neither children are of divorced parents. Both men and women contribute equally to intergenerational transmission.[147] Amato and Bruce Keith have noted that children of divorced parents are more likely to marry at younger age, cohabit, and experience higher levels of economic hardship. They become more pessimistic about lifelong marriage and develop more liberal attitudes toward divorce.[148] The increase in probability of a marriage ending in divorce could also be due to the difficulties the child experienced with their parents' divorce. If children see their parents' marriage eventually ending in divorce, they could assume that divorce is the way every marriage ends.[149] One study has even found that this occurs especially when the parental marriage had a low level of conflict, such parents may end marital relationships simply because they are less committed to marriage and may transmit this value to their offspring.[150] All these factors could raise susceptibility to divorce.

Premarital Pregnancy

There is also persistent evidence that premarital pregnancy is related to a higher rate of divorce. Research results have repeatedly shown that premarital pregnancy is associated with a higher rate of divorce. The most important factors explaining

144 Segrin, "Intergenerational Transmission of Divorce," in *Cultural Sociology of Divorce...*, 576.

145 Paul R. Amato and Jacob Cheadle, "The Long Reach of Divorce: Divorce and Child Well-being Across Three Generations," in Journal of Marriage and Family 67/1 (2005): 191.

146 Paul R. Amato, "The Impact of Family Formation Change on the Cognitive, Social and Emotional Well-Being of the Next Generation," in The Future of Children 15/2/ (fall, 2015): 76.

147 Strong and Cohen, *The Marriage and Family Experience ...*, 484.

148 Paul R. Amato and Bruce Keith, "Parental Divorce and the Well-Being of Children: A Meta-Analysis," in Psychological Bulletin 110/1 (1991): 29.

149 Amato and Bruce Keith, "Parental Divorce and the Well-Being of Children ..., 29.

150 Ambert, *Divorce: Facts, Causes & Consequences...*, 14-15.

these results include short periods of courtship and lack of preparation for family life.[151]

Sexual Dissatisfaction

Sex is an important aspect of marital union and its non-fulfilment causes serious repercussion in marital adjustment. If spouses are unable to establish satisfying sexual relationship, marriage is in danger. Sexual relationship is not merely a physical activity but includes other factors such as physical, psychological, and emotional aspects. In a study done by S. Pothen, it is found that among many other factors responsible for serious conflicts between spouses, one of the most important factors was sexual maladjustment.[152] Sexual needs is one of the inherent basic needs of couples and marital relations. Abraham Maslow puts this need among the basic survival needs. It can be said that although a happy marital life is partly related to the sexual relation, this relationship may be the main cause of happiness or lack of happiness in marital life. If sexual needs are not met, it may lead to feelings of deprivation, frustration, and lack of safety leading to disintegration of the family. Impotency and frigidity of either party to consummate marriage pose danger for the couple, which may eventually lead to divorce.

Extra Marital Affair/Infidelity

Extra marital relation is a major cause of marital disruption. According to a survey conducted by the British National Survey of Sexual Attitudes and Lifestyle, "extramarital sex is considered always or mostly wrong by 79 percent of men and 84 percent of women."[153] An extramarital relationship may be a symptom of an unhappy relationship and provide the proverbial "last straw" in the decision to divorce, or it may be the cause of the marital breakdown. Even happy relationship can be ended by a casual, meaningless one-night stand. The sense of betrayal, hurt and mistrust on discovering a spouse's infidelity undermines the marriage and results in divorce. Infidelity can be so profoundly humiliating and hurtful that it not only raises the possibility of divorce but leads to major depression and anxiety, which further destroys the marriage.[154] "Infidelity is a Trojan horse that gets inside relationships based on love and destroys them. Now that marriage is focused on the bond between two people and their mutual happiness, having an affair is a direct attack on the premise of their relationship," says Abigail Trafford.[155]

---

151 Guttman, *Divorce in Psychosocial Perspective...*, 27.

152 Pothen, *Divorce: Its Causes and Consequences*..., 140.

153 Cited in Wendy Stainton Rogers and Rex Stainton Rogers, *The Psychology of Gender and Sexuality: An Introduction* (Berkshire: Open University Press, 2004), 187.

154 Clarke-Steward and Cornelia Brentano, *Divorce: Causes and Consequences*..., 45

155 Abigail Trafford, *Crazy Time: Surviving Divorce* (New York: Harper and Row Publishers, 1974), 89.

Infertility

Infertility or barrenness may also lead to divorce. Husband and wife may blame each other for their childlessness. In some instances, the attitudes and behaviour of parents and in-laws become an important aspect of the problem, particularly when the desire for children is strong. The Hindu philosophy stressed on the necessity for a couple to have children. If a married woman does not bear children, she is deprived of sacramental rights in social life. In fact, in Hindu philosophy having a child is considered a fundamental biological need fulfilled through marriage.[156]

Domestic Violence and Abuse

Violence and abuse can take many forms such as physical, sexual, psychological, emotional, and economic. Violence is one of the significant factors causing women to leave marriage and thus contributes to the higher rate of divorce. Since 2000, there has been an increase in the number of studies considering domestic violence as a risk factor for divorce. A number of studies have found that domestic violence is a primary reason given by couples for seeking divorce. Domestic violence is a significant predictor of divorce.[157]

Having discussed the causes of divorce, the subsequent discussion deals with the psychosocial wellbeing of divorced women.

Psychosocial Wellbeing

Many researchers and scholars consider divorce as a major life-changing event with many negative impacts that require a significant redefinition of life. It produces a range of effects on the overall wellbeing of the individuals. These transitions have been shown to create a wide range of effects. The prevalence of divorce in today's society makes it imperative to thoroughly investigate the wellbeing of the divorcees. A number of researchers have found that divorcees suffer from economic hardships, poorer health, experience more depression, less happy and less satisfied with life, divorce may significantly benefit some others in their health and wellbeing especially those in abusive and unsatisfying/unhappy marriages and in achieving goals not attainable while married. Nonetheless, divorce changes individuals and their life situations. There is a need to explore and understand how divorced women cope and adjust to their post-divorce lives.

Howard Clinebell had written insightfully on wellbeing in his book, *Well Being: A Personal Plan for Exploring and Enriching the Seven Dimensions of Life.* His seven dimensions include spiritual wellbeing, mental wellbeing, physical wellbeing, relationship wellbeing, work wellbeing, play wellbeing, and the wellbeing of the world, which are inherently interconnected and intertwined.

156 Choudhary, *Divorce in Indian Society...*, 55-56.

157 Sandra M. Smith and Kyle C. Horst, "Domestic Violence," in *Cultural Sociology of Divorce: An Encyclopaedia*, vol.1 edited by Robert E. Emery (California: Sage Publications, 2013), 397.

All seven dimensions are important and have implications for divorced women's wellbeing.

First, spiritual wellbeing is about "wholeness nurturing spirituality involves enjoying a growing intimacy with the divine spirit of love and liberation."[158] It incorporates healthy religious beliefs, practices, values and institutions that energize and enrich all aspects of human's life. This dimension addresses an individual's need for purpose, guidance, meaning, and values. *Second*, mental wellbeing represents the profound interdependence of the mind and body that manifests itself on the mental and physical health. Mental wellbeing incorporates problem solving, creativity, clarity in thinking, service, and productivity. *Third*, physical wellbeing reflects the physical health which is evidenced by the ability to experience situations without pain, to effectively function with adequate energy, to be responsible for caring oneself and to nurture other areas of wellbeing such as mental and spiritual wellbeing. *Fourth*, relationship wellbeing represents the most important factor for healing and general wellness. This dimension incorporates the need for nurturing and love, for giving and receiving, for empowering others and for creating interpersonal bonds without which a person's entire wellbeing suffer. Establishing loving relationships enhance higher wellness levels. In order to enhance wellness and healing, "love needs to embody mutual respect, integrity, open communication, and mutual commitment to each other's full becoming."[159] *Fifth*, work wellbeing includes that satisfies the thirst for purpose. This dimension addresses the need for fulfilling a purpose in one's vocation. Self-worth, satisfaction, and personal fulfilment are all related to the individual's ability to serve the community in a meaningful way. *Sixth*, play wellbeing acknowledges that play provides the individual with laughter, cheer, energy and balance. It is the ability to successfully play that provides the needed healing and revitalization to meet the demands of other dimensions. *Finally*, wellbeing of our world reflects an individual's perspective in living in a healthy environment and protecting natural resources. This final dimension incorporates a broad overview of the world, a desire for wellbeing for all, adequate health care, interdependence, political participation, and the recognition of institutions as potential resources for meeting needs beyond the self.[160]

These seven dimensions are holistic and provide a framework for exploring various aspects of health and wellbeing including the multifaceted individual and perspectives of the world. According to Clinebell, "wholeness and wellbeing is not the absence of brokenness. Instead it is what you choose, at the center of your life, to do with your brokenness."[161] Taking a cue from Clinebell's understanding

158 Howard Clinebell, *Well Being: A Personal Plan for Exploring and Enriching the Seven Dimensions of Life* (San Francisco: Harper San Francisco, 1992), 7.

159 Clinebell, *Well Being: A Personal Plan for Exploring and Enriching...*, 8.

160 Clinebell, *Well Being: A Personal Plan for Exploring and Enriching...*, 7.

161 Clinebell, *Well Being: A Personal Plan for Exploring and Enriching...*, 4.

of wellbeing this section examines the impact on the overall wellbeing of divorced women encompassing multidimensional areas such as physical, mental, psychological/emotional, social, economic, and spiritual/religious wellbeing. This multidimensional approach is crucial because divorce touches all aspects of a person's life.

Physical Wellbeing

Traditionally, health has been defined negatively only as the absence of disease or illness. This notion of health as a disease-free state was based on the assumption that health and disease were objective and observable phenomena. This understanding of health leads to the development of anatomy, bacteriology, and physiology. Health was therefore defined solely in terms of absence of disease, symptoms and signs or problems.[162] With the definition of the WHO, health came to be viewed in a more positive and holistic understanding and not just absence of illness or infirmities but a state of wellbeing in which physical health is only one aspect.

During the 1960s and 1970s, ecological and relative notion of health emerged, a perspective different from the traditional and holistic approach. This perspective conceives health as a more relative concept and gives greater emphasis on the interrelationships between the environment and the individual's quality of life based on an evaluation of a person's level of functioning and adaptation to the environment. Health is seen as an adequate functional capacity, which allows an individual to carry out one's duties and responsibilities or in terms of certain quality of life, which enables a person to live happily, successfully, fruitfully and creatively.[163] This definition is based on the understanding that the natural environment is essential to support life, health, and wellbeing. There has been no consensus among scholars in defining health, however data from studies of children and adolescents suggests that health is essentially defined in four major notions such as "Health Practices," "Not Being Sick," "Feeling Good" and "Being Able to Do the Desired and/or Required Activities."[164]

Marital status and health have attracted research interest for many years with the earlier studies focusing on different mortality rates of married and unmarried adults. Many scholars have tried to establish the mechanism between marital status and health. Two major theories that have been used for understanding better health among married adults are marriage protection theory and marriage selection theory. The former posits that marriage is health protective through varied pathways including social regulation, social integration, and greater economic resources. Married people have more advantages in economic resources,

162 Evely Boruchovitch and Brigitte R. Mednick, "The Meaning of Health and Illness: Some Consideration for Health Psychology," in Psico-USF 7/2 (July-December, 2002): 176.

163 Boruchovitch and Brigitte R. Mednick, "The Meaning of Health and Illness…, 176.

164 Boruchovitch and Brigitte R. Mednick, "The Meaning of Health and Illness…, 177.

social and psychological support, and support for healthy lifestyle.[165] Marriage strengthens social integration, provides a source of instrumental support for tasks like household chores and increase economic resources. The presence of a spouse may also discourage risky behaviour.[166] Protection theory also suggests reduction in behaviours that are detrimental to health such as smoking, heavy drinking, and substance abuse by providing social and psychological support.[167] The latter theory posits that healthier people get married and remain married whereas less healthy people either do not get married or are more prone to separation or divorce.[168] Spouses are selected into marriage based on the absence of physical and mental disability and also on the range of health related characteristics such as emotional stability, risk taking personality, income, and physical appearance.[169] Noreen Goldman contends that "spouses may be selective for better health not only through the direct exclusion of mentally and physically ill persons from marriage, but also through a wide range of selection criteria including income, physical appearance, risk-taking behaviour, health related habits such as smoking and excessive drinking and emotional stability."[170] Most researchers conclude that there is a protection as well as selection model associated with marriage and health.

Many theorists suggest that marital dissolution is the most devastating life stressor and divorce takes a toll on the physical health. It is a stressful process that, beyond the termination of a long-term relationship, includes the impact it has on children, involvement of family and friends and societal disapproval. These factors may easily exacerbate loneliness, distress, damage to self-esteem and stress brought on by the dissolution of the relationship.[171] According to Amato, divorce is correlated with higher health and mortality risk. However, the link between divorce and mortality is highly co-relational, it is difficult to say with absolute certainty whether those who are at risk tend to get divorced or that unhealthy individuals or those with propensities for high risk behaviours such as smoking, drinking, risk taking are more likely to get divorced. A third alternative might be that divorce eliminates stress-buffering factors that promote good health,

---

165 Megan Beckett and Marc N. Elliot, "Does the Association Between Marital Status and Health Vary by Sex, Race, and Ethnicity?" in *Labor and Population Program*, Working Paper Series 02-08 (September, 2002): 3.

166 Beckett and Marc N. Elliot, "Does the Association Between Marital Status..., 5-6.

167 Lee A. Lillard and Linda J. Waite, "Till Death Do Us Apart: Marital Disruption and Mortality," in The American Journal of Sociology 100/5 (March, 1995): 1131-1132.

168 Charlotte A. Schoenborn, "Marital Status and Health: United States, 1999-2002," in Advance Data from Vital and Health Statistics Number 351 (December 15, 2004): 3.

169 Heather L. Koball et al, "What Do We Know About the Link Between Marriage and Health," in Journal of Family Issues 31/8 (2010): 1019.

170 Noreen Goldman, "Marriage Selection and Mortality Patterns: Inferences and Fallacies," in Demography 30/2 (1993): 190.

171 Erber and Maureen Wang Erber, *Intimate Relationships: Issues, Theories, and Research*..., 270.

life enhancing, health-promoting force that provides them with life support mechanism.[172]

Numerous studies have shown advantages of being married on health of an individual and that married adults have lower rates of mortality, morbidity, and mental disorders relative to divorced or widowed. Recent literatures have found that household composition and living arrangements associated with marital status may partially explain the differences in health status among various marital status groups.[173] A number of studies have found that compared to married women, divorced women have more health problems and higher death rates. Unhappiness and stress increase over time for people who get divorced. However, decrease in physical wellbeing actually begins even before the divorce.[174] These studies support the idea that divorce itself and the immediately preceding period of time cause much of the distress leading to physical health problems.

Research from a large sample of divorcing Norwegian suggests marital dissolution as a cause of stress and poor health. This study also provides support which proposes that poorly adjusted individuals whose personality characteristics predispose them to be relationship risk are more likely to get divorced.[175] Arne Mastekaasa has found dramatic increase in stress and decline in feelings of subjective wellbeing. However, even well adjusted and healthy people get divorced.[176] According to Anson, marriage offers protective factors that promote health and longevity and proposed three health benefits of marriage. *First*, marriage provides social integration through social ties that satisfy intimacy needs. *Second*, marriage provides clearer social roles for couples, which in turn lead to reductions in risk taking and other unhealthy behaviours. *Third*, it bestows higher social status. Thus, divorce has combined effect of increased stress level and the elimination of the protective benefits of marriage. Even in cases where divorce is amicable, couples lose marriage's mortality protection. Thus, because of added stress along with the elimination of positive buffering agents, divorce has detrimental effects on health and wellbeing.[177] Divorce weakens health and longevity. It also increases behavioural, emotional, and psychiatric risks including suicide.[178] A consistent

172 Cited in Erber and Maureen Wang Erber, *Intimate Relationships: Issues, Theories, and Research…*, 269.

173 Manoj K. Pandey, "Association Between Marital Status and Health: Examining the Role of Age and Gender," in *ASARC Working Paper* (2009/10): 3.

174 Gene H. Starbuck and Karen Soucier Lundy, *Families in Context: Sociological Perspective* (New York: Routledge, 2016), 420.

175 Erber and Maureen Wang Erber, *Intimate Relationships: Issues, Theories, and Research …*, 270.

176 Arne Mestekaasa, "Marriage and Psychological Well-being: Some Evidence on Selection into Marriage," in Journal of Marriage and the Family 2/2 (July, 2005): 907.

177 Cited in Erber and Maureen Wang Erber, *Intimate Relationships…*, 270.

178 Patrick F. Fagan and Aaron Churchill, *The Effects of Divorce on Children* (Washington D.C: Research Synthesis, 2012), 2.

finding is that married people enjoy better physical and mental health than those who are not married or divorced. One of the explanations for the link between marriage and health is that healthy people are more likely to marry and less likely to divorce. However, some researchers have suggested that marriage itself seems to improve health. In short, married women are better off than non-married or divorced in terms of physical health and quality of life.

Mental Wellbeing

Traditionally, mental wellbeing has been defined by a lack of symptom distress such as depression, anxiety and other symptoms of mental disorder neglecting aspects of positive functioning.[179] However, over the years, the term has taken a more positive definition. According to the WHO, mental health is, "a state of well-being in which every individual realizes his or her own potential, can cope with the normal stresses of life, can work productively and fruitfully, and is able to make a contribution to her or his community."[180] Mental wellbeing has been increasingly recognized as more than just an absence of distressful symptoms but includes positive qualities an individual possess that can lead to mental wellbeing.[181] Corey L. M. Keyes has operationalized mental health as a "syndrome of symptoms of positive feelings and positive functioning."[182] Mental health is also the presence of sufficiently high levels of wellbeing that constitutes the condition, which he calls "flourishing" mental health.[183] These definitions affirm that mental health is a complete state but not merely the absence of mental illness.

Carol D. Ryff and Keyes have proposed a theoretical model of mental wellbeing encompassing six distinct dimensions of wellness: Self-Acceptance is a positive evaluation of oneself or a positive regard a person has for oneself. Personal Growth is a sense of continued growth and dynamic process in which the individual perpetually strives to realize personal potential, is open to new experiences and it is a continuous state of development and possibilities as a person. Purpose in Life refers to having an orientation and purpose in life or the belief that one's life is purposeful and meaningful. Positive Relations with Others denotes that an individual is having satisfying and intimate relationships and is able to feel empathy, mutual affection, intimacy, and being interested in the

179 C. L. M Keyes and J. L. Magyar-Moe, "The Measurement and Utility of Adult Subjective Well-being in Positive Psychological Assessment," in *A Handbook of Models and Measures,* edited by S. J. Lopez and C. R. Synder (Washington DC: American Psychological Association, 2003), 422.

180 Summary Report on Promoting Mental Health, Concepts, Emerging Evidence, Practice (World Health Organization, Geneva, 2011), 10.

181 Krista Moe, "Factors Influencing Women's Psychological Well-Being Within a Positive Functioning Framework" (Doctoral Dissertation, University of Kentucky, 2012), 1.

182 Corey L. M. Keyes, "The Mental Health Continuum: From Languishing to Flourishing in Life," in Journal of Health and Social Behaviour 43 (June, 2002): 208.

183 Keyes, "The Mental Health Continuum: From Languishing to Flourishing in Life..., 208.

wellbeing of others. Environmental Mastery is the capacity to manage one's life and the surrounding world effectively. Autonomy refers to the individual's ability to navigate obstacles and completes tasks on his/her own, being independent and self-determined.[184] In order to test the theory, they conducted a confirmatory factor analyses with data from a national representative sample of adults, aged 25 and older, who participated in telephone interviews and validated the proposed multidimensional structure.[185] Thus, they developed a new model of positive functioning and defined it as a multidimensional construct as well as the degree to which individuals perceive themselves to be functioning well in these six major areas of life.

Resonating Ryff and Keyes's model, Marie Jahode observes that positive mental health includes one or more of the following six aspects of individuals: the degree of personal integration achieved by the individual; the degree of autonomy achieved by the person; the adequacy of the person's perception of reality; the degree of environmental mastery achieved by the person; the attitudes shown by the person toward his/her own self; the style and degree of a person's self actualization.[186]

Recent researches have suggested that divorced individuals exhibit more mental health symptoms such as depression and anxiety, more health problems and more substance abuse and have greater risk of mortality.[187] Yet, research on differences in mental health consequences of divorced men and women is ambiguous. M. Gahler has found that women experience lowest mental wellbeing shortly before and after the divorce whereas men experience lowest mental wellbeing after several years post-divorce.[188] L. Strohschenin, P. McDonough, D. Monettec and Q. Shoabhave proposed that losing a marital partner has a greater impact on psychological distress than gaining one; they postulate that mental health responses to marital change are similar for men and women in the short term, but diverge at some point. Men recover at a more rapid rate than women.[189]

184 Carol D. Ryff and Corey Lee M. Keyes, "The Structure of Psychological Wellbeing Revisited," in Journal of Personality and Social Psychology 69/4 (1995): 720.

185 They further proposed the need to probe people's sense of whether their lives have purpose, whether they are realizing their given potential, what is the quality of their ties to others, and if they feel in charge of their own lives. Ryff and Corey Lee M. Keyes, "The Structure of Psychological..., 720.

186 Marie Jahoda, *Current Concepts of Positive Mental Health* (New York: Arno Press, 1980), 23, 24.

187 Paul R. Amato, "Research on Divorce: Continuing Trends and New Developments," in Journal of Marriage & Family 72/3 (June, 2010): 652.

188 Michael Gahler, "Life After Divorce: Economic, Social and Psychological Well-Being Among Swedish Adults and Children Following Family Dissolution," in Swedish Institute for Social Research Reports 2 (1998): 17.

189 L. Strohscheni et al, "Marital Transitions and Mental health: Are There Gender Differences in the Short-Term Effects of Marital Status Change?" in Social Science and Medicine 61/11

However, Amato reports that mental health consequences are comparable for both divorced men and women.[190] Recent studies indicate that declines in mental health associated with divorce do not rebound overtime, perhaps because the divorcees have lost the resources provided by marriage. The persistence of diminished mental health may result from cumulative negative effects of enduring chronic problems such as financial strain and single parenting, which are associated with divorce.[191]

The extent to which marital dissolution undermines mental health also depends on the quality of marital relationship. The negative mental health consequences of divorce are notably weaker for those exiting an unsatisfying and unhappy marriage. In fact, in some cases divorce may boost mental health or at least appears to be no worse than remaining in a long-term toxic marriage. Daniel D. Hawkins and Booth feel that, "Unhappily married people may have greater odds of improving their well-being by dissolving their low-quality unions as there is no evidence that they are better off in any aspect of overall well-being than those who divorce."[192] Pre-existing mental health problems also affect marital disruption. P. Butterworth and B. Rodgers have suggested that in couples where one partner reported poor mental health, greater rates of marital disruption occurred.[193] Terrance Wade and David Pevalin have found that there is a much higher prevalence of mental health problems among the divorced. They also contend that such problems are evident even before the marital disruption indicating that there is a correlation between mental health and divorce and that it goes both ways. Linda Waite and Maggie Gallagher have also found that when people get married there is a substantial improvement in their mental health, but when they divorce their mental health also declines.[194]

Economic resources have positive impact on mental health and the married have more economic resources than the divorced, which is primarily derived from the dual-earning potential of the married. One particular reason that divorce undermines mental health is that marital dissolution typically results in reduced

---

(2005): 2397.

190 Amato, "Research on Divorce: Continuing Trends and New Developments..., 656.

191 Debra Umberson, Mieke Beth Thomeer and Kristi Williams, "Family Status and Mental Health: Recent Advances and Future Directions," in *Handbook of the Sociology of Mental Health,* edited by Carol S. Aneshensel, Jo C. Phelan and Alex Bierman (New York: Springer Science + Business Media, 2013), 410.

192 Daniel H. Hawkins and Alan Booth, "Unhappily Ever After: Effects of Long-Term, Low-Quality Marriages on Well-Being," in Social Forces 84/1 (2005): 445.

193 P. Butterworth and B. Rodgers, "Mental Health Problems and Marital Disruptions: It is the Combination of Husband and Wives' Mental Health Problems That Predicts Later Divorce?" in *Social Psychiatric Epidemiology* 43 (2007): 760.

194 Linda J. Waite and Maggie Gallagher, *The Case for Marriage: Why Married People are Happier, Healthier and Better Off Financially* (New York: Random House Inc., 2000), 65.

economic resources particularly for women.[195] Overall most researchers agree that marriage has positive influence on mental health and that marital dissolution has a negative effect.

Psychological/Emotional Wellbeing

Psychological/emotional consequences of divorce have been confounded with the psychopathological aspects because there can be an overlapping, if these consequences are severe and have the possibility of leading to mental illness. Some scholars put together emotional/psychological and psychopathology consequences in the same category, yet for this study they are treated as conceptually different.

Emotional/psychological wellbeing refers to the "emotional quality of an individual's everyday experience—the frequency and intensity of experiences of joys, stress, sadness, anger and affection that make one's life pleasant or unpleasant."[196] According to E. Diener and R. E. Lucus, "Emotional wellbeing refers to general life satisfaction and positive feelings such as happiness, interest, and pleasure in life."[197]

Sociologists have long recognized the interplay between social structural, social psychological and social factors that contribute to gender and marital status differences in emotional wellbeing. They have produced an impressive body of empirical work on the relationships among marital status, emotion and emotional wellbeing and distress. In fact, marriage, as associated with significantly higher levels of emotional distress, is one of the most oft-cited findings from the sociologies since the 1970s. For instance, studies repeatedly show that the married reported lower levels of generalized distress than their non-married or divorced counterparts do. These positive feelings and greater emotional wellbeing of married women is attributed by most sociologists to social causation. On the contrary, social selection hypothesis posits that persons who enjoy more frequent positive feelings and higher levels of emotional wellbeing are more likely than persons who experience more frequent distress to become or remain married in the first place.[198] In the past two decades, sociologists have evaluated the social causation and selection hypotheses by assessing degree to which marital status transitions result in changes in emotion. Several longitudinal studies suggest that getting married results in a significant decrease in negative feelings as well as symptoms of

195 A. M. Shapiro, "Explaining Psychological Distress in a Sample of Remarried and Divorced Persons," in Journal of Family Issues 17 (1996): 190.

196 Daniel Kahneman and Ashton Acton, "Issues in General Science and Scientific Theory and Method: 2011 Edition," in *Proceedings of the National Academy of Sciences* 107/38 (September, 2010): 1.

197 E. Diener and R.E. Lucus, "Personality and Subjective Well-being," in *Annual Review of Psychology* 54 (1991): 403.

198 R. W. Simon, "Mental Health and Emotions," in *Handbook on the Sociology of Emotions: Volume 2*, edited by Jan E. Stets and Jonathan H. Turner (Heidelberg: Springer Science + Business Media, 2012), 433.

depression whereas being divorced and widowed results in a significant increase in negative feelings and experience emotional distress.[199] These findings clearly support the social causation hypothesis of the relationship between marital status and emotional wellbeing.

On the other hand, there are also some supports for the social selection argument. For instance, based on national data, Robin W. Simon has found that persons who reported more symptoms of depression were significantly more likely to experience subsequent divorce than persons who reported fewer symptoms of emotional distress.[200] This and other findings indicate that complex social causation and selection processes are both involved in the relationship between marriage and emotional health.

Blair Wheaton has found that under certain condition that is high level of chronic marital stress, divorce or widowhood actually improve emotional health. He argues that for this group of people, divorce or widowhood represents "stress relief."[201] It is possible that non-married adults are less distressed than persons in highly stressful and or dissatisfying marriages offering escape from chronically stressful situations. Moreover, persons who are single by choice may enjoy the same level of emotional wellbeing as their married counterparts. In a study conducted by Bharti Sharma on the relationship between divorce and its impact on emotional health with passage of time and its effect on different age groups suggests that both older and younger women experience enormous amount of anxiety and depression.[202] The findings are in consistence with earlier studies suggesting that divorce is a stressful experience and puts an immense amount of strain on divorced women. The breakup of conjugal relationship is more distressing for women as they feel that they defy the norms set by the society. Divorce thus leads to lower self-esteem in women and hinders their ability to become positive role models often accompanied by feelings of helplessness, anger, depression, guilt, loneliness, and other negative emotions. Women whose self-esteem gets affected start to think that this happened to her only because she is not a good person, which leads to self-destruction and in turn leads to depression and feelings of anger and insecurity.[203] J. F. Hilliwell and R. D. Putman have found that the status of marriage was significantly associated with emotional

---

199 Jennifer Caputo and Robin W. Simon, "Physical Limitation and Emotional Wellbeing: Gender and Marital Status Variations," in Journal of Health and Social Behaviour 54/2 (2013): 242.

200 Robin W. Simon, "Revisiting the Relationship among Gender, Marital Status and Mental Health," in American Journal of Sociology 107/4 (January 2002): 1068.

201 Blair Wheaton, "Life Transitions, Role Histories and Mental Health," in American Sociological Review 55/2 (April 1990): 210.

202 Sharma "Mental and Emotional Impact of Divorce on Women..., 129.

203 Sharma "Mental and Emotional Impact of Divorce on Women ..., 130.

wellbeing and being divorced or widowed showed negative connections to life satisfaction.[204]

Research on the emotional wellbeing of divorced women reveals inconsistent findings. On life-stress indices, divorce is second only to death of a spouse in its potential impact.[205] Although, signs of emotional distress are indicated by both sexes following divorce, women experience significantly greater stress than men do. The relationship between low emotional status and mental and physical illness has been well documented. Many studies have concluded that most divorced women experience moderate to high levels of emotional distress at some point. Divorced women are more likely to have fears of an impending nervous breakdown, more likely to seek psychotherapy and less satisfied with their lives.[206] Divorced women especially with custodial children have consistently been found to experience higher rates of depression and psychiatric illness relative to married women.[207]

Several writers have attempted to theorize about divorce effect on psychological wellbeing including social scientists. There is a growing literature on the relationship of marital status to psychological wellbeing and a substantial number of empirical studies show the effects of marital disruption, particularly women. Many scholars suggest that divorce is associated with increased level of psychological distress, lower levels of psychological wellbeing including lower happiness, more symptoms of psychological distress and poorer self-concepts.

Divorce undermines psychological wellbeing because losing a spouse is stressful and is often accompanied by financial hardships especially for women.[208] Amato also asserts that "Compared with married, divorced individuals experience more psychological distress, poorer self-concepts, lower levels of psychological well-being, lower levels of happiness, more social isolation, less satisfying sex lives, and more negative life events."[209] Kristi Williams and Alexander Dunne-Bryant have posited that the impact of marital dissolution on psychological wellbeing varies by whether or not women have young children and that the negative consequences

---

204 J. F. Helliwell and R. D. Putman, "The Social Context of Wellbeing," in International Journal of Wellbeing 1/2 (2004): 359.

205 Martha B. Straus, "Divorced Mothers," in *The Different Faces of Motherhood*, edited by Beverly Birns and Dale Hay (New York: Springer Science + Business Media, 1988), 229.

206 Straus, "Divorced Mothers…, 229.

207 Clark-Stewart and Brentano, *Divorce: Causes and Consequences…*, 27.

208 Cited in Hyeyoung Woo, "Parental Status and Psychological Wellbeing Among Midlife Adult Women Using the Life Course Perspective" (Doctor of Philosophy Dissertation, The University of Texas, Austin, 2008), 43.

209 Paul R. Amato, "The Consequences of Divorce on Adults and Children" in Journal of Marriage and Family 62/4 (November 2000): 1272.

of marital dissolution are greater for women with young children.[210] Noncustodial mothers, whether voluntary or involuntary face difficulties following separation from their children, such as isolation, loneliness, guilt, depression, and rejection. Even voluntary noncustodial mothers are likely to feel rejected by their children and worry about the long-term effects of their decision on the development of the children.[211] Thus, divorce impact negatively on the emotional wellbeing particularly for women.

Social Wellbeing

The positive link between marriage and physical and psychological wellbeing is well founded, but there has been a paucity of research on whether or not marriage is associated with social wellbeing. Although, many studies have been done on social wellbeing using objective criteria, objective and societal-level indicators such as Gross Domestic Product (GDP) and behavioural measures such as community or organizational participation and membership, which reflect only the relative propensity of communities and societies, generally operationalize it. Measuring social wellbeing as individual or subjective perceptions level has not been given much attention.[212]

The study of individual perception level of social wellbeing is based on the premise that there is a distinction between public and private life with each having its own requests and challenges. While the leading conceptions of human functioning portray wellbeing primarily as a private phenomenon through measures of depression, distress and anxiety, individuals are embedded and integrated in social structures and community and face numerous social tasks and challenges. Hence, inclusion of social wellbeing becomes imperative in understanding optimal human functioning.[213] Keyes defines social wellbeing as "the appraisal of one's circumstances and functioning in society."[214] He proposes social wellbeing as characterized by five dimensions: Social integration model is the evaluation of the quality of one's relationship to society and community. In other words, it represents a good relation to the community and society that gives the feeling of belongingness. Social acceptance model refers to a positive view on other people and the ability to accept others as they are and believe that others are capable of kindness and that people are industrious. Social contribution refers to the evaluation of one's social value including the belief that one is a vital

---

210 Kristi William and Alexandra Dunne-Bryant, "Divorce and Adult Psychological Well-Being: Clarifying the Role of Gender and Child Age," in Journal of Marriage and Family 68/5 (December 2006): 1179.

211 Guttmann, *Divorce in Psychosocial Perspective: Theory and Research…*, 111.

212 A. Shapiro and Corey Lee M. Keyes, "Marital Status and Social Well-Being: Are the Married Always Better Off?" in Social Indicator Research 8/8 (2008): 33.

213 Corey Lee M. Keyes, "Social Well-Being," in *Social Psychology Quarterly* 61/2 (1998): 122.

214 Keyes, "Social Well-being …, 122.

and valuable member of society with something of value to contribute to the world, a concept akin to efficacy and responsibility. Social actualization implies the belief that society has the potential for positive change. Social coherence is the perception of the quality, organization, and operation of the social world with interest in the social environment and interaction.[215]

The WHO has identified social wellbeing as a key component in an individual's overall health. "Health is a state of complete physical, mental, and social well-being and not merely the absence of disease or infirmity."[216] According to James S. Larson, "the key to deciding whether a measure of social well-being is part of an individual's health is whether the measure reflects internal responses to stimuli—feelings, thoughts and behaviours reflecting satisfaction or lack of satisfaction with the social environment."[217] Similarly, A. Shapiro and Keyes pointed out that, social wellbeing has two faces: social adjustment and social support. The former refers to the subjective satisfaction with relationships or the performance of social roles. The latter refers to the quality and number of persons an individual trusts and can rely and also as the degree to which one is needed and matters to others and society.[218] Thus, social wellbeing can be understood as an individual's appraisal of one's social relationships, how others react to them, and how they interact with social institutions and communities.

Shapiro and Keyes have investigated the influence of marital status and marital history on individual level social wellbeing employing representative samples of adults in the US. The benefits of marriage have been explained through its status as a structural form of social support. "Marriage represents a social contract that bounds individuals together in an intimate relationship that can be stress-buffering and socially integrative."[219] Put it differently, marriage confers social integration to persons providing them with feelings of belonging and purpose. Marriage promotes an individual's sense of social wellbeing.[220] In their attempt to understand the social wellbeing on an individual level, they employed social causation and selection explanations. Social causation or strain/crisis theory suggests that marital status differences in social wellbeing stem from the strains and concomitant network disruptions associated with marital disruption. Divorce is also associated with economic distress especially for women affecting their social participation as many forms of social participation involve money. Married persons are also more socially enmeshed in supportive network than non-

215 Keyes, "Social Well-being ..., 122-123.

216 Frank P. Grad, "Constitution of the World Health Organization," in *Bulletin of the World Health Organization* (2008): 984.

217 James S. Larson, "The Measurement of Social Well-being," in Social Indicators Research 28/3 (1993): 286.

218 Shapiro and Corey Lee M. Keyes, "Marital Status and Social Well-Being..., 331.

219 Shapiro and Corey Lee M. Keyes, "Marital Status and Social Well-Being..., 330.

220 Shapiro and Corey Lee M. Keyes, "Marital Status and Social Well-Being..., 330.

married persons are since marriage represents a social contract and members feel a sense of belonging, purpose, and permanence. The selection explanation suggests that marital status differences in wellbeing are not the result of a casual effect of being married or unmarried, but rather from the differential selection of those individuals with high wellbeing into marriage and those with low wellbeing out of marriage. Since there is an interconnection of physical, psychological and social wellbeing, it is assumed that people with avoidant personalities or with mental or physical illness are more likely to report having problem maintaining social relationships and may lead to perceived lower social wellbeing.[221]

Several studies have been helpful in understanding the selection theory. For instance, Mestekaase has found that subjective wellbeing and life satisfaction predicted the probability of eventual marriage among Norwegians.[222] Additionally, early life experiences associated with social wellbeing has a potential impact on the probability of marriage and divorce. In a study conducted by L. Davis et al. it was found that many divorced women reported history of depression and problematic relations with the family of origin.[223]

Social identity theory posits that establishing a positive social identity fosters a sense of individual wellbeing, reduce depressive symptomatology and enhance self-esteem. Even when an individual's identity is threatened by factors such as stigma, discrimination and violence, which result in numerous negative psychological and physiological stress responses, people who have high social identity, experience least distress.[224] John Donne's infamous line "no [person] is an island" has been widely quoted by many scholars. Sigmund Freud has also asserted the need for interpersonal relationship the motive of which is derived from sex drive and from the filial bond.[225] Maslow in his hierarchy of needs theory has proposed "love and belongingness needs" as one of the needs of hierarchy.[226] Bowlby's attachment theory also suggests the need to form and maintain relationships.[227] Hence, the need to belong is a popular theory among many psychologists and psychotherapists. It is a powerful, fundamental, and

221 Shapiro and Corey Lee M. Keyes, "Marital Status and Social Well-Being..., 333.

222 A. Mastekaasa, "Psychological Wellbeing and Marital Dissolution: Selection Effects," in Journal of Family Issues 12 (1994): 208.

223 L. Davis, W. R. Avison and D. D. McAlpine, "Significant Life Experiences and Depression among Single and Married Mothers," in Journal of Marriage and the Family 59 (1997): 299.

224 Renate Yesseldyk, Kimberly Matheson and Hymie Anisman, "Religiosity and Identity: Toward an Understanding of Religion From a Social Identity Perspective," in *Personal and Social Psychology Review* 12/1 (January, 2010): 64.

225 Sigmund Freud, *New Introductory Lectures on Psycho-Analysis and Other Works*, trans. by James Strachey, vol. xxii (London: The Hogarth Press, 1981), 82.

226 Abraham Maslow, "The Theory of Human Motivation," in *Psychological Review* 50/4 (July 1943): 370.

227 Bowlby, *Loss, Sadness and Depression...*, 41.

extremely pervasive motivation.[228] Unsatisfied needs may lead to pathology including medical and psychological. Thus, "people who lack belongingness exhibit pathological consequences beyond mere temporary distress."[229]

Social support correlates with subjective wellbeing. A research in Israel has found that life satisfaction was higher in people with strong social support network.[230] An individual's social context has a significant impact on the life course and outlook. Social context also involves social and cultural norms and the environmental circumstances of one's immediate community. For instance, divorced women are less adversely affected when they live in communities where divorce is commonplace and consequently socially acceptable. In this way, the social perceptions of the acceptability of divorce may partially determine the impact of divorce on one's psychological and emotional wellbeing. It is also possible that the availability of social support accounts for the influence of the social context.[231] Taken together, these findings suggest that change in social life is one of the most important transitions in the life of adults and establishing social support and engaging in social activities help people compensate for losses associated with divorce.

Almost all the researches have shown loneliness to be a universal human condition experience by divorcees. Their social life is adversely affected especially during the initial period of one to three years following divorce.[232] Social connectedness with family, friends, and neighbours provide a source of companionship and stability, offering protection against negative consequences. Researchers believe that people who experience love and support tend to resist unhealthy behaviours and feel less stressed.[233] Social support offers fellowship and comfort in times of stress, suffering, and sorrow, diminishing the impact of anxiety and other negative emotions.

---

228 Roy F. Baumeister and Mark R. Leary, "The Need to Belong: Desire for Interpersonal Attachments as a Fundamental Human Motivation," in Psychological Bulletin 117/3 (1995): 497.

229 Baumeister and Mark R. Leary, "The Need to Belong..., 497.

230 Duane P. Schultz and Sydney Ellen Schultz, *Theories of Personality* (Boston: Cengage Learning, 2013), 398.

231 Daniel Hickman, "The Social Context of Divorce and Its Impact on Adolescent psychological Well-being" (An Honors Thesis, Cornell University, 2007), 3.

232 Raschke "Divorce," in *Handbook of Marriage and the Family*..., 611.

233 Shobhna Joshi, Shilpa Kumari and Madhu Jain, "Religious Belief and Its Relation to Psychological Well-being," in Journal of the Indian Academy of Applied Psychology 34/2 (July 2008): 349.

Economic Wellbeing

Economic wellbeing has been defined as the financial resources that a family has and the transactions that occur from these finances.[234] P. J. Smock, W. D. Manning and S. Gupta have measured economic wellbeing as amount of personal income and the amount of income that is spent on needs.[235] In the above discussion, it has been noted that socio-economic factors increase the risk of divorce. In turn, divorce also increases the risk of poverty particularly for women. Divorce results in a decline in the standard of living for all parties involved, but the turn down is larger for women than for men.[236]

In spite of the fact that economic status of women had been raised and that many women are increasingly relying on their own earnings, not all married women are economically self-reliant in the event of divorce. Studies of economic wellbeing of divorce come to the forefront as the economic wellbeing of divorced women declines to a great extent. This disparity has been brought into sharp focus by the plight of divorced women during the 1970s and 1980s.[237] Most of the debate around economic consequences of divorce is focused on gender inequalities and the consistent finding from the literature is a sharp gender differences in terms of financial outcomes following marital disruption. Explanations for the gender economic inequalities typically highlight four risk factors for women such as higher economic need and restricted earning capacities in the presence of children; risk of receiving insufficient child support and maintenance; disproportionate loss of income which is usually not fully compensated by spousal maintenance and human capital deficits resulting from gender specific specialization in the division of labour during marriage.[238] Researchers estimate that on an average divorced individuals would need more than 30 percent increase in income to maintain the same standard of living they had prior to divorce.[239]

Many researchers have found that women suffer a drastic drop in their income and standard of living. Lenore J. Weitzman's studies on women who had

234 D. M. Fergusson, L. J. Harwood and A. L. Beautrais, "The Measurement of Family Material Well-being," in Journal of Marriage and the Family 43/3 (1981): 715-725.

235 P. J. Smock, W. D. Manning and S. Gupta, "The Effect of Marriage and Divorce on Women's Economic Wellbeing," in American Sociological Review 64 (1999): 794.

236 Andrea H. Beller and John W. Graham, "Variations in the Economic Well-Being of Divorced and Their Children: The Role of Child Support Income," in *Horizontal Equity, Uncertainty, and Economic Well-Being,* edited by Martin David and Timothy Smeeding (Illinois: University of Chicago Press, 1985), 471.

237 Peterson, Women, Work, and Divorce..., 5.

238 H. J. Andress and M. Brockel, "The Economic Consequences of Divorce in Germany: What has Changed Since the Turn of the Millennium? Comparative Population Studies," in *Comparative Population Studies* 40/3 (2015): 12.

239 Alan J. Hawkins and Tamara A. Fackrell, J. D., *Should I keep Trying to Work it Out: A Guidebook for Individuals and Couples at the Crossroad of Divorce* (Utah: Np, 2009), 109.

been divorced for a year found that women suffer extreme economic crisis in the first year following divorce. This decline is especially severe for women with children, women who were married for longer period of time and women who married men from middle class. While the average divorced women experience a 73 percent drop in her standard of living, divorced men experience a 42 percent increase. Even after making alimony and child support payments, divorced men have more income after divorce than before divorce. Thus, Weitzman rightly concludes that divorce is a major cause of the impoverishment for women and children and that "we may well arrive at a two-tier society with an underclass of women and children."[240]

Other studies confirm Weitzman's conclusions regarding women's economic plight after divorce. It is widely acknowledged that divorce is more common among low-income couples. Yet, even after controlling their initially low income, divorce women are worst off, on average than married women. One National study, The Panel Study of Income Dynamics, has found that fewer than half of divorced women received alimony or child support payments. Even for those who receive payments, it provides for less than half the basic needs of the mother and children. Divorced women especially those with children, are more likely to become poor and remain poor over a period of years. Consequently, divorce typically leads to a dramatic decline in the standard of living especially mother-custody families, pushing them below the poverty line.[241] A recent research done by H. J. Andress and M. Brockel also have reported a similar result in German context where women's household income one year post divorce amount to only two thirds of their former husband's income.[242] Conversely, some studies on long term consisting of women who had been divorced for more than five years suggest that some women achieve at least a partial recovery from the financial disaster post-divorce.[243] Nevertheless, numerous studies have shown that the economic costs of divorce fall more heavily on women. They experience a sharper decline in household income and greater poverty risk.

Richard R. Peterson has explained the effects of divorce using individualist and structural models of labour market outcomes. This approach attempts to consider explicitly the constraints that family roles place on women's work careers. According to him, the effects of divorce on women's work career depend on a woman's work and family history prior to divorce. Pre-divorce work experiences

240 Lenore J. Weitzman, *The Divorce Revolution—The Unexpected Social and Economic Consequences for Women and Children in America* (New York: The Free Press, 1985), 504.

241 Amato and Bruce Keith, "Parental Divorce and Adult Well-Being: A Meta-Analysis...," 43.

242 H. J. Andress and M. Brockel, "Income and Life Satisfaction after Marital Disruption in Germany," in Journal of Marriage and Family 69 (2007): 506.

243 Peterson, *Women, Work, and Divorce...*, 6.

have a strong effect on women's economic outcomes after divorce.[244] Divorce also has a strong and immediate impact on women's labour supply.[245] Rosabeth Kanter also argues that women's greater burden of family responsibilities is a major reason for their disadvantage position in the labour market. Divorced women's work career has been affected by family responsibilities during marriage. After marriage, many women continue to have responsibility to take care of children.[246]

Various studies show that divorced women are being deprived and discriminated with limited access to resources. In both developed and developing countries, female-headed household have different socio-economic and demographic characteristic relative to their male-counterparts. Data across different countries indicate that female-headed families live in poverty.[247] In any given society, feminization of poverty is closely linked to the economic and social policy regime and also trends in women's employment and household headships.[248] "[F]or men, poverty is often the consequence of unemployment and a job is generally an effective remedy, while female poverty often exists even when a woman works full time... Virtually all women are vulnerable—a divorce or widowhood is all, it takes to throw many middle-class women into poverty."[249]

Various studies in Indian context indicate that female-headed families suffer grave economic consequences. For instance, a study done by Institute of Social Study Trust, New Delhi concludes that female-headed households suffer greater economic problems as compared to male-headed families.[250] Thus, there is a general decline in financial position especially for divorced women and they suffer from deprivation and discrimination.

Spiritual/Religious Wellbeing

Spiritual wellbeing is regarded as the fourth dimension of health. In a study on spiritual health, defining and measuring the 4th dimension of health, spiritual health is defined as "a state of being where an individual is able to deal with day-

244 Women who were homemakers and women who have many children find it more difficult to make adjustments to work after divorce. Early decision about work and family has a significant effect on later work and family outcomes, which in turn differentially position women to cope with the effects of divorce. In the event of divorce, women's work histories, not their early life plans, are more important determinants of their ability to support themselves. Peterson, Women, Work, and Divorce..., 106.

245 Peterson, *Women, Work, and Divorce...*, 108.

246 Cited in Peterson, *Women, Work, and Divorce...*, 3.

247 Ranjan Vardhan, "Single-Parent Families and Public Policy," in *Marriage and Family in India,* edited by Jasmeet Sandhu (Jaipur: Rawat Publications, 2016), 238.

248 Valentine M. Moghadam, "The "Feminization of Poverty" and Women's Human Rights," in *Social and Human Sciences* 2 (July, 2005): 6.

249 M. Gimenez, "The Feminization of Poverty: Myth or Reality?" in Insurgent Sociologist 14/3 (1987): 7.

250 Cited in Vardhan, "Single Parent Families and Public Policy..., 240.

to-day life issues in a manner that leads to the realization of one's full potential, meaning and purpose of life and fulfilment from within. Such a state of being is attainable through self-evolution, self-actualisation, and transcendence."[251] In the past few decades, many social scientists have attempted to define, theorize, and study religiousness and spirituality, but the ways in which these two are conceptualized and used are inconsistent in the research literatures. Some scholars have used the term spirituality loosely equating with religious activity while others see religion as one dimension of spirituality. The conceptions of religiousness and spirituality in the social scientific studies are diverse. M. Argyle and B. Beit-Hallahmi define religiousness as "a system of beliefs in a divine or superhuman power and practices of worship or other rituals directed towards such power."[252] Although there have been diversity of opinions regarding religiousness and spirituality, for the purpose of this study, spiritual and religious will be used in a broader concept to mean both personal beliefs and relationship with God and institutional beliefs and activities including attendance at services, performances of rituals, church membership and allegiance etc. encompassing both the personal and the institutional. "An organized belief system that include shared, institutionalized moral values, practices, involvement in a faith community, and for most, beliefs in God or a Higher Power."[253]

Rapson Gomez and John W. Fisher have defined spiritual wellbeing as,

> A state of being, reflecting positive feelings, behaviours, and cognition of relationships with oneself, others, the transcendent and nature, that in turn provide the individual with a sense of identity, wholeness, satisfaction, joy, contentment, beauty, love, respect, positive attitudes, inner peace and harmony, and purpose and direction in life.[254]

There is an increase interest in the study of effects of religion on the psychosocial wellbeing. A number of clinical and epidemiological studies have shown that people who are religiously committed have less psychological distress who handle depression better than the uncommitted ones. Other longitudinal studies have suggested that those who attend religious service regularly leads to less psychological distress and depression in different spheres of life.[255] Persons

251 Neera Dhar, S. K. Chaturvedi and Deoki Nandan, "Spiritual Health, The Fourth Dimension: A Public Health Perspective," in WHO South East Asia Journal of Public Health 2/1 (January-March, 2013): 3.

252 M. Argyle and B. Beit-Hallahmi, *The Social Psychology of Religion* (London: Routledge & Kegan Paul, 1975), 1.

253 F. Welsh, *Spiritual Resources in Family Therapy* (New York: The Guilford Press, 2008), 5.

254 R. Gomes and J. W. Fisher, "Domains of Spiritual Wellbeing and Development and Validation of the Spiritual Well-being Questionnaire," in Personality and Individual Differences 35 (2003): 1976.

255 Joshi, Shilpa Kumari and Madhu Jain, "Religious Belief and Its Relation ..., 345.

with higher spiritual strivings tend to have greater purpose in life, greater personal happiness, better life satisfaction and higher level of wellbeing and a fewer negative psychosocial consequences of traumatic life events.[256] According to Krause and Van Tran, religious involvement is a crucial psychosocial factor that counteracts the adverse effects of stress on feelings of self-esteem and mastery.[257] Similarly, a research conducted by David R. Williams at al. have also suggested that religion is a potent coping strategy that facilitates adjustment to the stress of life.[258] Religious identification and positive psychosocial health is also associated with support from members of the community, which may foster positive outcomes. Supportive communities of believers might fulfill an individual's need for belongingness,[259] which Roy F. Baumerster and Mark R. Leary called a "fundamental human motivation."[260] Besides, individuals also benefit when they accept religion as a guiding belief and principle that offers a worldview entailing life purpose and meaning because these two factors are intertwined that neither faith alone nor communities alone, but rather "communities of faith," fosters the greatest well-being."[261] The relationship between religiousness and mental health has been conceptualized in varied ways. Personal religiousness has been viewed both as a contributor to mental health and as an outcome of one's mental state. Seward Hiltner opines that, "Religion does have a constructive influence for health in the widest and deepest sense."[262] Thus, it is evident that religion plays a significant role on happiness and overall sense of personal wellbeing.

Human beings are spiritual beings. Spirituality can be seen from traditional understanding as an expression of religiosity in search of the sacred. From humanistic point of view, spirituality is seen as devoid of religion. Health is also increasingly seen as having multifaceted dimensions reporting the relationship of spirituality with physical, mental, emotional, social, and vocational wellbeing. In this vein, John Fisher points out that spiritual health is one of the "fundamental dimensions of people's overall health and well-being, permeating and integrating all the other dimensions of health."[263] According to him, spiritual health is a dynamic state of being which is reflected in the quality of relationships that people have in four domains of spiritual wellbeing. First, personal domain in

256 Joshi, Shilpa Kumari and Madhu Jain, "Religious Belief and Its Relation ..., 345.

257 Cited in David R. Williams et al., "Religion and Psychological Distress in a Community Sample," in Social Science and Medicines 32/11 (1991): 1259.

258 Williams et al., "Religion and Psychological Distress in a Community Sample...," 1260.

259 Williams et al., "Religion and Psychological Distress in a Community Sample...," 1260.

260 Baumeister and Mark R. Leary, "The Need to Belong: Desire for Interpersonal Attachments as a Fundamental Human Motivation"..., 499.

261 Williams et al, "Religion and Psychological Distress in a Community Sample...," 1260.

262 Seward Hiltner, *Religion and Health* (New York: The Macmillan Company, 1947), 22.

263 John Fisher, "The Four Domains Model: Connecting Spirituality, Health and Wellbeing," in Religions 2 (2011): 17.

which persons interrelate with the self, such as meaning, purpose, and values in life. Second, communal domain has in-depth interpersonal relationships between self and others including love, justice, hope and family in humanity. Third, environmental domain refers to connecting with the nature for the physical and biological world with a sense of awe, wonder, and unity with the environment. Fourth, transcendental domain is related to something or someone beyond the human relationship level such as cosmic force, transcendent reality, or God and involves faith towards adoration and worship of the source of mystery of the universe.[264] For him, enhancement of spiritual wellbeing depends on developing healthy relationship in each of these domains. In other words, all these four spiritual wellbeing dimensions cohere to determine the global wellbeing of a person.[265] His theoretical model was tested to validate its reliability with a self-rating questionnaire called Spiritual Well-Being Questionnaire. Consistent with the proposed model in his quantitative analysis, Fisher has found that people live with harmony within relationship with oneself (personal), others (communal), nature (environment) and God (or transcendental other).[266]

R. Elliot Ingersoll also has developed spiritual wellbeing as a ten dimensional construct. *First* is the conception of the absolute/divine, which is described as reflecting a personal image or experience of the absolute. The *second* domain is meaning which expresses as a sense that life is worth living and purposeful as well as a sense of being at peace. The *third* domain is connectedness referring to the relationship with other people, God and with the environment. *Fourth*, mystery, this dimension measures a person's comfort level and ways of dealing with the ambiguities and uncertainties of life. Spiritual freedom, the *fifth* domain is associated with the sense of freedom from internal and external compulsions and willingness to make a commitment. *Sixth*, experience/ritual dimension includes healthy spiritual rituals and practices. *Seventh* domain is forgiveness; this dimension shows a person's inclination of giving and receiving forgiveness. The *eighth* dimension is hope, which reflects the person's belief that one's sufferings are not in vain or going to last forever and it reflects the sense of being safe in life. The *ninth* dimension is knowledge/learning, this dimension shows the increased interest in getting knowledge of self and other things in the environment, and the *last* domain is present-centeredness, which depicts one's ability to be aware of the present moment.[267]

As stated earlier, spiritual wellbeing has received much interest in the health care settings as it improves strategies for managing stress and positively

---

264 Fisher, "The Four Domains Model: Connecting Spirituality, Health and Wellbeing…," 17.

265 Gomez and John W. Fisher, "Domains of Spiritual Well-Being and Development...," 1975-1976.

266 Gomez and John W. Fisher, "Domains of Spiritual Well-Being and Development…," 1975.

267 R. Elliott Ingersoll, "Refining Dimensions of Spiritual Wellness: A Cross-Traditional Approach," in Counseling and Values 42 (1998): 157-159.

influence immune, cardiovascular, hormonal and nervous systems.[268] Many researchers have shown that spiritual wellbeing has a number of positive as well as negative impacts. On the positive side, spiritual wellbeing relates to meaningful goals in life, social support, ideal body weight, and psychological and relational scales, it also has an overall life satisfaction. On the negative side, it is related to substance abuse, anxiety, depression and other maladaptive behaviour. These empirical findings highlight the importance of spiritual wellbeing as a practically useful concept. Spiritual wellbeing is conceptualized as a two dimensional construct consisting of both vertical and horizontal. The vertical dimension being an individual's wellbeing in relation to God or higher power and the horizontal dimension focuses on how well a person is adjusted to self, community, and the surroundings. Studies have shown that religion, as a coping mechanism is highly effective in dealing with various life stressors.

Employing a combination of religious and problem solving strategies to manage stress is considered one of the most efficient and adaptive approaches. Moreover, religious coping generally results in positive outcomes and better psychological functioning in the individuals.[269] With the growing emphasis on the positive impact of religious based approaches in therapeutic endeavours W. E. Fiala, J. P. Bjorck and R. L. Gorsuch have developed a scale called Religious Support Scale to measure individuals' perceived support from God, consisting of three distinct yet related subsections: support from God, support from the congregation and support from the church leadership. The result was that all three types of support are linked to lower scores of depressions, higher scores on psychological wellbeing and distinct increase in life satisfaction. Moreover, perceived support from God was rated significantly higher than general support, indicating that for Christians religious support may be appraised more highly than social support. Thus, religious support as perceived by Christians statistically predicts a higher quality of functioning.[270]

Another study conducted in the Western Cape by A. P. Greeff and I. N. Ritman focusing on the resilience in single-parent families, suggest that , "People who have faith use it to enhance their resilience."[271] From these studies, it is apparent that religious affiliation and activity can aid in alleviating the stress in coping with a different serious stressor including divorce. Spiritual wellness is

---

268 Francesco Chirico, "Spiritual Wellbeing in the 21st Century: It's Time to Review the Current WHO's Definition?" in Journal of Health and Social Science 1/1 (2016): 11.

269 J.P. Bjorck, "Faith, Coping and Illusory Control: Psychological Constructs with Theological Ramifications," in Journal of Psychology and Christianity 26/3 (2007): 197.

270 W. E. Fiala, J. P. Bjorck and R. L. Gorsuch, "The Religious Support Scale: Construction, Validation and Cross-Validation," in American Journal of Community Psychology 30 (2002): 763.

271 A.P. Greeff and I. N. Ritman, "Individual Characteristics Associated with Resilience in Single-Parent Families," in Psychological Reports 96/1 (2005): 36.

an important component that can enhance the quality of life and wellbeing of divorcees to develop to the maximum level of human potential.

Conclusion

The theoretical approaches to divorce help in understanding and interpreting the experiences divorce women go through although there is no one simple explanation. The different theories presented above provide a strong foundation from which to conduct divorce research. While divorce is always a unique, personal, and subjective experience, there are common denominators within the process of most divorce. The discussion presents several theoretical models through which some of the denominators can be understood. The critical discussion of these theories provides not only with a theoretical spectrum from which to consider the proposed psychosocial wellbeing of divorced women but also with the necessary background for understanding the need for, and the conceptual assumptions of the theory. While all the above mentioned theories drive home important and unique insights, they are not without limitations especially when used exclusively in studying divorce.

It also examines the many facets of divorce and the factors that contribute to divorce. It is important to note that many factors contribute to divorce including marrying at young age or age of marriage, cohabitation, remarriages, socio-economic status, growing secularization, rapid social mobility, dowry, child marriages, rising expectations of marriage, increase in work and family demands, premarital pregnancy, sexual dissatisfaction, extra-marital affair, infertility and domestic violence and abuse etc. All these factors destabilize the couple's relationship and may eventually contribute to divorce.

Divorce is a complex issue that must be viewed in its physical, mental, psychological/emotional, social, economic and religious/spiritual context as all these factors are intertwined. Divorce is not caused by single factor, but it involves multiple levels. The effects of divorce on physical health, mental and emotional/psychological wellbeing have been extensively documented. Divorce has always been linked to economic distress particularly for women, which in turn affect their social participation. All these factors are interwoven for example the health effects of divorce have been attributed to the economic hardships and material conditions experience by women when marital relationship dissolves and to the loss of social network. Divorce causes irreparable harm to all persons involved especially women that lead to decline in their spiritual wellbeing. Though it might show beneficial for some individuals in some cases, overall it causes a temporary decrease in an individual's quality of life and from which they might never fully recover. Poverty and economic hardship loom large especially for divorced women. Examining the different causes of divorce provides a useful complement and is necessary for a fuller understanding of the divorce process. Compared to married women, divorced women have poorer physical and mental health. They also experience social isolation, which include feeling of loneliness, unhappiness, and lower self-esteem. Thus, the negative link between divorce and physical, mental, psychological/emotional, social, economic, and spiritual/religious wellbeing is well established.

Chapter 2

Divine Wholeness For All

Introduction

The preceding chapter dealt with the theoretical appraisal on divorce and psychosocial wellbeing. It has been noted that divorced has strong implications on the physical, mental, psychological/emotional, economic, social and spiritual/religious wellbeing for women. Considering that it is a crucial ministerial challenge, this chapter attempts to give the biblical and theological foundation of the wellbeing of divorced women. The church is not immune to the issue of divorce. It has never been an easy one and has deep theological, moral, and personal ramifications. The voices of the divorcees are rarely heard in the church and their experiences are seldom considered in doing theology, though they raise new theological, moral, and spiritual questions. There is a need for re-reading biblical and theological interpretation locating in the experience of the divorced women. Just as the church responds to various issues concerning people in the margins, it needs to address the crisis divorcees' face. Only when the church listens to the cries of divorcees, can it discern the true ministerial praxis among them. How can the existence of such pain and suffering, which disrupts human relationships resulting in denial of human wholeness and wellbeing, be understood in the context of all knowing and all-powerful compassionate and loving God? What does it mean to experience shalom, to experience the loving, forgiving, liberating and justice seeking God who liberated the people of the Hebrew and whose resurrection is the hallmark of Christian faith in the midst of human brokenness and pain, failure, loneliness, emptiness and alienation?

Biblical Foundations

Wellbeing and wholeness is a predominant feature in biblical and theological domain. Human wholeness and health can be considered as one of the integral themes of the Bible. Health and wellbeing in biblical teaching encompasses physical, mental, emotional, social, economic, and spiritual aspects. While in the Old Testament, health and healing is understood as restoration, the New Testament carried forward the concept of health and wellbeing in a more comprehensive manner fully expressed and illustrated its significance particularly manifested in the life and ministry of Jesus Christ, which is predominated by healing and restoration. The concept of wellness or wellbeing is the centre of the gospel. Healing consistently involves not only the physical aspect but the renewal of relationship with God and fellow human beings. In light of this scriptural understanding, healing can be understood as a process of bringing or restoring wholeness and sound functioning in every aspect of human life.

The Old Testament

Wholeness and abundant life is the will of God for all people. "A person may be described as healthy when he (sic) exhibits that state of body and mind in which all the functions are being discharged harmoniously."[272] In fact, the concept of wholeness and completeness forms the basic foundation of the Hebrew word salom, which can be translated as "wholeness,"[273] "completeness"[274] and "peace."[275] Thus, health is not just one particular aspect but wholeness and completeness of being in itself and in relation to God, to fellow human beings as well as to the world. John Wilkinson says that shalom in the OT illustrates the concept of wellbeing par excellence. It is a recurring theme referring to a holistic wellbeing, which can be linked to qualitative life possibilities. "The usage of the word in the OT is to denote the presence of wholeness, completeness, and well-being in all spheres of life whether physical, mental and spiritual or individual, social and national."[276] In Hebrew understanding, shalom is not just the absence of war rather it is a dynamic condition of wholeness and fulfilment in all aspects of life. It carries different dimensions such as completeness, wholeness, soundness, wellbeing, peace, justice, salvation and prosperity because shalom entails living

272 R. K. Harrison, "Healing, Health," in *Interpreters Dictionary of the Bible*, vol. 2 edited by Katharine Doob Sakenfeld (Nashville: Abingdon Press, 2008), 541.

273 William Lee Holladay, ed., *A Concise Hebrew and Aramaic Lexicon of the Old Testament* (Grand Rapids: William B. Eerdmans Publishing Company, 1971), 371.

274 F. Brown, S. R. Driver and C. A. Briggs, *A Hebrew and English Lexicon of the Old Testament* (Oxford: Clarendon Press 1972), 1022.

275 John Wilkinson, *Health and Healing: Studies in New Testament Principles and Practice* (Edinburgh: The Handsel Press Ltd., 1980), 3-8.

276 Wilkinson, *Health and Healing...*, 4-5.

in covenantal relationship with God and others.[277] It often occurs as inquiries about one's welfare (Gen. 29:6; 37:14; Exodus 18:7). It thus, "includes everything necessary for healthful living including good health, a sense of wellbeing, good fortune, the cohesiveness of the community, relationship to relatives and their state of being, and anything else deemed necessary for everything to be in order."[278]

The word `salvation' is also very closely related to the Latin word for health. "Be perfect just as your heavenly father is perfect" (Matt. 5:48). The Greek word for perfect is *teleios* meaning, "to be brought to completion, to maturity, to wholeness."[279] The early church understood the experience of the risen Christ in terms of health and wellness. God cares about human wellbeing and flourishing and Christ's saving work entails human flourishing. This concern finds its expression in the term "salvation" which is seen as liberation from economic injustice, oppression, alienation, and despair. God's salvific actions and providential activities of the wellbeing of individuals and society are recorded in many instances in the OT. The Bible talks about happiness, joy, wellbeing, fulfilment, wholeness, and flourishing. The very nature of God's redemption in Jesus Christ who promised abundant life, human flourishing and wellbeing are a function of God's saving work. This redemptive act is denied to divorce women due to patriarchy in many cases.

There are many instances in the bible where God intervenes when human beings are oppressed and treated unjustly based on gender, race, status, and class. God intervenes when people are in crisis and desperate situation expressed in many ways in the OT in the form of theophany, divine speech, visions, dreams etc. The book of Exodus is one classic example where God shared the pain of the people in their affliction and expressed his compassion that resulted in their delivery from oppression. God acts on their behalf to deliver them from the hands of the oppressors. In the words of Walter Brueggemann, "God is now physically mobilized to be present in the midst of the trouble."[280] God acted as the protector of the people, showed concerned for their wellbeing, and liberated them from the bondage of slavery. Salvation results in healing of human brokenness and restoration of health and wholeness. God's salvation and healing strategy is enacted through the deliverance of God's people from slavery. God's redeeming act of Israel can be described as shalom because the result is fullness of life.

277 Tammy R. Williams, "Is There a Doctor in the House," in *Practicing Theology: Beliefs and Practices in Christian Life*, edited by Miroslav Volf and Dorothy C. Bass (Grand Rapids: B. Eerdamans Publishing Co., 2002), 100.

278 Claus Westermann, "Peace [Shalom] in the Old Testament," in *The Meaning of Peace*, edited by Perry B. Yoder and Willard M. Swartley (Elkhart: Institute of Mennonite Studies, 2001), 49.

279 Jeffrey D. Lee, "Toward a Theology of Wellness," in *All Shall Be Well: An Approach to Wellness*, edited by William S. Craddock Jr. (New York: Church Publishing, 2009), 18.

280 Walter Brueggemann, *A Social Reading of the Old Testament: Prophetic Approaches to Israel's Communal Life* (Minneapolis: Fortress Press, 1994), 112.

In a world where the weak and powerless has little or no protection and rights, God fought for them. The theology of liberation is strongly emphasized in the exodus event. The social situation is changed from oppression to freedom. The book of exodus speaks of liberation from oppression. The Bible testifies that the Divine participates in history to defend those who are victims of power like the widows, slaves, and children. God is depicted not only as hearing the groans of the people but also committed to bring justice and liberation from their pain and suffering. God protects the poor and establishes the rights to those who are being oppressed by acting on behalf of the weak and the vulnerable. Yahweh is the God who brought Israel out of Egypt. Through the exodus event, God revealed himself as the saviour of the oppressed.

Repeatedly, God is projected as the provider and protector of widows and orphans. Israel is called to defend widows (Jeremiah 7:6; 22:3), and mistreatment of widows is often given as an example of sin (Job 24:21; Psalms 94:6). The concern is derived from the fifth commandment and enlarged to be a community responsibility. Like the widows, the orphan and the poor, divorced women also fit in within the broader category of those worthy of special attentions and protections. The crisis and brokenness experience by divorced women can be interpreted as human suffering to which God responds with compassion and healing. It is a cry of the oppressed because of patriarchy, inequalities and injustice. Without listening to their cries, the church cannot develop ministry among the victims. Speaking about the exclusion of marginalized people, Wati Longchar says,

> From the margins, they bring firsthand knowledge of the suffering that accompanies exclusionary practices as well as unmask the forces that work against God's will in the world. Through their lives and struggles for life, they hold forth what God wants in the world while also bringing a reservoir of hope, resistance, and perseverance that is needed to remain faithful to the promised reign of God.[281]

Those who suffer alone can provide a solution. Thus, those who suffer injustice and oppression are the subjects of God's special attention and concern. God revealed among the people of the margins and their cries become God's cry.[282] God intervenes when injustice prevails and human beings are in desperate and hopeless situations.

The exodus narrative provides a description of identity and human dignity. It talks about how the Israelites were liberated from slavery, oppression and suffering and were given identity and human dignity as a nation under the divine guidance and protection. The term 'nation' is inclusive of all irrespective of gender and social conditions. Therefore, the identity, dignity, salvation, liberation, and

281 Wati Longchar, *Transforming Cultures and Praxis: Engaging Peoples in the Margins* (Kolkata: PTCA, 2017), 106.

282 Longchar, *Transforming Cultures and Praxis: Engaging Peoples in the Margins...*, 105.

redemption are assured to all including divorced women. Redemption means liberation and salvation. Divorce represents shattered dreams and brokenness and there is a significant interplay between culture, religion, and power relations such as status, rights, position, and role that contribute to this problem. God's response to this sinfulness is liberation, unity and equality and this understanding relate to the overall biblical witness of salvation.

Therefore, the church must be an extension of God's presence and salvation to those who are experiencing brokenness and sense of rejection and betrayal that resulted in broken relationship. The church must take a holistic approach by reflecting God's purpose for all creation and live out the prophetic and shepherding role, which includes healing, nurturing, caring, fellowship, peace, and reconciliation towards divorced women.

The New Testament

The Bible affirms that God became flesh. God became Immanuel and gave his life for the downtrodden people. He touched, cared, loved, and worked for the liberation of the excluded, discriminated, stigmatized, and marginalized. The biblical mandate to care for widows and orphans translates directly into the call for action in aiding those in vulnerable situations including divorced women is carried forward in the NT. God's concern for human wellbeing, wholeness and flourishing is exemplified through the revelatory coming of Jesus Christ whose mission is to establish God's reign on earth.

The exodus story of liberation is also reflected in the life and ministry of Jesus. Analogues to the exodus liberation story are depicted in Jesus' healing ministry recorded in the Gospels. Jesus' ministry such as healing people of their infirmities, forgiving their sins and working towards bringing hope and liberation to those who are oppressed by the rigid political, social and religious institutions are all liberation and salvific acts. The passage that best captures the Exodus liberation event is Luke 4:18-19 where Jesus proclaims: "The spirit of the Lord is upon me, because he anointed me to bring good news to the poor. He has sent me to proclaim release to the captives and recovery of sight to the blind, to let the oppressed go free, to proclaim the acceptable year of the Lord's favour." Jesus inaugurates his ministry by describing in terms of those who are poor and oppressed. Through his coming there will be role reversal based on Kingdom's teaching. The liberation motif and the Nazareth manifesto reveal God's option to the victim of unjust system.

Jesus was very much concerned for the wellbeing of people particularly of women. The special place of women in the life and ministry of Jesus reveals concern for their wellbeing. The Samaritan Woman in John 4:1-26 gives a vivid illustration.

The story has attracted numerous attentions ranging from the traditional interpretation where the woman was seen as inferior, sinful, immoral in search of a man for sexual gratification, a threat in the community and living on the fringes of the society. She is projected as intellectually incompetent in comprehending Jesus' theological discourse, infamously known for her irregular conjugal situation. The fact that she was alone at the well without any female company at an inappropriate time substantiated with the details of having had five husbands all put together as evidence to define her as immoral and deviant. Christian feminist theologians have dismissed such one-sided judgmental interpretation and sought to reinterpret the story by paying careful attention to the socio-historical context. The traditional sexiest interpretation does not take into account the possibility of having run out of water so that she was desperately in need to fetch water immediately or it was a coincidence that she happened to be there when Jesus was there.[283]

Contrary to the popular reading, feminist writers see the woman as a knowledgeable person who engaged in a theological discourse with Jesus. She is also recognized as a spokesperson, a missionary, and a mediator between Jesus and her community. Nevertheless, besides the liberating description, feminist readers also acknowledge the victimization and disparagement of her character in the text. Feminist writers see her as victim of oppression and marginalization on account of being a Samaritan and a woman. She remains nameless and without identity all throughout the narration. While she was described as married five times and was living with someone who was not her husband (vv. 17-18) nothing was mentioned why her conjugal relationships with her former husbands failed. Perhaps the woman might have been widowed, had been a wife in levirate marriage or as a second wife in a polygamous marriage or perhaps she was a bonded servant or a slave,[284] or abandoned five times and is now dependent on another man for survival because to be accepted in the community, women had to be married. Conceivably, she was a five-time divorcee or some of the marriages might have ended with the dead of a husband. Divorce in that era was a unilateral right of the husband and the wife cannot divorce her husband. "In the OT law, the initiative in instituting divorce proceedings lay entirely with the husband (Dt. 24:1-4). There is no hint of a divorce being initiated by a wife. This is in keeping with the double standard which characterized Israel as well as most of its contemporaries in the Mediterranean region."[285] Gail R. O'Day maintains that "there are many possible reasons for the woman's marital history…Perhaps the woman…is trapped in the custom of levirate marriage and the last male in the family refused to marry her"[286] Since the text did not mention any details about her age, it is also possible

283 Surekha Nelavala, "Jesus Asks a Samaritan Woman for a Drink: A Dalit feminist Reading of John 4," in Lection Difficilior 8/1 (2007): 17.

284 Ronnie Sim, "The Samaritan Woman in John 4," in Journal of Translation 2/1 (2015): 20.

285 C. R. Taber, "Divorce," in *The Interpreter's Dictionary of the Bible Supplementary Volume,* edited by Keith Crim (Nashville: Abingdon Press, 1976), 244.

286 Gail O'Day, *The Word Disclosed: John's Story and Narrative Preaching* (St. Louis: CBP, 1987), 41- 42.

that the woman was old and had outlived her five husbands and she probably gave up on legal marriage contracts and live with a man who is not her husband or perhaps she had been deserted by five husbands and she became a victim.[287] In the words of Luise Schottroff, "The Samaritan woman is described as a woman in an extreme situation of sexual exploitation. The man with whom she now lives did not even offer her the security of a married contract."[288] These possibilities are strengthened by the fact that she was able to convince her community about her encounter with Jesus and the transformation that took place.

Many scholars have affirmed Jesus' deep sensitivity and radical initiative in crossing gender, ethnicity, and moral boundaries in order to reach out to the Samaritan woman that brings about liberation. In her analysis of the text from dalit feminist perspective, Surekha Nelavala proposes a transformative liberation.[289] Jesus' approach towards the woman was neither judgmental nor moralistic. E. Haenchen argues that whoever postulates that Jesus was moralistic and judgmental towards the woman have misunderstood the text.[290]

Jesus' attitude is centred on the social, cultural and personal wellbeing of women, which is reflected in the way he treated the Samaritan woman, and the woman caught in adultery. He challenged all aspects that were defined and controlled by men under a patriarchal structure. His attitude to divorce challenged the prevalent norms that favoured the male dominated society and thus helped establish equality and justice. Jesus respected the dignity of human person especially that of women and liberated them from their degraded and humiliated status in a context where women have been silenced and dehumanized for centuries by the patriarchal hegemony.

The Bible speaks of human flourishing in a very significant way, which is a function of God's redemptive act. Throughout both the OT and the NT, God is at work redeeming the broken, sinful and rebellious people saving them from oppression and injustice. Human life in fullness is a central part of the biblical teaching on salvation and redemption. Healing thus consistently involves not only the physical aspect, but also the renewal and restoration of relationship with God and fellow human beings. In light of this scriptural understanding, healing can be understood as a process of bringing or restoring wholeness and sound functioning in every aspect of human life. The biblical mandate demands protection of the stigmatized divorced women.

---

287 Christine Lienemann-Perrin, "The Biblical Foundation for Feminist and Participatory Theology of Mission," in International Review of Mission 95 (January, 2004): 20.

288 Luise Schottroff, "The Samaritan Woman and the Notion of Sexuality in the Fourth Gospel," in *What is John*, vol. II, edited by Fernando Segovia (Atlanta: Scholars Press, 1998), 174.

289 Nelavala, "Jesus Asks a Samaritan Woman for a Drink...," 17.

290 E. Haenchen, *John 1: A Commentary on the Gospel of John*, trans. by Robert W. Funk (Philadelphia: Fortress Press, 1984), 221.

Theological Foundations

The experience of divorced women raises disturbing theological and moral questions. Profound human pain and suffering always raises theological questions and divorced women experience is no exception. How can human suffering be understood in relation to the all-knowing and all-loving God? What does it mean when a particular group of people is prevented from full participation in the fundamental aspects of Christian faith and life? What does it mean to experience the love of God for a person whose faith is obliterated by the experience of divorce? The challenge for Christian theology in the midst of human despair is to develop ways to provide koinonia for divorced persons to restore a sense of self and connection to the Christian community and to attain wholeness and wellbeing. Christian theology will remain incomplete if it remains silent on the issues that divorcees face. There is a need for theology in which God is perceived as fellow sufferer, companion, healer, and great comforter as a divine power that is not dominating of controlling. This nature and power of God is effectively revealed in God's redemptive act and creation of human in God's own image.

Theology of the Image of God

Genesis 1:26-28 announces that all human beings are created in the image of God. The intrinsic dignity of each human being is founded in his/her creation in the image and likeness of God. This dignity reaches its peak and its fulfilment in the person of Jesus who recognized and honoured the dignity of the people he came into contact with regardless of their status. In a context where the church is confronted with many questions and dilemmas, the church should be aware of how the traditional reading of Biblical texts may create a distorted, exclusive image of God. Every person has an inherent dignity irrespective of one's social standing. The creation narrative affirms the inviolable dignity of the human person, which implies rights conferred by the Creator.

For centuries, the creation narrative has been a central point of contention for Christian understanding of man and woman. Patriarchal anthropology sees women as lower beings and many androcentric theologians runs the threads of patriarchal thought. The creation narratives have been used to subjugate women by placing Adam/male as superior. Such arguments were based on the assumption that Adam was created before Eve and that the woman was created as a helpmate. Rosemary Radford Reuther criticises classical Christian theologians particularly Augustine, Aquinas, Luther, and Barth who had uncritically promoted such patriarchal anthropology. To quote:

> Although, Augustine concedes women's redeemability and hence her participation in the image of God, it is so overbalanced by her bodily representation of inferior, sin-prone self that he regards her as

> possessing the image of God secondarily. The male alone possesses the image of God normatively.[291]

Aquinas accepted a biological theory of women's inferiority by adopting the Aristotelian definition of woman as a "misbiggotten male."[292] Such distorted interpretation has denied women as bearing full image of God. Feminist reading of the creation account challenged such androcentric interpretation and advocated an egalitarian ideology. Ruether has criticized such male bias construction of theology and asserted equality of both male and female as created in the image of God. She contends that,

> Whatever denies, diminishes, or distorts the full humanity of women is, therefore, appraised as not redemptive. Theologically speaking, whatever diminishes or denies the full humanity of women must be presumed not to reflect the divine or an authentic relation to the divine, or to reflect the authentic nature of things, or to be the message or work of an authentic redeemer or a community of redemption.[293]

Similarly, Phyllis Trible argues that there is no justification to read the creation of Adam before Eve, the word Adam refers to "humanity" and not a male individual. Moreover, the passage is clear that "the human" was originally created as a non-gendered being and was only divided into two genders later.[294] In the same vein, Letty Russell postulates that "the image has to do with the totality of the human person in relation to God, and as such is not reducible to one or another quality such as rationality, spirituality, or even sexuality...but rather as the one who shares "identity, mutuality and equality."[295] For Russell, "The act of creating woman and man is an act of creating helpers who are companions for each other. It fulfills the need for life-in-community. As God is partner to humanity, men and women are to be partner to one another."[296] If man's superiority is claimed based on the order of creation, it would mean that human beings are inferior to the animals and plants which were created before them. Allison J. Young invalidates male superiority. She posits:

> In order to be equal, man and woman would have to be created at the same time, both from the dust. Indeed, based on the order of creation presented in Genesis 2:18-25, namely that animals were created before

291 Rosemary Radford Ruether, *Sexism and God-Talk* (Boston: Beacon Press, 1983), 95.

292 Ruether, *Sexism and God-Talk*..., 96.

293 Ruether, *Sexism and God-Talk*..., 18-19.

294 Phyllis Trible, *God and the Rhetoric of Sexuality: Overtures to Biblical Theology* (Augsburg: Fortress Press, 1978), 88.

295 Letty M. Russell, *Becoming Human* (Philadelphia: The Westminster Press, 1982), 65-66.

296 Russell, *Becoming Human*..., 70.

> human, one could just as easily conclude that Eve, created after Adam from his flesh, superseded him and became his superior."[297]

Marsha M. Wilfong also observes that the woman as a helpmate has been misunderstood as menial helper or inferior by androcentric interpretations. On the contrary, it attests to the fact that helper is someone more powerful and stronger than the one being helped. For instance, in the OT, it refers to God as the helper and where it does not refer to God it refers to the superior whom the person helped could rely. Thus, the status of the helper rather brings it "down to the level of the one being helped, so as to affirm the equality between them.[298] Similarly, Samuel Terrain posits,

> ...woman is created a help and succor to man's loneliness. Far from denoting the idea of service in a subordinate position, the word "help"('ezer) is generally applied to God who is par excellence the succor of those in need and in despair. Woman is not a mere tool of physiological or psychological delight. She fulfils a function of creative complementariness.[299]

Therefore, Randy Maddox rightly proposes that, "a truly inclusive doctrine of humanity would not only defend the equality of humanity as male and female, it would emphasize the social-relational nature of humanity as created in the Image of God—male and female."[300] Moreover, the essence of humanity is to maintain "a loving relationship with God, others, self, and the created order. While such an ability would involve reason, will, conscience, it "humanizes" these isolated capabilities by placing them in the service of relationality."[301]

The Bible has encapsulated the highest norms for Christians. However, a faulty interpretation and selective literalism of these norms within patriarchal structures has contributed and resulted in discrimination of many marginalized groups including divorced women. Evangeline Anderson-Rajkumar has expressed the point sharply in this regard:

> The Bible is one of the most used and perhaps also, one of the most misused/abused books we've ever had in the history. The Bible is used as authority for the formation of Christian faith in God through the person of Jesus Christ and for shaping values like justice and peace

297 Alison J. Young, "In Likeness and Unity: Debunking the Creation Order Fallacy," in Priscilla Papers 23/2 (2009): 12.

298 Marsha M. Wilfong, "Genesis 2:1-24," in Interpretation 42/1 (1988): 59.

299 Samuel Terrein, "Towards a Biblical Theology of Womanhood," in *Religion in Life* (autumn 1973): 324.

300 Randy L. Maddox, "Toward an Inclusive Theology: The Systematic Implications of the Feminist Critique," in Christian Scholar's Review 16 (1986): 20.

301 Maddox, "Toward an Inclusive Theology...," 19.

> for the whole creation. The Bible is used when we recognize it as a witness to a living God—who has created redeemed and ever sustains this world out of love. The Bible, however, is misused when exclusive claims of salvation and discrimination against fellow human beings are legitimized on the basis of class, race and gender are upheld as "Biblical."[302]

Furthermore, Ruether argues that the divine presence manifests the true created nature of humans. It had not been lost in the Fall but distorted and silenced by hegemonic ideologies and social system of oppression. Through Christ the divine nature is revealed anew and to overcome the distorted system. She asserts:

> The mission of Christ was to restore the original equality of all humans in the image of God, overcoming the sinful systems of domination of male over female, master over slave. But the churches have betrayed this mission, creating new justifications of these evils. Far from violating divine law, the equality of women is no more than the restoration of God's original plan for human relations.[303]

Christian feminist writers reinvent and assert the egalitarian paradigm claiming equal standing and equal right for all humanity as created in the image of God. They countered the androcentic anthropology where women were considered subordinate in creation. Such claims are being discredited and are regarded as unbiblical and sinful. Feminist theologies deconstruct such unjust and distorted ideology, and assert the authentic human nature, and essential humanity for everyone, the fullness of life.

In view of these considerations, the full acceptance of all humans including divorced women within the imperative that all are created in the image of God forms pastoral theological approach. Christians should affirm the full image bearing humanity including divorced women. The image of God in human reveals the covenantal relationship of the creator and the creation. The creation narrative is a powerful theological theme to relate in the life of divorced woman who are challenged of their very existence by human made barriers, and on many instances denigrate them to a lower being in the hierarchical order of God's creation. The fact of the matter is that they are equals and deserves justice, love, inclusion and compassion from the church and society. The compassionate care of God is revealed in the incarnation of God through Jesus Christ. This compassionate nature of God should motivate the church and the society to look at the divorced women through the lens of God's care for the broken humanity.

---

302 Evangeline Anderson-Rajkumar, "New Eyes, New Reading, New Woman: Feminist Hermeneutics," in *Feminist Hermeneutics,* edited by Lalrinawmi Ralte and Evangeline Anderson-Rajkumar (Delhi: IWTI/ISPCK, 2002), 106.

303 Rosemary R. Ruether, *Introducing Redemption in Christian Feminism* (Sheffield: Sheffield Academic Press, 1998), 58.

Theology of Redemption

Human beings create unjust structures built on false ideology. Patriarchy is an unjust structure and ideology manipulating religion, culture, and even God. In this view of life, there is always a dualistic structure of human values. Social power structure is organized in which the others are defined as inferior, not intelligent, weak, incapable, unclean and impure, uncivilized, backward and primitive. Thus, subjugation of the other is not divine will.Such false presuppositions, beliefs, and institutions are created by the powerful to protect their vested interests. Divorced women struggle for justice needs to be located within this framework. One needs to understand the feminist struggle to redefining redemption within this structure.

Redemption and salvation is the central message of Christian faith. The son of God came to this world to redeem the people from the bondage of sin and destruction. The purpose of the incarnation is to redeem the people and restore them to their original condition, which was destroyed by sin. For Augustine, "Christ is the center of salvation history; Adam marks the beginning of human history in so far as it is characterized by sin and death."[304] In the NT, redemption refers to both deliverance from sin and freedom from captivity. Any consideration of the Christian concept of salvation must take place in the context of human suffering. Sin and its resultant disruption of the whole order of creation necessitate a reordering. Jesus Christ sacrificed his life for humanity and brought about redemption by setting people free from enslavements, psychological and emotional disturbances, and spiritual crisis. What does salvation and redemption, a concept central to Christian theology mean to those divorcees who are going through crisis and brokenness? This question leads to the reflection of the meaning of the saving act of Christ. Salvation and redemption of humanity is centered upon Christ the liberator. This implies the universality of the salvific will of God with the church as the mediator of salvation. Jesus Christ has brought newness of life to humankind and to all creation, assurance, redemption from wrong and the establishment of right relationship with God and fellow humans. For Dietrich Bonheoffer, at the heart of Christian message is the obligation to be a person for other person, "As Christ bears our burdens, so ought we to bear the burdens of our fellow-men (sic)."[305] Just as the fall of Adam, was the ruin of the whole creation, redemption through Jesus Christ results in the salvation of all humanity. Christ's act of salvation and redemption can be understood in terms of liberty.

While Christian feminists acknowledge that the full and final expression of salvation is eschatological, they also affirm the biblical notion that Jesus Christ has conquered evil and that "deliverance from evil is available in a real, albeit preliminary, sense in this world. Though sin is subtle and pervasive, it is not

304 M. Lamberigts, "Competing Christologies: Julian and Augustine on Jesus Christ," in Augustinian Studies 36/1 (2005): 175.

305 Dietrich Bonheoffer, *Testament to Freedom: The Essential Writings of Dietrich Bonheoffer* (San Francisco: Harper Collins, 1995), 80.

inescapable."[306] Christian feminists reject the understanding of redemption and salvation only in terms of eschatology or a future event. In an attempt to stress the here-and-now aspect of salvation, they underscored its holistic and social dimensions. They posit, "Conversion is never simply an inner "spiritual" affair. Rather, it is a turning of the entire person from a dehumanizing way of life to a liberating and serving way of life. Such a turning will involve the reorienting of one's self-understanding and one's relationship to other persons (justice) and nature (care)."[307] Russell observes,

> The message of salvation as expressed in the Bible and heard among the nations today cannot be reduced to one simple formula. It is not simply focused on "individual salvation," nor on social salvation. This gift of the liberating power of God's love is experienced in different situations and times, in various ways. Yet, in spite of the situation variability of its description, it is clear that salvation has to do with new joy and wholeness, freedom and hope that is experienced in the lives of individuals and communities as a gift of God. This message of liberation is good news for those of our age who are searching for freedom, for meaning, for community, for authentic existence as human beings.[308]

Redemption and salvation are never simply personal but encompass social as well as ecological component. Feminist theologians critiqued traditional understanding of sin which is largely seen in connection to sex and women. As a result, women are being subjugated and marginalized. In this regard, Kwok Pui-lan has made a compelling point, "Women are not just sinners; they are the sinned against too. Many Asian women suffer as outcasts of their society, not because of any innate human depravity or moral deficiency, but because of the social and institutional violence that dehumanizes and marginalizes them."[309] Many marginalized groups of people including divorced women who are in such a state of dehumanized condition sincerely long for acceptance and deliverance. In order to address this issue and bring about a renewed state they need redemption and salvation as envisioned by Pui-lan,

> Redemption comprises, therefore, not only personal and spiritual reconciliation with God, but also from liberation from bondage, the opportunity to develop one's potential, the well-being of one's family and community, the freedom from warfare and other forms of

306 Russell, *Becoming Human...*, 82.

307 Maddox, "Towards an Inclusive Theology...," 21.

308 Letty M. Russell, *Human Liberation in a Feminist Perspective* (Philadelphia: The Westminster Press, 1974), 106.

309 Kwok Pui-lan, *Introducing Asian Feminist Theology* (Cleveland: Pilgrim Press, 2000), 80.

> violence, the availability of life-sustaining eco-system and a sense of hope and security for the future.[310]

For Elisabeth Schussler Fiorenza, "the empty tomb as a symbol of salvation holds up women's agency as valuable in the on-going work of Jesus."[311] Since the empty tomb denotes Christ as resurrected from the dead and who is living among and with us, this provides the assurance of salvation not in suffering but in life beyond and through resurrection. For Fiorenza,

> Connecting the cross to salvation by means of the empty tomb allows us to reclaim this space of resurrection for women's meaning-making today in the face of dehumanization and oppression. Feminist Christological discourses can take seriously the spaces of the brutal victimization of women and other nonpersons and at the same time claim wo/men's agency in either collaborating with or transforming such spaces of death.[312]

This promotes the idea of delegitimizing the inhumane treatment of women and promises of a life beyond suffering through the salvation extended to us through the Christ in one's personal experiences.[313] "Liberation theologians emphasize sin as the refusal to give others room to breathe and live as human beings."[314]

For feminist theologians, redemption means liberating women from all unjust social structures and ideologies. Feminist theologians also take issue with Christology based on masculine concept of God and masculine idea of authentic humanity. Such understanding of Christianity denies women as they "can never 'image Christ' since they cannot imagine either the male God or the masculine humanity of Christ."[315] Such androcentric understanding of Christ excludes women as redeemed by Christ. Feminist theologians reclaim Jesus of the Gospel who actively engaged in dismantling social and patriarchal hierarchy, who preaches good news to the poor and marginalized, liberation of the captives and takes the side of the victims of oppression including women. Jesus is understood as redeemer of women and people who are in the margins; Jesus entered their condition, became a victim himself, and suffered with them. "It is not Jesus' suffering and death, but his life as a praxis of protest against injustice and solidarity in defense

---

310 Pui-lan, *Introducing Asian Feminist Theology...*, 81.

311 Elisabeth Schussler Fiorenza, *Jesus: Miriam's Child, Sophia's Prophet* (New York: Continuum, 1994), 126.

312 Fiorenza, *Jesus: Miriam's Child, Sophia's Prophet...*, 124-125.

313 Amy Chapman, "Suffering Our Way to Salvation: Ivone Gebara, Elisabeth Schussler Fiorenza, and the Adequacy of the Cross as a Symbol for Women," in Lumen et Vita (June 2011): 17.

314 Russel, *Human Liberation in a feminist Perspective...*, 112.

315 Ruether, *Introducing Redemption in Christian Feminism...*, 66.

of life that is redemptive. We need to imitate Jesus, not by acquiescence to being crucified, which represents the victory of oppression who sought to silence him, but in his protest against evil and his defense of life."[316] Jesus' suffering with the oppressed group is understood as a factor in the process of redemption but not as the means of redemption. The pain and suffering that Jesus took upon himself is to resist the oppression of unjust social system.

> Suffering is the factor in the redemptive process, but not as a means of redemption, but as the risk that Jesus took and that we take when confronting and denouncing unjust systems whose beneficiaries resist change. But, the efficacious means and process of redemption is not more victimization, but conversion, the changing of persons and systems from violence and injustice to loving and life-giving relations.[317]

The traditional ecclesiologies have promoted an ideology to justify the patriarchal nature and structure of the church that have resulted in dehumanizing and victimization of women. Feminist ecclesiology describes the church ministry as healing the victimized women from their suffering and brokenness under patriarchal church order and empowering them to participate in the struggle to destroy the ideology of domination or their liberation and solidarity. As Russell envisions:

> The vision women have for the Church is that it could be a sanctuary, a place of safety for all who enter, and especially for those who are the most marginal, weak and despised of any community...and the welcome extends to those of all races, ages, nationalities, genders, sexual orientations, all creatures and creation itself as the Church becomes a place where there is intent to heal and to live out God's justice rather than harm and promote the privilege of the few.[318]

The challenge to interpret the meaning of redemption and salvation calls for action by relating the experience of freedom and liberation among the oppressed groups. Human redemption will take place only when there is justice and equality. Is the church an agent of liberation of excluded people or simply another dimension of their oppression? The church may not exclude tax collectors or haemorrhaging women, but what about the divorcees? As theologian Gustavo Gutierrez puts it, the quest of Christianity should be driven by "the human being who is not considered human by the present social order—the exploited classes, marginalized ethnic groups and despised cultures. Our question is how to tell

316 Ruether, *Introducing Redemption in Christian Feminism...*, 67.

317 Ruether, *Introducing Redemption in Christian Feminism...*, 67.

318 Letty M. Russell, "Hot-house Ecclesiology: A Feminist Interpretation of the Church," in Ecumenical Review 53/1 (2001): 52.

the non-person that God is love."[319] There has been a shift in understanding the concept of redemption from individualistic and otherworldly to social and worldly hope. Ruether captures this idea when she says, "redemption is about the transformation of self and society into good, life-giving relations, rather than escape from the body and the world into eternal life."[320]

There is no record of divorced persons being defellowshipped in the NT, even when church discipline was done for other reasons; it was a form of pastoral care. Contemporary church discipline is more of a punishment. In some churches, the persons responsible for divorce are being defellowshipped, shunned, or excommunicated. In this regard, Bruce Parmenter asserts that if church discipline is required, it is not pastoral care unless Christian community and its representatives are willing to become involved, listen to the complexity of the marital dilemmas, feel the pain of the real situation, offer concern out of deep sense that all human beings live in a fallen world. Pastoral caregivers also have decision to make and sometimes the choice is between "coming alongside" or "passing by on the other side."[321] In response to the question who is my neighbour? in the well-known parable The Good Samaritan (Luke 10:29-37) Jesus spoke of a man travelling from Jerusalem to Jericho who fell among thieves who was robbed, wounded and left half-dead on the road. His dignity had been devalued. The action of the Samaritan, 'moved by compassion' restores the dignity of the victim and provides him with what is needed. The final word of Jesus in the parable is addressed also to the church: "go and do the same." The divorcees are struggling for a life of dignity. They may feel broken, hurt, injured, and alone. The church should take the place of the Good Samaritan and listen to the fears, nurse the wounds and bandage the broken hearts of the divorcees and restore them to wholeness.

Another view is to remember Jesus' injunction, "The Sabbath was made for humanity, not humanity for Sabbath" meaning that the seventh day should serve the good of people and not be a legal noose around the neck. Marriage, like the Sabbath was made for human beings to bring fulfilment for both spouses and not persons for marriage. Where that is not happening, God has shown to be more than forgiving and understanding. In this age of many failing marriages, the church needs to be courageous and compassionate enough in dealing with those who have failed in their marriages. There are numerous stories where Jesus went against the Sabbath institution of his day to care for individuals who were being oppressed by it. If the way in which Jesus dealt with the adulterous woman "neither do I condemn you" is any indication Jesus Christ would have us deal even with the guilty party of a divorced with compassion, grace and mercy rather than

319 Gustavo Gutierrez, *A Theology of Liberation: History, Politics and Salvation* (Lima: CEP, 1971), 62.

320 Ruether, *Introducing Redemption in Christian Feminism…*, 64.

321 Bruce Parmenter, *Christians Caught in the Divorce Trap: Helping Families Recover from Divorce* (Missouri: College Press Publishing Company, 1995), 89.

a judgmental attitude. The church ought to set example in dealing with divorcees in a redemptive manner.[322]

James G. Emerson, Jr., speaks of the needs of persons rather than the need of the church to maintain the status quo. He believes that divorcees carry a burden of guilt and need "realized forgiveness.[323] Marriage can die; realized forgiveness affirms this reality, but moves beyond it to forgiveness, which frees persons from the sin of broken marriages. Weaver appeals to the church to be redemptive in its response to persons and families experiencing divorce, to help them return to the life of the church. "The church must be an advocate for the divorcees, affirming their equality with others in the sight of God and prophetically critiquing social, cultural prejudices within and without the church."[324]

Conclusion

The chapter has investigated the biblical and theological foundation of wellbeing. Holistic understanding of wellbeing is derived from divine wholeness and reflects God's desire for all creation. When injustice and oppression prevail, God takes the side of the oppressed. God is concerned about the vulnerable section of the society. God warned the oppressors that God is on the side of the oppressed, the weak, and the defenseless. In the light of this, the theological approach to the wellbeing of divorced women is grounded in the theology of the image of God and theology of redemption. The church must develop a redemptive outlook toward divorced persons. Regardless of their failure in their marital life, the church is called to be a community that meets all people where they are, even in their sin and failure, with the message of the grace of God. Focusing attention on this ministry must become a crucial task of the church if it is to meet the challenge of the divorcees in the society and to restore their wellbeing. The dignity of divorced women needs to be defended and promoted. If God's redemption is the restoration of full humanity then Christian theology should be centered on practical outworking of true human flourishing both individually and corporately. Christian theology must be informed and motivated by such understanding without which the pursued of human flourishing is unbiblical. Seeking justice, equality, flourishing, and peace is not an option but a divine mandate.

322 Andreas J. Kostenberger and David Jones, *God, Marriage, and Family: Rebuilding the Biblical Foundation* (Illinois: Crossway, 2010), 52.

323 James G. Emerson, Jr., *Divorce, The Church and Remarriage* (Philadelphia: Fortress Press, 1977), 11-32.

324 T. Craig Weaver, "A Niebuhrian View of Divorce" (Master's Thesis, Wake Forest university, 1982), vi.

Chapter 3

Empirical Data Analysis

Introduction

This chapter presents the tables and interpretation of the data obtained through empirical study in order to examine in depth the psychosocial wellbeing of divorced women in contrast with married women. Subjective Wellbeing Inventory (SWBI) and Personal Wellbeing Index Scale were employed together with the socio demographic details to explore its influence on divorced women.

The data was collected with the help of structured questionnaire comprising of both open and closed ended questions. The questionnaire was administered individually to the respondents, who provided the information personally and for some the investigator took the help of volunteers. A pilot study was conducted among forty women comprising equal numbers from both the experimental and control group in Dimapur and Wokha. After the validation of the tool, the data was collected between October 2017 and February 2018. The collected data was categorised, coded, and fed into the computer for analysis. Statistical Package for Social Sciences (SPSS) version 22 software was employed to analyze the data.

Chi square test, independent sample t test, and Pearson's correlation analyses were employed to compare the groups of subjects as well as to correlate the dimensions of wellbeing. Level of significance was fixed at 0.05.

Likert type statements with 5 points were employed for measuring wellbeing, they were coded as 1-Strongly agree, 2-Agree, 3-Undecided, 4-Disagree, 5-Strongly disagree. Wellbeing had six subscales namely, physical wellbeing, mental wellbeing, emotional/psychological wellbeing, social wellbeing, economic wellbeing, and religious/spiritual wellbeing. Each subscale had about 15 to 18 closed ended questions comprising of both negative and positive statements and an open-ended question at the end of each segment. Negatively worded statements were reverse coded before taking the summated scores of dimensions of wellbeing. The total score ranged from 15 to 90.

The following tables show the distribution of samples between the groups and the percentage of the total sample size of 300. Socio-demographic details of both groups are compared and presented in Tables 1-3 and Figures 1-4.

Socio-Demographic Details of the Subjects

The following data present the socio-demographic details of the respondents. The Experimental group (EG) comprised of divorced women and the Control group (CG) comprised of married women.

Age

The table shows that 72.7% in the experimental group belongs to the age group of 31-45, while 21.3% belongs to the age group of 46 and above and only 6.0% falls within the category of 18-30 years of age. In the control group 66.7% falls within the age group of 31-45 and 22.0% were within the age group of 46 and above and only 11.3% belongs to the age group of 18-30. Majority of the women in both groups belong to the age group of 31-45 and there is no significant difference between the two groups.

Education

The table below shows that 30.0% in the experimental group were high school pass, 25.3% were graduates, 22.0% had pre-university education, and 12.0% below high school and only 10.7% were post-graduates. Among the control group 43.3% were graduates, 21.3% were postgraduates, 20.7% had pre-university education, 12.0% were high school pass and only 2.7% below high school.

Occupation

Occupation includes four categories such as self-employed, government employed, private employed and unemployed. The table shows that in the experimental group 36.0% were government employed, 33.3% were private-employed, 16.0% self-employed and 14.7% not employed. In the control group 29.1% were government employed, 26.4% unemployed, 25.0% private employed, and 19.6% self-employed.

Income

Income includes seven categories to assess the economic status of the respondents. The table shows that in the experimental group 47.7% had monthly income below 10,000, 20.7% had 10,001-15,000, 10.7% had monthly income of 30,001-40,000, 9.3% had 20,001-25,000 monthly income, 6.7% 15001- 20,000 another 6.7 had 25,001-30,000 monthly income and only 3.3% had monthly income of 41,001 and above. In the control group 27.0% had 30,001-40,000 monthly income, 18.9% had 41,001 and above and 18.2% had 24,001-30,000, 15.5% had 20,001-25,000 monthly income, 8.8% had 10,001-15,000, 6.8% had 15,001-20,000 and only 4.7% had below 10,000.

Type of Residence

The table shows that 42.7% in the experimental group lived in their own houses, 10.7% indicated any other, 6.7% lived in service quarters and 4.0% lived in rented house. In the control group 52.0% lived in their own houses, 24.0% lived in service quarters and another 24.0% lived in rented house.

Table 1: Comparison of Socio-demographic Details of groups

Variables		Group				Chi-square value	p – value
		Divorced Women		Married Women			
		No	%	No	%		
Age (in years)	18-30	9	6.0	17	11.3	2.864	0.239
	31-45	109	72.7	100	66.7		
	46 and above	32	21.3	33	22.0		
Place	Wokha	37	24.7	37	24.7	0.027	0.999
	Mokokchung	37	24.7	37	24.7		
	Kohima	38	25.3	38	25.3		
	Dimapur	38	25.3	38	25.3		
Education	Below High School	18	12.0	4	2.7	32.954	0.001
	High School Pass	45	30.0	18	12.0		
	Pre-University	33	22.0	31	20.7		
	Graduate	38	25.3	65	43.3		
	Post Graduate	16	10.7	32	21.3		
Occupation	Self-employed	50	33.3	29	19.6	14.202	0.003
	Govt.employed	54	36.0	43	29.1		
	Private employed	22	14.7	37	25.0		
	Unemployed	24	16.0	39	26.4		
Income (in Rupees)	Below 10,000	64	42.7	7	4.7	89.431	0.001
	10,001 – 15,000	31	20.7	13	8.8		
	15,001 – 20,000	10	6.7	10	6.8		
	20,001 – 25,000	14	9.3	23	15.5		
	25,001 – 30,000	10	6.7	27	18.2		
	30,001 – 40,000	16	10.7	40	27.0		
	41,001 and above	5	3.3	28	18.9		
Type of Residence	Own House	64	42.7	78	52.0	38.076	0.001
	Rented House	60	4.0	36	24.0		
	Service Quarters	10	6.7	36	24.0		
	Any Other	16	10.7	-	-		

In summary, it can be seen that majority of the women in both the groups belong to the age group of 31-45 years and it did not differ significantly between the groups (72.7 vs 66.7, p=0.239). Subjects in both groups were selected with equal proportion from the four places. Education, Occupation, Income and Type of Residence differed significantly between the groups. One-third of the divorced women (30%) had high school education, while more than 40% of the married women (43%) were graduates (p=0.001). Less than one-fifth of the divorced women (16%) were unemployed however more than one fourth of the married women (26%) were unemployed (p=0.003). More than 40% of the divorced women (42%) have income below 10,000 rupees, while only 5% of the married women have income below 10,000 rupees (p=0.001). Though majority of the women in both groups stay in their own house (43% vs. 52%), it is noticeable that about 10% of the divorced women mentioned "Any other" as their place of stay, which could be friend's/brother's/sister's houses. It is to be noted that none of the married women had mentioned "any other" as their place of stay (p=0.001).

Table 2: Comparison of Marriage and Illness Related Details of groups

Variables		Group				Chi-square value	p –value
		Divorced Women		Married Women			
		No	%	No	%		
Nature of Marriage	Customary Law/Civil Union	10	6.7	7	4.7	28.223	0.001
	Church Marriage	2	1.3	3	2.0		
		64	42.7	107	71.8		
	Elope	66	44.0	29	19.5		
	Consensual	8	5.3	3	2.0		
Type of Marriage	Arranged	31	20.9	40	26.8	1.42	0.233
	Love	117	79.1	109	73.2		
Duration of Marriage	< 5	43	28.7	26	17.3	17.767	0.001
	6 – 10	54	36.0	44	29.3		
	11 – 15	37	24.7	37	24.7		
	16 – 20	9	6.0	21	14.0		
	21 +	7	4.7	22	14.7		
Number of Children	1	29	22.7	34	23.6	8.363	0.015
	2-3	80	62.5	69	47.9		
	3 +	19	14.8	41	28.5		
Health Problems	Blood Pressure	28	33.7	34	54.0	26.205	0.001
	Diabetes	5	6.0	6	9.5		
	Thyroid	5	6.0	13	20.6		
	PCOD	4	4.8	3	4.8		
	Depression	41	49.4	7	11.1		

Nature of Marriage

The above table shows that 44.0% in the experimental group eloped, 42.7% had church marriage, 6.7% had customary marriage, 5.3% consensual and 1.3% had low/civil marriage. In the control group, 71.8% had church marriage, 19.5% eloped, 4.7% had customary marriage, 2.0% consensual and another 2.0% law/ civil marriage.

Type of Marriage

In the experimental group, 79.1% had love marriage and 20.1% had arranged marriage whereas in the control group, 73.2% had love marriage and 2.8% had arranged marriage.

Duration of Marriage

The table shows 36.0% in the experimental group were married for 6-10 years, 28.7% were married for 5 years, 24.7% were married for 11-20 years, and 4.7% were married for 21 years and above. In the control group 29.3% had been married for 6-10 years, 24.7% had been married for 11-15 years, 17.3% had been married for 5 years, 14.7% had been married for 21 years and above, and 14.0% had been married for 16-20 years.

Number of Children

The table shows 62.5% in the experimental group had 2-3 children, 22.7% had one child, and 14.8% had more than 3 children. In the control group, 47.9% had 2-3 children, 28.5% had more than three children, and 23.6% had one child.

Health Problem

The table shows 49.4% in the experimental group suffer from depression, 37.7% had blood pressure, 6.0% had diabetes, another 6.0% had thyroid and 4.8% had PCOD. In the control group 54.0% had blood pressure, 20.6% had thyroid, 11.1% depression, 9.5% diabetes and 4.8% PCOD.

In summary, it can be seen that nature of marriage, duration of marriage, number of children and the type of health problems differed significantly between the two groups. It can be seen that about half of the divorced women (44%) had eloped while majority in the control group had a church wedding (72%). About one-third of the control group women (29%) were married for more than 15 years compared to only 10% of the divorced women who were married that long; also about one-third of the women in control group had more than 3 children (29%) while majority of the divorced women had 2-3 children (63%). More than half in the control group (54%) had blood pressure while about half of the divorced women (49%) had depression as their major health issue.

Details, which are specific to divorced women like Custody of Children, Visitation rights etc. are graphically represented below.

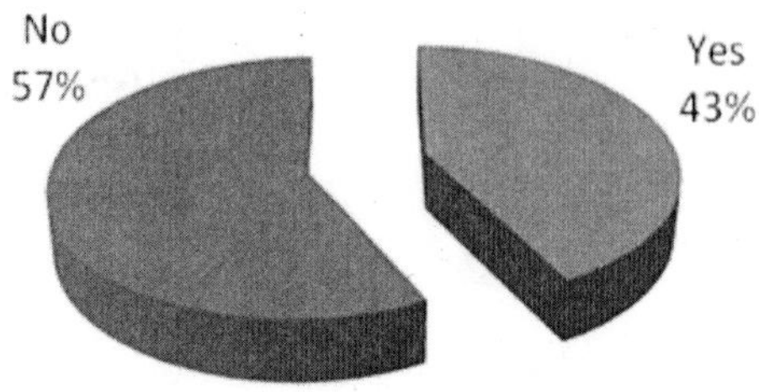

Figure: 1a Custody of Children

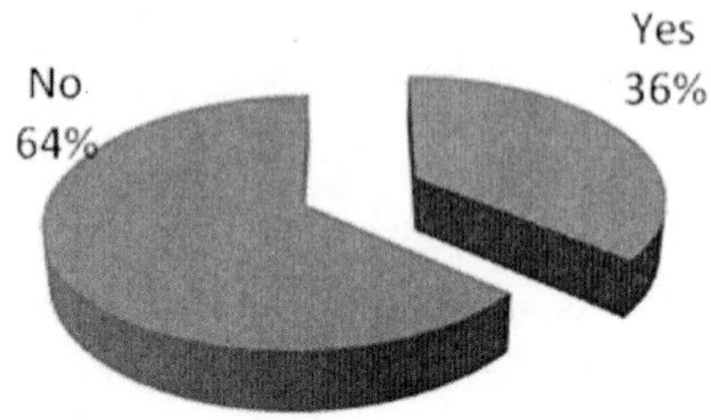

Figure: 1b Visitation Rights

It can be seen that majority of the divorced women stay alone (n = 45), they do not have custody of the children (57%), and majority do not enjoy visitation rights (64%).

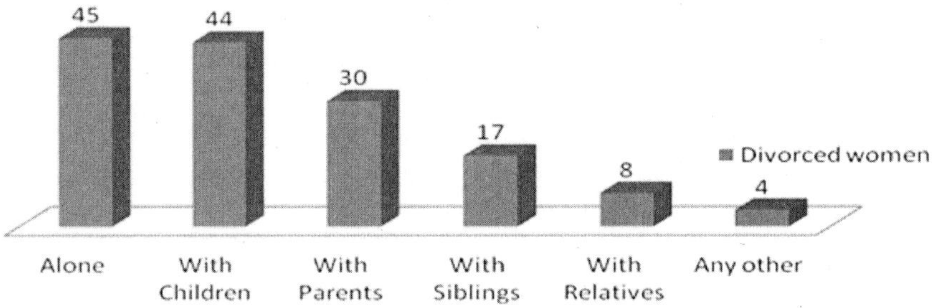

Figure: 1c Residing with

Details, which are specific to married women, are graphically represented below.

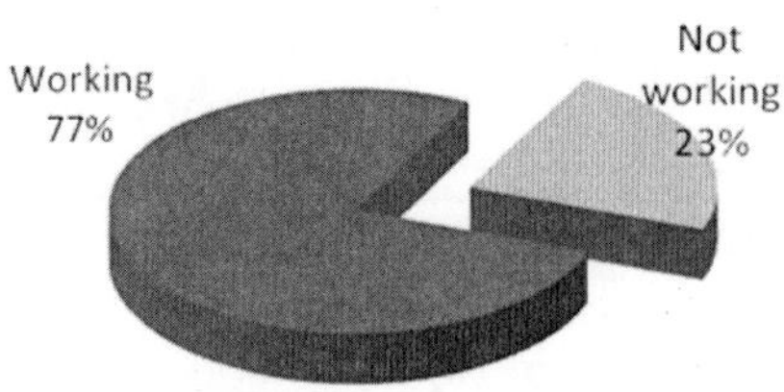

Figure: 2a Husband's employment staus

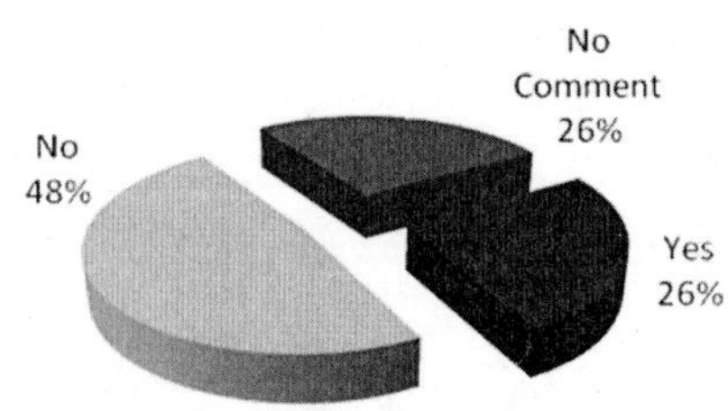

Figure: 2c Ever considered divorce ?

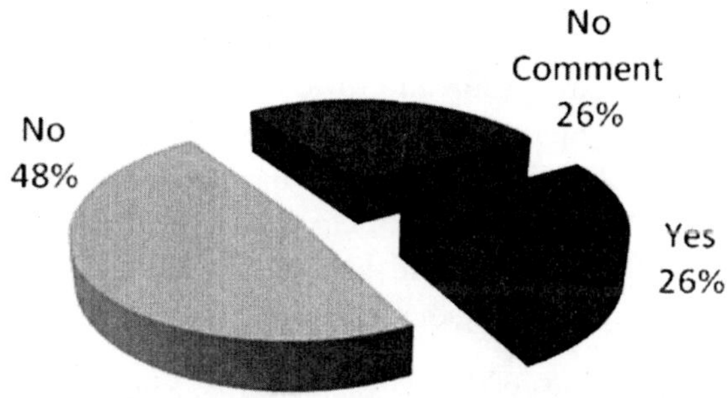

Figure: 2c Ever considered divorce ?

It can be seen that majority of the married women had a working spouse (77%) who also took care of the expenses (51%). It is to be noted that about one fourth of them had considered divorce (26%) while half of the women gave no comments (48%) on this aspect.

Comparison of Psychosocial Wellbeing between the Experimental and Control Group

The main focus of this study is to examine the psychosocial wellbeing of divorced women, and to compare it with married women of similar ages. To assess the wellbeing of divorced women multidimensional domains such as physical, mental, emotional/psychological, social, economic, and spiritual/religious areas were studied.

Table 3: Comparison of Wellbeing between groups

Dimensions of Wellbeing	Study Groups		t- value	p-value
	Divorced women (n= 150)	Married women (n= 150)		
	Mean ± SD			
Physical Wellbeing	47.23 ±10.85	55.53± 9.35	7.095	0.001
Mental Wellbeing	53.30± 10.12	60.03± 7.60	6.513	0.001
Emo/Psy Wellbeing	54.75 ± 12.80	64.02 ± 8.53	7.379	0.001
Social Wellbeing	54.31 ± 10.20	59.37 ± 7.05	5.345	0.001
Eco Wellbeing	49.61 ± 10.23	55.07 ± 7.70	5.223	0.001
Rel/Sp Wellbeing	57.51 ± 13.30	63.90 ± 9.05	4.868	0.001

Table 3 shows the comparison of wellbeing between the two groups in the six areas under investigation using independent sample t-test for equality of means. Women in the experimental group and the control group differed significantly on their scores of physical, mental, emotional/psychological, social, economic, and religious/spiritual wellbeing. It can be seen that wellbeing scores are significantly lower for divorced women in all six dimensions.

It can be seen from the table below that dimensions of wellbeing are positively inter-correlated with each other.

Table 4: Relationship among Variables

COMBINED N =300		MWB Total	EPWB Total	SWB Total	EWB Total	RSWB Total
PWB Total	Pearson Correlation	0.649**	0.627**	0.378**	0.442**	0.360**
	p-value	0.001	0.001	0.001	0.001	0.001
	N	300	300	300	300	300
MWB Total	Pearson Correlation		0.749**	0.587**	0.496**	0.507**
	Sig. (2-tailed)		0.001	0.001	0.001	0.001
	N		300	300	300	300
EPWB Total	Pearson Correlation			0.658**	0.644**	0.587**
	Sig. (2-tailed)			0.001	0.001	0.001
	N			300	300	300
SWB Total	Pearson Correlation				0.571**	0.619**
	Sig. (2-tailed)				0.001	0.001
	N				300	300
EWB Total	Pearson Correlation					0.547**
	Sig. (2-tailed)					0.001
	N					300

**. Correlation is significant at the 0.01 level.

At the end of each segment, the subjects were asked to express their concerns in relation to the six domains under investigation. This section quantifies the open-ended responses.

Table 5: Physical Health Problems

Physical Health Concern	Group	
	Divorced women	Married women
	No. (%)	
Physically Weak	61 (41)	52 (35)
No Major Concern	53 (35)	82 (55)
No Comment	36 (24)	16 (10)

The above table indicates 41% in the experimental group reported physically weak and 35% in the control group rated as physically weak. 35% in the experimental group did not have any major health concerns whereas in the control group 55% did not have any major health concerns. 24% in the experimental group and 10% in the control group did not comment.

The table below shows 4.7% in the experimental group were able to make decisions and 15.3% in the control group were able to make decision, 28.6% in the experimental group reported difficulty in making decision whereas only 13.4% in the control group faced difficulty in making decision, 15.4% in the experimental group reported to be mentally stressed whereas no one in the control group reported to be mentally stressed, 24.0% in the experimental group does not have any major concern with regard to their mental processes 56.0% in the control group cited no major concern and 27.3% in experimental group and 15.3% in the control group did not give any comment.

Table 6: Mental Health Concern

Mental Health Concern	Group	
	Divorced Women	Married Women
	No. (%)	
Able to make decisions	7 (5)	23 (15)
Difficulty in making decision	43 (29)	20 (13)
Mentally Stressed	23 (15)	0
No Major Concern	36 (24)	84 (56)
No Comment	41 (27)	23 (15)

Table 7: Emotional/Psychological Health Concern

Emotional/Psychological Health Concern	Group	
	Divorced Women	Married Women
	No. (%)	
Emotionally Strong	9 (6)	35 (23)
Emotionally Weak	55 (37)	0
Sad and Worried	32 (21)	5 (4)
No Major Concern	10 (7)	83 (55)
No Comment	44 (29)	27 (18)

The above table indicates 6.0% in the experimental group and 23.4% in control group rated themselves as emotionally strong, 36.7% in experimental group and 0.0% in control group rated themselves as emotionally weak, 21.4% in the experimental group and 3.5% in control group reported being sad and worried, 6.8% in the experimental group and 55.1% cited no major concern. 29.1% in the experimental group and 8.0% in the control group did not comment.

Table 8: Social Concern

Social Concern	Group	
	Divorced Women	Married Women
	No. (%)	
Good Social Life	31 (21)	60 (40)
No Social Life	47 (31)	22 (15)
Social Exclusion and Stigma	44 (29)	1 (1)
No Major Concern	14 (9)	36 (24)
No Comment	14 (9)	31 (20)

The above table shows 20.8% in the experimental group and 40.0% in the control group have good social life, 31.4% in the experimental group and 15.0% in the control group does not have social life, 29.0% in the experimental group and 0.7% in the control group experience social exclusion and stigma, 9.4% in the experimental group and 24.0% in the control cited no major concern, 9.4% in the experimental group and 20.3% in the control group did not comment.

Table 9: Economic Concern

Economic Concern	Group	
	Divorced Women	Married Women
	No. (%)	
Economically Stable	12 (08)	42 (28)
Economic Instability	53 (35)	0
No Major Concern	38 (25)	78 (52)
No Comment	47 (31)	30 (20)

The above table shows 8.0% in the experimental group and 28.0% were economically stable, 35.3% in the experimental group and 0.0% in the control group face economic instability, 25.5% in the experimental group and 52.0% in the control group did not have any major concern with regard to their economic wellbeing, 31.3% in the experimental group and 20.0% in the control group did not comment.

The table no. 10 shows 28.0% in the experimental group and 50.6% in the control group rated themselves as spiritually strong, 40.0% in the experimental group and 14.6% in the control group rated their spiritual wellbeing as weak, 13.3% in the experimental group and 15.3% in the control group did not have any major concern and 18.7% in the experimental group and 19.3% in the control group did not comment.

Table 10: Spiritual Concern

Spiritual Concern	Group	
	Divorced Women	Married Women
	No. (%)	
Spiritually Strong	42 (28)	76 (51)
Spiritually Weak	60 (40)	22 (15)
No Major Concern	20 (13)	23 (15)
No Comment	28 (19)	29 (19)

Table 11: Post Divorce Concern

Post-Divorce Concern	EG
	No (%)
a. Shame b. Hopelessness c. Guilt	25 (17)
a. Economic instability b. Future/Family insecurity c. Loneliness	66 (42)
a. Single Parenting b. Bitterness c. Anger	20 (13)
No Major Concern	19 (13)
No Comments	20 (13)

The above table shows 44.2% divorced women go through economic instability, future insecurity and loneliness, 17.2% experience shame, guilt and hopelessness, 13% face problem in the area of single parenting and experience bitterness and anger, 12.6% did not have any major concern and 13.0% did not comment.

Table 12: Concern in Married Life

Concerns in Married Life	CG
	No. (%)
a. Economic instability b. Future/Family insecurity c. Loneliness	23 (15)
a. Misunderstanding b. Abusive husband c. Completely different mindset	24 (16)
a. Lack of respect b. Lack of trust c. Incomplete without children	12 (8)
a. No strong family bond b. Adjustment problem c. Health issues creates tension at home	17 (11)
No Major Concern	45 (30)
No Comments	29 (19)

The table shows 15.3% married women cited economic instability, family insecurity and loneliness, 16.0% cited misunderstanding, abusive husband and completely different mindset, 8.0% cited lack of respect, lack of trust and incomplete without children, 11.4% cited no strong family bond, health issues creating tension at home and adjustment problem, 30.0% cited no major problems and 19.3% did not comment.

Table 13: Positive Experience Post Divorce

Positive Experience Post Divorce	CG
	No. (%)
a. Independent and Happy b. Closer with God c. Managing life better	51 (34)
a. Empowering b. No abuse and torture c. Stronger relation with children	40 (27)
a No family burden b. Inner peace and satisfaction c. Helping others in similar situations	21 (14)
No Comment	38 (25)

The table shows 34.0% divorced women are independent and happy, feel that they are closer with God and are able to manage life better post-divorce, 26.7% mentioned being empowered, no abuse and torture and stronger relation with children, 14.0% no family burden, inner peace and satisfaction and helping others in similar situation, 25.3% did not comment.

Table 14: Positive Experience in Married Life

The table below shows 32% have closer relationship with God and manage life better and extended family support, 26.7% experience happiness, supportive husband and children and life satisfaction, 7.3% experience care, concern and mutual respect, 13.3% cited companionship, sharing and solving problems together in their married life, 20.7% did not comment.

Positive Experience in Married Life	CG
	No. (%)
a. Closer with God. b. Managing life better c. Extended family support	48 (32)
a. Happy with married life b. Supportive husband and children c. Satisfaction	40 (27)
a. Care b. Concern c. Mutual respect	11 (7)
a. Companionship b. Sharing c. Solving problems together	20 (13)
No Comment	31 (21)

Interpretation of Data in relation to the Hypothesis

The core focus of the study is to analyse psychosocial wellbeing of the divorced women. In order to assess their levels of wellbeing, two standardised scales were employed covering the six domains: physical, mental, emotional/psychological, social, economic and religious/spiritual wellbeing.

There are six sub-hypotheses formulated in order to assess psychosocial wellbeing of divorced women. The following section discusses the findings of the study in relation to the hypotheses.

Sub-Hypothesis One: *It appears that divorced women experience decline in physical wellbeing compared with married women.* The study result proves that there is a significant difference between the two groups.

Sub-Hypothesis Two: *It appears that divorced women experience decline in mental wellbeing compared with married women.* The result proves that there is a significant difference between the two groups.

Sub-Hypothesis Three: *It appears that divorced women experience decline in emotional/psychological wellbeing compared with married women.* The study result proves that there is a significant difference between the two groups.

Sub-Hypothesis Four: *It appears that divorced women experience decline in social wellbeing compared with married women.* The study result proves that there is a significant difference between the two groups.

Sub-Hypothesis Five: *It appears that divorced women experience decline in economic wellbeing compared with married women.* The study result proves that there is a significant difference between the two groups.

Sub-Hypothesis Six: *It appears that divorced women experience decline in religious/spiritual wellbeing compared with married women.* The study result proves that there is a significant difference between the two groups.

Conclusion

The study provides evidence to support the hypotheses that divorced women experience lower wellbeing in all the six areas under investigation as compared to married women. The succeeding chapter deals with the analysis of the major findings.

Chapter 4

Divorce and Its Negative Impact on Women's Psychosocial Wellbeing

Introduction

The preceding chapter presented the empirical data on psychosocial wellbeing of divorced women. This chapter presents the summary of the major findings with reference to the hypotheses formulated for the study and compares the research finding with other research to strengthen the findings.

Major Research Findings

The major research findings are divided into two sections: socio-demographic details, and psychosocial wellbeing.

Socio-Demographic Background

This section covers the socio-demographic details of the subjects under investigation from the empirical data. There is a slight variation in the demographic details between the two groups.

Details in experimental group include age, educational qualification, age at marriage, nature of marriage, type of marriage, duration of marriage, duration of divorce, number of children, custody of children, visitation rights, current occupation, monthly income, type of residence, currently living with and health issues.

Details in control group include age, educational qualification, age at marriage, nature of marriage, type of marriage, duration of marriage, ever considered divorce, number of children, husband's employment, person responsible for financial expenses, current occupation, monthly income, type of residence, leisure time and health issues.

The study suggests the effect of demographic factors on the wellbeing of divorced women. Factors such as educational qualification, age at marriage, monthly income, and health problems were found to be associated with the lower wellbeing of divorced women.

Age

The age of the subjects did not differ significantly between the two groups. Majority of the respondents in both the experimental (72%) as well as control group (67%) fall in the age group of 31-45 years. The sample with regard to age shows that more than half of the respondents are in their mid-life.

Educational Qualification

The levels of education differed significantly between the two groups under investigation. 30% in the experimental group falls in the category of high school pass, 25% graduates and 22% pre- university whereas in the control group 43% falls in graduate level, 21.3% post graduate and 20.7% in the pre-university. The finding shows that divorced women are less educated than compared to married women suggesting that women holding higher educational level have lower divorce risk. In other words, less educated women have higher divorce rates than better educated women. Low educational level is a strong predictor of divorce. A recent study done by Dietrik Boertien and Juho Harkonen in the United Kingdom found that there is a strong impact of educational level of women on divorce risk. Educated women have more stable marriages.[325] Another study conducted in India by Pramchand Dommaraju confirms that marriage among higher educated are more durable and the difference between higher educated and lower educated women has widened over time.[326] Some authors had also proved the negative correlation between divorced women level of education and wellbeing as well. Yet, there is no general consensus among researchers and scholars. According to the economic theory of family, educational level of the wife increases the risk of divorce as better education gives women more economic opportunities outside the marriage making it easier to leave the union.[327]

---

325 Dietrik Boertien and Juho Harkonen, "Less Education More Divorce: Explaining the Inverse Relationship Between Women's Educaion and Divorce," in Demographic Research 38/41 (2018): 1256.

326 Pramchand Dommaraju, "Divorce and Separation in India," in Population and Development Review 42/2 (June, 2016): 195.

327 Gary S. Becker, Elizabeth M. Landes and David E. Bloom, "An Economic Analysis of Marital Instability," in Journal of Political Economy 85 (1977): 1147.

Age of Marriage

The mean age of marriage in the experimental group is 25.13 and in control group, the mean age is 27.48. The t-value of -4.430 and the p-value of 0.001 indicate that there is a significant difference between the two groups and divorce is concentrated among younger women. This confirms many other findings that there is a strong association between women's age at first marriage and marital stability.[328] A recent study conducted in the US focusing on different race and ethnicity found that as age of marriage increases, marital instability decreases. The reason was that women entering into marriages at the young age do not have better informed choices in the marriage market.[329] Thus, the younger a person is at the time of marriage decrease stability of marriage, and has negative effect on divorce risk is well founded.

Nature of Marriage

In the experimental group, 44% of them eloped and 42.7% had church marriage whereas in the control group 71.8% had church marriage and only 19.5% eloped. The chi-square value at 28.223 and the p-value at 0.001 indicate that there is a significant difference between the two groups in terms of the nature of marriage. Little less than 50% in the experimental group did not have church marriage.

Type of Marriage

In the experimental group, 79.1% had love marriage, only 20.0% had arranged marriage, in control group 73.2% had love marriage, and 26.8% had arranged marriages. The chi-square value is fixed at 1.42 and the p-value of 0.233 shows that there is no significant difference between the two groups. Majority of the women in both the experimental and control groups had love marriage.

Occupation

The finding shows 36% of the respondents in the experimental group were government employed, 33.3% were self-employed, 14.7 % were private employed, and 16% were unemployed. In the control group, 29% were government employed, 26.4% were unemployed, 25 were private employed, and 19.6 were self-employed. Less than one fifth of the divorced women (16%) were unemployed whereas in the control group more than one-fourth of them were unemployed (26%). The data suggests that divorced women's quality of life and wellbeing is determined to a large extent by their professional status and economic

328 Bryan Strong, F. Christine DeVault, Theodore. F. Cohen, *The Marriage and Family Experience: Intimate Relationships in a Changing Society* (Belmont: Thomson Wadsworth, 2011), 112.

329 Evelyn L. Lehrer and Yeon Jeong Son, "Women's Age at First Marriage and Marital Instability in the United States: Differences by Race and Ethnicity," in Demographic Research 37/9 (August, 2017): 231.

standing. Women who are fulltime employed and are in better financial position demonstrate higher wellbeing than those women who are not employed.

Duration of Marriage

In the experimental group 36% of the respondents were married about 6-10 years, 28.7% less than 5 years, 24.7% 11-15 years whereas in the control group 29.3% were married between 6-10 years, 17.3% less than 5 years and 24.7% 11-15 years. The chi-square value is 17.767 and the p-value 0.001. This shows that there is a significant difference between the two groups. Divorce is concentrated among women who had been married for less than 10 years as more than 50% falls in the category of 6-10 and less than five years.

Duration of Divorce

The mean duration of divorce was fixed at 7.16 and the standard deviation is ±5.15. Only those women who had been divorced for more than two years and have not been remarried were included in the research.

Considered Divorce

About 48% of them have not considered divorce at any point in time whereas 26% of them had considered divorce and 26% did not make any comment.

Number of Children

In the experimental group, 62.5% had 2-3 children, 22.7% one child and 14.8% more than 3 children while in the control group 47.9% had 2-3 children, 28.5% had more than 3 children and 23.6% had only one child. The chi-square value is 8.363 and the p-value 0.015. This shows that there is a significant difference between the two groups.

Custody of Children

Majority of the divorced women (57.5%) does not have custody of children and only 42.5% have custody of children.

Visitation Rights

Majority (63.8%) of the divorced women do not have visitation rights of the children and only 36.2% have visitation rights.

Income

In the experimental group 42.7% have a monthly income of less than Rs. 10,000/, 20.7% earns less than 15,000/-, 10.7% earns between 30,000 and 40,000/- whereas in the control group 27% earns between 30,000 and 40,000/-, 19% earns more than 40,000/- and only 18.2% earns about 25,000-30,000/-. The chi-square value of 89.431 and the p-value of 0.001 show a significant difference between the two groups. Most of the divorced women have lesser monthly income compared with married women. The data shows that although only 16% of the divorced women were unemployed little less than half of the divorced women earn less than 10,000/- per month. Most of the participants in the experimental group were low earners based on their average monthly household income. Divorced women's wellbeing was also considerably influenced by their financial situation. The study reveals a statistically strong correlation between financial position and divorced women's wellbeing. The more satisfied they are with their financial standing the better their wellbeing is.

Residing With

About 30% of the divorced women reside alone, 29.7% with children, 20.3% with parents, and 11.5% with siblings. About 10% of the divorced women mentioned "any other" as their place of stay but none of the married women had mentioned "any other" as their place of stay.

Health Problems

There is a significant difference between the two groups. The data indicate that in the experimental group 49.4% suffer from depression, 33.7% suffer from blood pressure, 6.0% diabetes and another 6.0% thyroid whereas in control group 54% have blood pressure and 20.6% have thyroid problem and only 11.1% suffer from depression. Nearly half of the women in experimental group reported suffering from depression indicating a serious concern as they struggle quite substantially. Divorce confers risk for poor health outcome. A research conducted by Pooja Rathi and J. P. Pachauri in Meerut, India on the impact of divorce on physical health status suggests that divorce has a negative impact on general health status, health behaviour and the life expectancy of women. It is also reported that many of the subjects experience depression and other health related issues post-divorce.[330]

In the above discussion, comparison was made between the socio-demographic status and its impact on divorced women's wellbeing. The data reveals a significantly lower wellbeing in divorced women. Married women are found to have better quality of life and wellbeing. The analysis of the data obtained proved that the quality of life and wellbeing of divorced women has negatively affected as compared to women in experimental group in most of the domains. Several studies have also shown that socio-demographic factors affect the wellbeing of divorced women.

In this study, level of education of women remained a strong predictor for divorce. Women who are not well educated are more likely to divorce compared to educated women. Similarly, women belonging to lower economic status also suffer more divorce. This result is consistent with other studies. Women with low

330 Pooja Rathi and J. P. Pachauri, "Problems Faced by Divorced Women in their Pre and Post-Divorce Period: A Sociological Study with Reference to District Meerut," in Journal of Pharmacognsy and Phytochamistry 7/1 (2018): 210.

level of education, women in low economic status, women who are not employed were greatly disadvantaged and diminished their wellbeing post-divorce. Poorer wellbeing outcomes in divorced women are the results of factors such as lack of education, financial problems, and issues of unemployment or underemployment. Hence, it is not surprising that divorced women suffer from higher depression problems. Thus, improving education of women and girls in particular could be an appropriate strategy.

Psychosocial Wellbeing

The hypothesis that divorce leads to decline of physical, mental, emotional/ psychological, social, economic, and religious/spiritual wellbeing of women was proven to be true in the study. The research shows a significant difference between the experimental and control group. Divorced women scored lower in all the six areas under investigations.

Poor Physical Wellbeing

Data of the physical wellbeing shows a significant difference between the two groups. Divorced women rated their physical wellbeing poorly. The data shows that divorce is characterized by disturbed sleep, health deterioration, tiredness, and loss of appetite, loss of weight often accompanied by weakness, being worried about their health, experiencing pains in some parts of the body, giddiness, disturbed sleep, physical weakness and being uncomfortable with their physical appearance. Women in the experimental group responded negative to their overall health satisfaction.

The t test analysis presented in table 3 reveals a significant difference on the score of physical wellbeing. Divorced women obtained a lower mean value and standard deviation of 47.2 ±10.85, whereas in the control group the mean and the standard deviation was 55.53±9.35. Moreover, the t-value of -7.095 and the p-value of 0.001 clearly indicate that there is a significant difference in the physical wellbeing between the two groups.

Divorced women are found to have more physical problems as compared with the married women although majority of the subjects fall under the same age group. The first sub-hypothesis that divorced women experience decline in physical wellbeing compared to married women is well supported. The findings confirm many other researches. For instance, Amato and Hohmann-Marriott found that married people tend to be better off than divorced in terms of physical health; divorced people are found to be unhappier, have poorer health and less satisfied in life.[331]

331 Paul R. Amato and Bryndl Hohmann-Marriott, "A Comparison of High-and Low-Distress Marriages that End in Divorce," in Journal of Marriage and Family 69/3 (2007): 630.

Depression and Stress

Many divorced women reported being depressed (49.4% table no. 2) and difficulty in making decisions (28.6%) and 15.4% reported being mentally stressed as mentioned in table 6. Divorced women experience inability to think rationally, not being able to accept oneself, not able to concentrate, not able to make decisions, not able to accept reality, not being able to appreciate themselves, not able to seek help when needed, depression, unable to cope with life challenges, not firm under stress, often tensed, mentally stressed, experience mental block, anxiety and tension. Divorced women also reported negative to being balanced in their intellectual and mental processes.

The mean and standard deviation for mental wellbeing was fixed at 53.30±10.12 in the experimental group, whereas in the control group the mean and standard deviation was fixed at 60.03±760. Moreover, the t-value of -6.513 and the p-value of 0.001 clearly indicate that there is a significant difference in the mental wellbeing between the two groups. The finding is in consistent with many others who had done similar research. According to a study done by Morten Blekesaune, divorce is associated with a number of negative mental health outcomes for individuals such as depression and anxiety. Divorce is also associated with very high level of distress.[332] A longitudinal study conducted in the US also found interconnection between most mental health problems and divorce. The authors have concluded that divorce leads to development of mental health problems.[333]

For Maslow, failure to meet needs at various stages of the hierarchy could lead to psychiatric illness or mental health issues. Individuals who do not feel loved or belonging may experience depression or anxiety. Lack of self-esteem or the inability to self-actualize may also contribute to depression and anxiety.[334] Depression is not just a low mood, but also a serious mental illness. People with depression find it difficult to function and do not enjoy activities that they previously enjoyed. Depression has serious repercussion on both physical as well as mental health.

Helplessness/hopelessness is one of the frequently proposed theories for depression. Originally, this model proposed that as a result of repeated exposure to uncontrollable aversive outcomes, individual may conclude that their behaviours have no effect on external events. The cognitive, affective, and behavioural correlates of these feelings are consistent with that of depression, including passivity in the face of challenge and lowered self-esteem. A person's attributions for the uncontrollable events are the primary determents of the helplessness/

332 Morten Blekesaune, "Partnership Transition and Mental Distress: Investigating Temporal Order," in Journal of Marriage and Family 70/4 (2008): 880.

333 K. William and A. Dunne- Bryant, "Divorce and Adult Psychological Well-being: Clarifying the Role of Gender and Child Age," in Journal of Marriage and Family 68 (2006): 1179.

334 Maslow, "A Theory of Human ...," 373.

hopelessness response pattern.[335] According to Susan Nolan-Hoeksema and Benito Jackson, depressed women display a self-questioning mode of coping with stress characterized by rumination rather than by active problem solving solution. They found that rumination was related to women's beliefs that they are responsible for maintaining positive relationship with others, and that they have relatively little control over important events in their lives.[336] Divorced women's depression may also be related to the traditional understanding of the role of male and female. Women are seen as good homemakers. Having internalized these messages divorced women may discredit themselves that their life is a failure since they could not adhere to the roles dictated by the society and culture, resort to self-hatred, and self-blame that further contributes to their depression which Aaron Beck termed it as "the cognitive basis of depression."[337] The accumulated effects of these gender-role socialization factors appear to contribute substantially to the depressive syndromes experience by divorced women.

Psychologically/Emotionally Weak

The mean and standard deviation for emotional/psychological wellbeing was fixed at 54.75 ±12.80 in the experimental group, whereas in the control group the mean and standard deviation was fixed at 64.02±8.53. Moreover, the t-value of -7.379 and the p-value of 0.001 clearly indicate that there is a significant difference in the emotional/psychological wellbeing between the two groups.

Table 7 shows that 36.7% women in the experimental group reported to be emotionally weak as opposed to none (0%) in the control group, 21.4% were sad and worried in the experimental group and only 3.5% in the control group reported to be sad and worried. While only 6.0% in the experimental group rated themselves as emotionally strong, 23.4% in the control group rated themselves as emotionally strong. Besides, 17.2% in the experimental group cited shame, guilt and hopelessness as one major concern post-divorce and about 13.0% experience bitterness and anger in the experimental group. Shame, guilt, low self-esteem, self-blame and feelings of worthlessness are some of the dominant manifestations of divorced women experience.

Subjects in the experimental groups reported lower emotional/psychological wellbeing as they responded negative to areas such as life interesting, happy with the present life, happy with things that they have been doing, can manage situation even when they do not turn out the way they expected, confident in coping with the future, confident in case of crisis they will be able to face it boldly, that things around them belong together and are integral parts of a common

335 Judith Woroll and Pamela Remer, *Feminist Perspectives in Therapy: Empowering Diverse Women* (New Jersey: John Wiley & Sons Inc., 2003), 161.

336 Susan Nolan-Hoeksema and Benito Jackson, "Mediators of the Gender Differences in Rumination," in Psychology of Women Quarterly 25/1 (2001): 37, 38.

337 Aaron Beck, *Cognitive Therapy and the Emotional Disorder* (New York: Meridian, 1976), 45.

force, experience moments of intense happiness, experience joyful feeling of being part of humankind as one large family. They reported in affirmative on areas such as being upset over minor things, easily upset when criticized, get upset easily if things do not turn out the way they expected, easily irritated and sensitive, sad without any reason, life is boring and uninteresting; worry about the future, life is useless and often lose temper over minor things.

A similar study conducted in Europe and the US on marital status and psychological/emotional wellbeing found that individuals who experienced a marital transition such as divorce reported an increase in psychological distress.[338] Several studies have shown that divorced individuals reported lower levels of psychological wellbeing and higher levels of depressive symptoms compared to their married counterparts. The positive effects of marriage and negative effects of divorce have been well documented.[339] These findings suggest that a stable marital status is beneficial for emotional/psychological health outcomes.

The finding corresponds to conclusions reached by different scholars. The emotional effect of women post-divorce has been consistently documented. Women experience feelings of self-blame, anger, guilt, fear, and hopelessness. Many divorced women experience shame and guilt, which is confirmed through the open-ended responses. Shame together with other negative emotions presents enormous challenges for divorced women. While shame may have appropriate and useful functions in the social relationships of an individual, it can also have very negative effects. Shame may also become pathological and destructive. Stephen Pattison opines that, "If shame becomes a constant experience, a perennial attitude of the self, a dominant mood or character trait, its effects can be negative. The habitually deeply shamed or shame-bound person is trapped, self-rejected, paralyzed, passive, and often depressed."[340]

Pattison distinguished between appropriate and acute shame and chronic dysfunctional shame. The former refers to protecting the inner self and integrity that inhibit the person from performing actions that might be destructive to the social relationship or the society; it is a necessary social attitude. The latter refers to shame that manifest symptoms such as "withdrawal, self contempt, inferiority."[341] He points out some of the pathological or chronic shame such as "a feeling of being dirty, defiled, unwanted," "something I want hidden surfacing", "feeling demeaned and put on view," "a sense of unworthiness and badness because of something that I have done," "my self feels diminished," "there is nowhere to hide," "feeling of exposure," "wanting not to be seen," "a sense of deep embarrassment,"

338 Paul R Amato and Spencer James, "Divorce in Europe and the United States: Commonalities and Differences across Nations," in Family Science 1/1 (January, 2010): 4.

339 Hawkins and Allan Booth, "Unhappily Ever After...," 446.

340 Stephen Pattison, *Shame, Theory, Therapy Theology* (Cambridge: Cambridge University Press, 2000), 7.

341 Pattison, *Shame, Theory, Therapy Theology...*, 82-83.

"not being good enough."[342] These are closely related to the divorced women experience of shame which is essentially related to self rather than attributing to the society. Many divorced women experience negative self-judgment. Pattison thus concludes that "Any experience that induce a sense of persistent inferiority, worthlessness, abandonment, weakness, abjection, unwantedness, violation, defilement, stigmatization, unlovability and social exclusion are likely to be generative of chronic shame."[343] "The self-rejected person who has internalized a sense of shame will find it difficult to trust and integrate herself within human relationship."[344] Shame and guilt also lead to social withdrawal as many of the divorced women reported social withdrawal and aloofness.

For Carl Goldberg, shame is "ironic" because the more intense it is, the more difficult it becomes to articulate or speak about it.[345] Shame thus leads to social isolation, which Leon Wurmser termed it as "radical abandonment" as the person stay aloof and loses social bonds.[346] Thus, shame leads to loneliness and alienating experiences. This sense of isolation may further lead to despair. Gershen Kaufman says that, "Shame can engulf the self, immersing the individual deeper into despair."[347] Shame is a distinctive psychologically associated feeling where a person "sense a total paralysis" which hinders the inability to move, act or do anything.[348] For divorced women shame is perceived as failure to measure up to what others expect or what one expects of oneself.

Some of the most pervasive psychological/emotional challenge that divorced women go through includes a deep sense of inferiority, shame, guilt, low self-esteem, worthlessness. Branden has rightly mentioned that,

> Self esteem is a powerful human need. It is a basic human need that makes an essential contribution to the life process; it is indispensable to normal and healthy development. It has survival value. Lacking positive self-esteem, our psychological growth is stunted. Positive self-esteem operates as, in effect, the immune system of consciousness, providing resistance, strength and the capacity for regeneration. When self-self-esteem is low, one's resilience in the face of life's adversities is diminished.[349]

---

342 Pattison, *Shame, Theory, Therapy Theology...*, 70.

343 Pattison, *Shame, Theory Therapy Theology...*, 108.

344 Pattison, *Shame, Theory Therapy Theology...*, 109.

345 Carl Goldberg, *Understanding Shame* (New Jersey: Jason Aronson, 1991), 86.

346 Leon Wurmser, *The Mask of Shame* (New Jersey: Jason Aronson, 1995), 6.

347 Gershen Kaufman, *The Psychology of Shame* (London: Routledge Publishers, 1993), 25.

348 Gershen Kaufman, *Shame: The Power of Caring* (Rochester: Shenkman Books, 1985), 58.

349 Nathaniel Brandon, *The Power of Self-esteem* (Deerfield Beach, FL: Health Communications, 1992), 9.

Social stigma and discrimination attached to divorce can be attributed to the negative emotional problems divorced women exhibit. Their sense of shame and worthlessness are shaped by their experiences of being looked at as deviant and thus diminish their self-esteem.

Another important manifestation of the sense of worthlessness of divorced women is guilt or self-blame. Jeffrey Kauffman points out a correlation between self-blame and injustice. To quote him,

> A disturbing and revealing psychic occurrence in acts of injustice is the self-blame of the victim. This is a very significant part of the psychology of injustice: the guilt and shame of the victim the violation of self by another wounds the victim in a way that arouses self-blame, with an intense, often hidden, shame. This is not an incidental aspect of the woundedness of injustice; injustice has a powerful tendency to fault the victim, perhaps based in the belief that I am responsible for what happens to me.[350]

Self-blame is a common occurrence among divorced women and the manner in which divorced women participate unconsciously to their own oppression is the result of internalized societal messages.

Diminished Social Wellbeing

The mean and standard deviation for social wellbeing was fixed at 54.31±10.20 in the experimental group, whereas in the control group the mean and standard deviation was fixed at 59.37±7.05. Moreover, the t-value of -5.345 and the p-value of 0.001 clearly indicate that there is a significant difference in the social wellbeing between the two groups. As many as 31.4% women in the experimental group does not have social life, 20.8% does not have good social life and 29.0% face social exclusion and stigma. In contrast, 40.0% in control group reported to have good social life and only 15.0% said that they do not have social life.

Social relations play a vital role in health and wellbeing. Subject in the experimental group reported lower social wellbeing compared to the control group as they responded negative to areas such as achieving social status they had expected, normally accomplish what they want to, feel good about the relationship they share with their children, consider family as a source of help in finding solutions to most of their problems, most of the members of the family are closely attached to one another, members of the family will look after them well, if they were seriously ill, confident that their relatives will help them out in case of emergency, confident that friends will look after them if they were seriously ill or met with an accident, relatives would help out in times of need, satisfied with their personal relationships with others, feel very much part of the

350 Jeffrey Kauffman, "Restoration of the Assumptive World as an Act of Injustice," in *Handbook of Restorative Justice: A Global Perspective*, edited by Dennis Sullivan and Larry Tifft (London: Routledge 2006), 228.

community and feel safe. On the contrary, they affirmed that they worry about the relationship they have with their children, often worry about the relationship they have with ex-husband, wish for more friends than they actually have and feel that they do not have real close friends. All these factors indicate that social support and family relationships decline post-divorce.

It is widely acknowledged that personal relationships and social support are crucial for one's health and wellbeing. Critical to the wellbeing of divorced women is associated with perceived closeness rather than its availability of contacts. Many divorced women reported that although they have many friends, they do not have real close friends to share their problems. Divorced women also may look for exclusion because in some cases they are being judged and considered dangerous sexual objects causing promiscuity as expressed by some of the subjects.

As is evident from the study, in the face of rejection, divorced women build wall around themselves. According to C. Koons and M. Anthony "They very often will withdraw into themselves, into their homes, and become reclusive, rejecting all attempts of others to reach out to them in a warm, caring, understanding relationship."[351] Much of the divorced women's discomfort in socializing with people and seclude themselves from the society is mainly because of the society's assumptions about them. These experiences match with what has been there in the literature regarding the negative social stigma that many divorced women encounter. It suggests that social stigma is organized around gender and the society views women as bearing the burden for successful or failed marital relationships.[352] Social stigma is another contributing factor that adversely impact divorced women, as there is a general perception that something is wrong with them. One study that examines the perception that people have of divorce concluded that divorcees were evaluated more negatively than married woman and men on four scales such as professional competence, interpersonal adjustment, psychological deviance and morality.[353]

The societal negative attitudes and reactions intensify divorced women's personal distress to a large extent as they experience social exclusion. Many of the respondents reported that they have lost many friends post-divorce. It may be because they either withdraw from friends or their friends reject/abandon them because of their status. Not only are the divorced women looked at by others as shameful but the divorced women view themselves as morally less worthy and as inferior to others. Divorced women internalized the societal messages and thus experience more shame, guilt that leads to social isolation. Loss of self-esteem

351 C. Koons and M. Anthony, *Single Adult Passages: Unchartered Stories* (Grand Rapids: Baker Publishers, 1991), 115.

352 Judy Root Aulette, *Changing Families* (Belmont: Wadsworth Pub., 1994), 56.

353 Mary A. Dolan and Charles D. Hoffman, "The Different Effects of Marital and Custodial Status on Perceptions of Mothers and Fathers," in Journal of Divorce & Remarriage 29/3 (2008): 55.

is also closely associated with shame, which is related to the sense of failure. Thus, divorced women who blame themselves for bad events experience a loss of self-esteem. Attribute bad events to internal causes that lead to feelings of incompetence in coping with future situations.

The data provides rich text revealing prejudice toward divorced women in Naga context. Cultural and religious emphasis on marriage and patriarchal gender role ideology contribute to the stigma and shame associated with divorce and prejudicial attitudes towards divorced women. They usually feel lonely and experience deficiency in social relationships, which eventually leads to poor mental health. About two thirds of the women reported being perceived negatively by society and having little or no social life after family disintegration. When a person experiences hopelessness, one's view of life narrows. Hopelessness includes losing the meaning and direction of life. Social support is found to be more for the married women than the divorced women. The devastating effects of divorce and its damage to women's sense of self-identity for Naga women can be attributed to the traditional understanding of women's identity largely through her roles as mother, daughter, and wife. Hence, the loss of these social roles inevitably implies the loss of identity or a loss of sense of selfhood for divorced women. They face the challenge of being judged and stigmatized about violating conventional or societal/cultural expectations. Marriage is often viewed as core aspects of a woman's identity. Hence, they experience social withdrawal and are ashamed and depressed.

A meta-analysis conducted by Elizabeth Krumrei et al. to assess the link between social relationships and post-divorce adjustment indicated that social relationship post-divorce is associated with higher levels of positive adjustment and lower level of maladjustment. This study shows the association of social relationship with positive post-divorce adjustment. It was found that network relationships promote all forms of positive adjustment including global adjustment, coping, overall happiness, wellbeing and life satisfaction.[354] Being part of the network relationships such as support group, church community or circle of friends are particularly important for healthy adjustment post-divorce as it may help divorced women to mobilize strength and promote personal growth.

Another study conducted by Shapiro and Keyes on the influence of marital status and social wellbeing using a representative sample of adults in the U.S. found that married women experience feeling of belonging and purpose and social integration that promote an individual's sense of wellbeing whereas divorced women experience decline in social network and relationships with others.[355]

Divorced women experience a deep sense of social alienation. This is a direct result of their personal and social experiences in the society that disparage them.

354 Elizabeth Krumre et al., "Post-Divorce Adjustment and Social Relationships: A Meta-Analytic Review," in Journal of Divorce and Remarriage 46/3-4 (2007): 145.

355 Shapiro and Corey L. M. Keyes, "Marital Status and Social Well-Being"..., 333.

Divorced women keep themselves aloof from the society and withdraw from significant areas of their social life, which may also hinder them from pursuing goals and interests that are meaningful to them.

Limited Resources/Economically Poor

The mean and standard deviation for economic wellbeing was fixed at 49.61±10.23 in the experimental group, whereas in the control group the mean and standard deviation was fixed at 55.07±7.70. Moreover, the t-value of -5.223 and the p-value of 0.001 clearly indicate that there is a significant difference in the economic wellbeing between the two groups.

Many of the divorced women have a monthly income of below 10,000/- (42.7%), another 20.7% has monthly income of less than 15,000/- and only a few earn about 40,000 and above, i.e., 3.3%. One significant issue that causes future insecurity and tension divorced women cited is economic instability (35.3%).

Divorced women scored lower in the economic wellbeing as they responded negative to areas such as satisfied with current financial situation, financially self-reliant, satisfied with standard of living, can sustain economic life without depending on anyone, present economic condition is stable, can handle a major unexpected financial expense, enjoy a fair share of family property, families provide financial assistance in times of need, friends and acquaintances provide financial assistance in times of need, future security and being satisfied with what they are earning. Divorced women reported financial stability as one of their major concerns, decline in living standard, in times of financial needs they do not have anyone to help them out, they do not earn enough for survival and having lots of debt. Conversely, women in the control group experience economic security in spite of the fact that many of them were not employed.

As shown in table 1, divorce rates are higher among less educated and lower income groups. For many divorced women, poverty is a threat to their survival. Many of them who are employed juggle work and household chores, which takes a toll on their physical, mental, emotional, and social wellbeing. Many custodial mothers face economic strains owing to the demands of single parenting and raising children single handedly on reduced budget.

Divorced women have substantially lower income. Following divorce there is usually a sudden loss of financial support and a consequent lowering of the standard of living. One key component that adversely affects divorced women and contributes to their suffering is lack of financial assistance. With no resources and income to meet their needs they experience insecurity and stress in terms of the economic factors. The problem is even greater for women who have custody of children. Some divorced women cited single parenting as one major problem. Many of them reported that life has been financially challenging because they had to fend for themselves and their children. Majority of those who have a job do not earn enough to run the family. However, for some the severity of this loss of financial support is lessened by their employment and other vocations that earn them a living. These women are able to experience a certain level of financial security and independence. Divorced women who are employed face fewer financial challenges compared to their unemployed counterparts. Most studies focusing on the economic consequences of divorce observe that women suffer from a decreasing level of economic wellbeing post-divorce. Numerous studies have confirmed that divorce has detrimental economic consequences for women. Smock, Manning and Gupta have asserted that divorce highlights the differences between men and women economically with women being more vulnerable outside of marriage.[356]

Many researches have shown that two-adult households tend to be much better off economically compared to household headed by women.[357] Studies that compare the experience of divorced men and women show that the economic experience of the divorced men differs from that of women. A study done in Canada found that women's income dropped by 30% following divorce.[358] Research conducted in Australia has similar findings, women experience disproportionate declines in household income post-divorce.[359] Increased financial worry and sole child parenting are two of the most cited stressors post-divorce.[360]

Poverty affects physical, mental and psychological/emotional health and social, relational and parental functioning. There is a high correlation between poverty and physical health. As is evident from the data, as many as 49.4% suffer from depression and 37.7% suffer from blood pressure in the experimental group.

The finding that divorced women suffer from economic wellbeing underscores women's status in the Naga society. Women's post-divorce economic hardship could be attributed to several interrelated factors. Social structural factors such as women's secondary position in the economy with no inheritance rights, personal factors such as women's education and training, whether she maintained a career or expected to be a homemaker and whether she dropped out of the work force to take care of the family. In many cases, marriage itself limits job options and earnings for women, marriage and parenthood are characterized by gender inequality in the division of labour. Even if women work outside the home, they tend to be the primary caretakers of children and do a larger share of nonmarket work. Many women in Naga society are integrally connected with

356 Manning, W. D Smock, S. Gupta, "The Effect of Marriage and Divorce" ..., 796.

357 John Scanzoni, *Contemporary Families and Relationships: Reinventing Responsibility* (New York: McGraw Hill Inc, 1995), 285.

358 Tahany M. Gadalla, "Impact of Marital Dissolution on Men's and Women's Incomes: A Longitudinal Study," in Journal of Divorce and Remarriage 50 (2008): 62.

359 David de Vaus et al., "The Economic Consequences of Divorce in Australia," in International Journal of Law, Policy and the Family 28/1 (2014): 7.

360 H. Wang and Paul R. Amato, "Predictors of Divorce Adjustment: Stressors, Resources, and Definitions," in Journal of Marriage and Family 62/3 (2000): 657.

and inseparable from their roles as wife who live for and to fulfil the needs of her husband and children. They usually do not have strong desire to be employed. Hence, the wife is dependent on the husband for economic support and when they get divorced women face serious economic crisis. Besides, many divorced women were married at a young age and hence lack the education to compete in the job market but often find themselves chiefly responsible for the need of the children. Little less than 50% that is 42.5% has custody of children that comes with additional responsibilities of physical, emotional and financial care of the children causing distress.

Divorced women with children are usually the main financial contributors of their children's wellbeing. There is no system in place for these women to receive any financial aid or assistance and in many cases; the women have to take care of the economic needs of the children single handedly with their own devices and initiatives for survival. Consequently, with no proper support system in place such as alimony and inheritance/property rights and child payment, divorced women bear the brunt. With looming economic instability, divorced women experience no sense of control over their lives and thus diminish their sense of wellbeing. All these factors put together to create women's economic status after divorce. What creates the vulnerability of the female-headed household to poverty is a pertinent question. Female-headed households are vulnerable because Naga women are attributed secondary status in the family as well as in the society. The sexual divisions of labour together with their secondary status in the society continue to place women in the disadvantaged position in the socio-economic structure.

Weakened Spiritual Wellbeing

The mean and standard deviation for religious/spiritual wellbeing was fixed at 57.51±13.30 in the experimental group, whereas in the control group the mean and standard deviation was fixed at 63.90±9.05. Moreover, the t-value of -4.868 and the p-value of 0.001 clearly indicate that there is significant difference in the religious/spiritual wellbeing between the two groups.

Many of the divorced women, i.e., 40% reported as spiritually weak and only 28% are spiritually strong. In contrast, 50.6% in the control group rated their spiritual wellbeing as strong and only 14.6% reported to be spiritually weak. About 34% of the divorced women reported that they have drawn closer to God post-divorce as indicated in table 13.

Many divorced women expressed discontentment in their spiritual/religious life and scored lower in their spiritual/religious wellbeing compared to the experimental group. They reported negative in areas such as trust in God, feel connected with God, faith helps them to cope with problems, peace within oneself, trust in faith for decisions, feel the love of God, God as companion in times of distress, look to God for insights and coherence, understand the meaning of life, feeing of sense of purpose in life, find strength and comfort in their faith or religious beliefs, satisfied with their religious life, attend church service, prayer meetings/fellowship groups regularly, read the Bible, pray at home regularly and comfortable to share their problems with the pastor and members of the church. The responses indicate that the absence of specific pastoral ministry to divorced women has affected negatively on their spiritual life although for some, belief in God serve as a coping mechanism.

Divorce experience often draws people closer to God while at the same time drive them further away from God. Many divorced women often feel alienated from the church. Majority of the women in the experimental group were reluctant to seek help from pastor or counselors because of their internalized sense of shame and fear of judgment. Even when they are in need of assistance, they avoid seeking help out of fear of being labelled or shame that result from this label. Some scholars have linked the experience of divorce to their religious beliefs. This also resonates with the experience of many divorced women. Lacking spiritual nourishment and support, many of the divorced women experience what C. C. Neuger termed as "damaged spiritual self-esteem" because they do not experience healing and wholeness of their brokenness and in their search for meaning.[361]

Strong religious/spiritual connection is said to help people lead a healthy lifestyle and give them a sense of meaning that provide comfort, social support and coherent framework of understanding and coping with difficult life situations. Religious beliefs can also serve as a coping mechanism that helps individuals deal with conflict and difficult life situations. Studies that have examined how divorce experience influences their religious attendance post-divorce controlling for their previous religious attendance show that divorce experience significantly reduces the likelihood of attending religious services.[362]

In many cases, divorce occurs at the backdrop in which marriage is seen as a sacred institution and hence it may be appraised in an intensely negative light. Spiritual aspect being a core dimension of life, divorce may often raise profound spiritual issues. Traumatic life experience such as divorce invalidates and challenges some spiritually based assumptions. Divorce can thwart one's religious/spiritual life and one such roadblock occurs when the events are interpreted as a violation of something sacred, which is termed as "spiritual trauma."[363] In an attempt to understand the role that spirituality plays in a potentially traumatic experience

361 C. C. Neuger, "Women's Depression: Lives at Risk," in *Women in Travail and Transition: A New Pastoral Care*, edited by M. Glaz & J.S. Moessner (Minneapolis: Fortress Press, 1991), 155.

362 Richard J. Jenks, Divorce, *Annulments, and the Catholic Church: Healing or Hurtful* (New York: The Haworth Press, 2002), 119.

363 Annette Mahoney, Elizabeth J. Krumrei and Kenneth Pargament, "Broken Vows: Divorce as a Spiritual Trauma and Its Implications for Growth and Decline," in *Trauma, Recovery, and Growth: Positive Psychological Perspectives on Posttraumatic Stress*, edited by Stephen Joseph and P. Alex Linley (New Jersey: John Wiley & Sons Inc., 2012), 105.

such as divorce, Annette Mahoney, Elizabeth J. Krumrei and Kenneth Pargament have proposed sacred loss and desecration as two conceptual model/spiritual struggles that divorcees may experience. The former is the experience that occurs when a person perceives the loss of something, which was once regarded with spiritual qualities as for instance "something I held as sacred is no longer present in my life"; "something of sacred importance in my life disappeared when this event took place." The latter refers to "perceiving sanctified aspect of life as having been violated." For example, a person may experience "something that was sacred to me was destroyed.[364]

They further propose three types of spiritual struggle that are consistent with divorced women experience such as divine, intrapersonal and interpersonal. First, divine spiritual struggle refers to the individual's relationship with God. A divorced person experiencing trauma and crisis may experience anger and doubt about God or feel being abandoned by God and start questioning God who is perceived as all loving and omnipotent for allowing a sacred aspect of one's life to be lost or violated. Divorcees may also reason that since their marriage did not work out as expected by God they deserved to be cut off from the presence of God. Second, intrapersonal spiritual struggle refers to the internal doubts and questions a person has about spiritual matters. In the case of divorce, being unable to live up to the expectation, a divorcee may be guilt ridden for breaking the vows and for violating the parameters that they believe surrounding marriage maybe unable to forgive themselves for breaking their vows that they have failed a sacred marriage that demands lifelong perseverance. Third, interpersonal spiritual struggles refer to the tension and conflict with family, friends, congregations, and communities. Such interpersonal crisis may occur when people in the congregation and communities are being judgmental and insensitive to the divorcees and fail to express appropriate levels of empathy. Interpersonal spiritual struggle may occur when the individuals feel being blamed or judged by the people. Thus, for some individuals, divorce may lead to cutting ties from one's religious community. In some religious circles, some divorcees have to pay the penalties as a consequence of getting divorced by being excommunicated from the church. Some even exclude divorcees from religious rituals. For example, in the Roman Catholic Church divorcees are barred from receiving communion.[365] In Baptist churches in Nagaland, they are excommunicated from the church.

Consistent with this theory the present research reinforces that divorced women experience spiritual trauma leading to greater distress. They withdraw from church activities and feel ashamed to go to church or any Christian gatherings. Divorced women reported that they do not feel comfortable sharing their problems with the pastors and church works and it has implications for the church as a community. The church neither provides support and assistance

364 Mahoney, Elizabeth J. Krumrei and Kenneth Pargament, "Broken Vows"..., 108.

365 Mahoney, Elizabeth J. Krumrei and Kenneth Pargament, "Broken Vows".., 108-109.

specific to coping with divorce that could facilitate effective coping responses nor offer any rituals to facilitate spiritual coping responses with the painful transitions. Unable to find healthy spiritual responses, divorced women experience spiritual crisis. Other studies have also shown clear and consistent links between spiritual struggle and greater psychological maladjustment and distress.[366] According to narrative theorists, people lend meaning to their lives by structuring their experiences into "micronarratives" encompassing life stories and "micornarratives" smaller stories.[367] When people get married, they believe that the union will last for a lifetime. The loss or violation of such sacred narratives disrupts the flow of one's life. Events such as divorce may be more painful when individuals cannot find religious teachings that help them make sense of the shuttering experience of the sacred story or enable them to construct a new story or to reconstruct a meaningful personal reality.

Nevertheless, crisis and trauma such as divorce can also help people to reformulate their sense of spiritual meaning, purpose, and direction. Some of the women in experimental group reported being connected to God and building stronger relation with God and identified faith in God as an important coping resource. Adaptive use of spiritual coping resources offers benefits to people to cope while facing different life challenges including divorce. Such strategies decrease emotional stress and increase spiritual growth and wellbeing. Life struggles motivates people to turn to their faith as a means to grow through their pain. Life traumas can also help people to reformulate their sense of direction, purpose, and spiritual meaning.

In spite of the many negative effects divorced women experience, some positive effects have emerged in the research. As many as 34.0% reported being independent and happy, drawn closer with God and managing life better, 26.7% reported being empowered, no abuse and torture, stronger relation with children, 14.0% experience no family burden, inner peace and satisfaction and helping others in a similar situation. 25.3% did not give any comment.

Conclusion

This section summarizes the major findings of the subject under investigation. The findings suggest that divorced women face physical, mental, emotional/psychological, social, economic, and spiritual/religious difficulties. The study further points out that divorced women in comparison to married women reported more complaints of being unhappy and worried about the different aspects of

366 Kenneth I. Pargament and G. G. Ano, "Empirical Evidences in the Psychology of Religion and Coping," in *Religious Influence on Health and Well-Being in the Elderly*, edited by K.W. Schaie, N. Krause and A. Booth (New York: Springer, 2004), 119.

367 Robert A. Niemeyer and Heidi Levitt, "Coping and Coherence: A Narrative Perspective," in *Coping with Stress: Effective People and Processes*, edited by C.R. Snyder (Oxford: Oxford University Press, 2001), 48.

their lives. Besides the socio-economic woes, many women in the experimental group pointed out the emotional problem and trauma they go through as a result of being a divorcee. Such negative emotions and experience adversely affect their overall wellbeing. The study also reveals that demographic factors also contribute to divorced women's wellbeing. Divorced women are susceptible to social stigma, emotional insecurity, and economic uncertainty, which in turn reduce their wellbeing. On the contrary, married women reported fewer complaints related to the domains under investigation and enjoy better quality of life and wellbeing.

The findings confirm that divorced women experience lower wellbeing. These findings also validate the theoretical considerations. Many researchers have established that divorce has significant implications for wellbeing particularly for women. Thus, based on the findings and the theoretical interpretations of wellbeing, it may be concluded that married women experience higher wellbeing than compared to divorced women. The findings underscore the need for effective pastoral care and counselling ministry. The succeeding chapter deals with the implications for pastoral care and counselling.

Chapter 5

A Liberative Pastoral Care and Counselling Paradigm

Introduction

The preceding chapters dealt with the psychosocial problems associated with divorced women and its negative impact on their wellbeing. The major findings reveal that divorced women experience higher psychosocial problems compared to married women. With more and more women experiencing divorce which require them not only to take decision that affect their immediate future but also impact their overall wellbeing in the long run, it is imperative to find ways to address the needs of divorced women. Based on the major findings of the study, this chapter draws implications for the ministry of pastoral care and counselling.

Implications for Pastoral Care and Counselling

Pastoral Care

Different scholars have variously defined pastoral care. According to William A. Clebsch and Charles R. Jaekle, "Pastoral care consists of healing acts done by representative Christian persons, directed toward the healing, sustaining, guiding, and reconciling of troubled persons, whose troubles arise in the context of ultimate meanings and concerns."[368] This definition locates three important tasks of pastoral care such as helping acts performed by a representative Christian

---

368 Clebsch and Charles R. Jaekle, *Pastoral Care in Historical Perspective...*, 4.

person to the troubled persons who are in need of healing, sustaining, guiding, and reconciliation that arise in the context of ultimate meanings and concerns.

For Alistair Campbell pastoral care is "that aspect of the ministry of the Church which is concerned with the well-being of individuals and of communities."[369]

Stephen Pattison, a well-known pastoral theologian defines pastoral care as,

> Activity within the ministry of the Church which is centrally concerned with promoting the well-being of individuals and communities. The ultimate aim of pastoral care is that of ministry as a whole...to increase love between people and between people and God. Its specific functions are healing, sustaining, reconciling, guiding, and nurturing.[370]

Pattison asserts that pastoral care does not simply confine within individualistic therapeutic settings, but it involves socio-political dimension where individuals are recognized as embedded within the society. He identifies the link between pastoral care and liberation theology and posits that the first function of pastoral care is to seek liberation from oppression.[371] Hence, in its broader sense, pastoral care may be defined as a ministry of seeking to liberate people from their oppression and to enable them to live in harmony with God as well as with others. This understanding of human flourishing and wellbeing is not confined only to the individual level, but a holistic vision of the person, a concept akin to shalom. Pattison's definition of pastoral care is more encompassing as it includes the wider concept of understanding a person's problem rather than confining only within the personal level.

Pastoral Counselling

As defined by the Association of Pastoral Counsellors, pastoral counselling is "a process in which a pastoral counsellor utilizes insights and principles derived from the disciplines of theology and the behavioural sciences in working with individuals, couples, families, groups, and social systems toward the achievement of wholeness and health."[372]

Clinebell posits, "Pastoral counselling, one dimension of pastoral care, is the utilization of the variety of healing (therapeutic) methods to help people handle

369 Alistair V. Campbell, "Nature of Pastoral Care" in *A Dictionary of Pastoral Care*, edited by Alistair V. Campbell (London: SPCK, 1987), 188.

370 Stephen Pattison, *Pastoral Care and Liberation Theology* (Cambridge: Cambridge University Press, 1994), 14.

371 Pattison, *Pastoral Care and Liberation Theology*..., 14.

372 Cited by Orlo Strunk, Jr. "A Prolegomenon to a History of Pastoral Counseling," in *Clinical Handbook of Pastoral Counseling*, vol. 1, edited by Robert J. Wicks, Richard D. Parsons and Donald Capps (New York: Paulist Press, 1985), 15.

their problems and crisis more growthfully and thus experiencing healing of their brokenness. Pastoral counselling is a reparative function needed when the growth of persons is seriously jeopardized or blocked by crisis."[373] Clinebell goes on to say that,

> Pastoral counseling is a response to the need for someone to really care for the troubled within the church fellowship and those numerous persons who have no church, but who turns to a minister for help when crisis strikes. A considerable percentage of those who seek a pastor's counseling are not a part of any meaningful fellowship. They are the alienated ones in the society. Their need for pastoral care is acute. Less obvious, but often no less painful, are the needs of those "lost within themselves in our own congregations." Thus, pastoral counseling has both an inreaching and an outreaching mission to persons in conflict and trouble, wherever they may be.[374]

This definition is true to the experience of divorced women as they experience alienation/exclusion from both the church and the society and experience acute crisis and loss. According to Jill L. Snodgrass,

> Pastoral counseling is a mode of clinical mental care that integrates the knowledge of psychology and the behavioral sciences with the wisdom of spirituality, religion and theology. The foci of pastoral counseling include the alleviation of symptoms, fostering increased coping, assisting with positive behavioral changes, promoting spiritual, economic, intellectual and physical well-being, improving relationship with self and others…[375]

In line with this definition, to best promote wholeness and wellbeing of divorced women, pastoral counselling is to help increase their coping skills, help them make positive behavioural changes and promote all aspects including physical, mental, emotional, social, economic, and spiritual life.

For Emmanuel Y. Lartey, "Counselling is the skilled and principled use of relationship to facilitate self-knowledge, emotional acceptance and growth and the optimal development of personal resources. The overall aim is to provide an opportunity to work towards living more satisfyingly and resourcefully."[376] He further suggests that pastoral counselling refers to the entire person and addresses

---

373 Clinebell, *Basic Types of pastoral Care and Counseling…*, 27.

374 Clinebell, *Basic Types of Pastoral Counseling…*, 41-42.

375 Jill L. Snodgrass, "Pastoral Counseling: A Discipline of Unity amid Diversity," in *Understanding Pastoral Counseling*, edited by E. A. Maynard and Jill L. Snodgrass (New York: Springer Publishing Company, 2015), 5-6.

376 Emmanuel Y. Lartey, *In Living Color: An Intercultural Approach to Pastoral Care and Counseling*, second edition (London: Jessica Kingsley Publishers, 2003), 82.

issues affecting the wellbeing of the individual. The aim of counselling is then to enable the counselees "to explore their thoughts, feelings and behavior; to reach clearer knowledge and understanding of themselves; and as a result find the strength and resources to cope more effectively with life."[377]

Seward Hiltner sees pastoral counselling as, "the attempt by a pastor to help people help themselves through the process of gaining understanding of their inner conflicts."[378] Hiltner position entails "emotional re-education" whereby the counselor helps people with their immediate problems by helping them find solutions to their problems in order to achieve optimal functioning.

Chris R. Schlauch visualizes pastoral counselling as "Counseling for the whole person, as an individual as well as part of a family and social unit, and as a whole person, body, mind and spirit, but with particular reference to the person's psychological, ethical and theological frame of reference."[379] In the same vein, Latrey claims, "pastoral counselors work alongside others in seeking the total well-being of all persons. This totality includes individual bodies, minds and spirits, families and other social units. It also brings psychological, social, ethical, and theological perspectives to bear upon all its concerns."[380] Thus, pastoral counselling embraces the whole person with their psychosocial dimensions as equally important to assist the person to achieve the optimal functioning and wellbeing.

According to Ezamo Murry, "Pastoral counseling arises from a crisis situation of the people. It is a caring ministry centered around an individual or group focused on a specific problem."[381] The ministry of pastoral care and counselling premised on the idea that every person in crisis might be enabled to experience fullness of life and wholeness.

Biblical and Theological Basis for Care and Counselling

Pastoral care is intrinsic to Christian tradition and linked to the biblical image of the shepherd. The OT imagery portrays God as the shepherd, the one who guides and protects the people. "He will feed his flock like a shepherd" (Isaiah 40:11), "The Lord is my shepherd" (Psalms 23). In the NT, Jesus is presented as showing compassion for the people who were like "sheep without shepherd" (Matt. 9:36). The image of Jesus as the good shepherd is prominent in the Fourth Gospel. Jesus informs his readers "I am the good shepherd" (John 10:14). Thus, in the

377 Lartey, *In Living Color: An Intercultural Approach to Pastoral Care and Counseling...*, 82-83.

378 Seward Hiltner, *Pastoral Counselling: How Every Pastor Can Help People Help Themselves* (Nashville: Abington Press, 1949), 19.

379 Chris R. Schlauch, *Faithful Companioning: How Pastoral Counseling Heals* (Minneapolis: Fortress Press, 1995), 223.

380 Lartey, *In Living Color: An Intercultural Approach to Pastoral Care and Counseling...*, 108.

381 Ezamo Murry, *An Introduction to Pastoral Care and Counseling* (ISPCK: New Delhi, 2016), 141.

company of the good shepherd, human souls find healing, comfort, nourishment, nurturance, restoration, and guidance. It also implies that Jesus as the shepherd offers guidance, protection and friendship. In its final section, Peter was charged with the responsibility to feed my sheep (John 21:17). Thus, pastoral care is at the heart of Christian ministry.

Pastoral care brings together the practical and spiritual aspects and was expressed historically as "the cure of soul" meaning care for others is the pastoral task of being "accountable for shepherding the inner life of the people through the crisis of emotional conflict and interpersonal pain towards growth in responsiveness towards God."[382] In the words of Edward E. Thornton, "Theology and pastoral care interpenetrate each other."[383] Hence, he defines the interdependency and interconnection of theology and pastoral care and counselling as "Pastoral care and counseling are forms of religious ministry which integrates the findings of behavioral science and theology in the effort to prepare the way for divine-human encounter in the midst of human crisis."[384] Thornton further asserts that the ultimate goal of pastoral care and counselling is experiencing of God's grace.[385] Thus, the role of pastoral care and counselling is to prepare a way for divine-human encounter amidst human crisis.

The Bible presents many situations that involve the ministry of counselling. In both the Old and the New Testaments, counselling settings are recorded. God has worked through people in the ministry of counselling. For instance, the book of Proverbs speaks of the benefits of counselling; Proverbs 12:15 instructs "Make plans by seeking advice." Psalms 55:13,14 recorded how much David enjoyed the counsel of a friend. Donald Capps uses the Bible's many literary genres such as wisdom, parable, or lament to address the different situations. The Psalms of lament not only respond to and help people through the grief process but also help free people from obtrusive pious expectations and allow them to be angry with God. In the New Testament, Jesus Christ had an extensive counselling ministry recorded particularly in the Gospels.

The life and ministry of Jesus depicts many of the counselor's attitudes towards the counselee as Murry puts it "the therapist's positive regard of the individual, the pent up emotion and cathartic experience, the concept of acceptance and the doctrine of divine justification of the sinner, the concept of disciplined listening and the idea of God as a patient listener."[386] The heart of the theology of pastoral care is Jesus' injunction in the form of an exhortation "you shall love

---

382 Thomas C. Oden, *Pastoral Ministry: Essentials of Ministry* (San Francisco: Harper & Row publishers, 1983), 187.

383 Edward E. Thornton, *Theology and Pastoral Counseling* (Philadelphia: Fortress Press, 1964), 15.

384 Thornton, *Theology and Pastoral Counseling...*, 27.

385 Thornton, *Theology of Pastoral Counseling...*, 38.

386 Murry, *An Introduction to Pastoral Care and Counseling...*, 79.

the Lord your God with all your heart, and with all your soul, and with all your strength, and with all your mind, and your neighbour as yourself" (Mark 12: 30, 31; Luke 10:27). This implies that the nucleus of pastoral role of the church is that Christians stand in relation not only with God but also to one another. At the heart of Christian ministry, pastoral ministry of care and counselling is understood as human flourishing and achieving life in all its fullness. Pastoral care ministry is a potentially transformative service of love and care that will assist the person to fully develop one's God given potential in relationships both vertically and horizontally.[387]

Pastoral Care Functions

In each historical epoch, the church has employed innovative ways of tackling different situations and meeting the needs of troubled persons. In the present increasingly diverse and conflicted society, pastoral caregivers must continue to develop new ways in order to remain relevant to the varying needs of the people and to carry out caring, healing, and growth nurturing ministry of wholeness and wellbeing. Many traditional approaches and caregiving shaped by old ways are no longer adequate to effectively deal with the new challenges and problems. Hence, there is a need to develop a new and innovative ways of handling different issues more effectively.

Several key pastoral care functions can be employed to achieve the desired result of human wholeness and wellbeing. The three aspects of shepherding perspective delineated by Hiltner where the shepherd's concern for the welfare of the persons are healing, guiding and sustaining to which reconciling was added by Clebsch and Jaekle and nurturing was conceptualized by Clinebell. Further Lartey has added liberating and empowering in his cross-cultural approach to pastoral care and counselling. All these aspects are important in dealing with divorced women in their distress.

Healing

Healing as understood by Hiltner implies wholeness. He defines healing as "involving the restoration of functional wholeness that has been impaired as to direction or timing."[388] Healing is "rebecoming", a restoration of a condition once obtained but then lost. It does not necessarily mean that the result of healing is the same in its condition that previously obtained except for the characteristic of wholeness.[389] Hiltner proposes that if the person's impairment/disability is due to

387 John Caperon, *A Vital Ministry: Chaplaincy in Schools in the Post-Christian Era* (London: SCM Press, 2015), 8.

388 Seward Hiltner, *The Christian Shepherd: Some Aspects of Pastoral Care* (Nashville: Abington Press, 1959), 19.

389 As for instance, a man who has lost one kidney is healed when the other kidney perform the work of two although in structure the new wholeness is not the same as that pertaining before

negative feelings, healing begins by acknowledging, accepting, understanding and assimilating those feelings and not only through verbal encouragement. Genuine acceptance and understanding of negative feelings help the person to assimilate the facts of his/her psychic life. If a person senses that he/she is accepted, the negative feelings that had been repressed will emerge into the open. Paul Tillich also posits this idea as "acceptance-in-spite-of."[390] Healing takes place only when the painful process of negative feelings has been assimilated and reconciled, otherwise healing becomes symptomatic and hence not holistic.[391] Hiltner contends that healing is capable of changing the total situation of a person. The goal of healing "involves restoration and functional wholeness in terms of possibilities opened up by pastoral counselling in an educative mode, one that draws out the feelings for examination and decision and that relies on the parishioner's inner resources for healing and well-being."[392] The concept of healing proposed by Hiltner is particularly relevant for divorced women as they are wounded and broken and are in need of healing. Through this function, restoration of wholeness that has been impaired may be achieved. Healing for divorced women entails interpreting the situation that provides meaning and transcends the situation.

Sustaining

Sustaining emphasizes on "standing by." Unlike healing, sustaining relates to those situations where the total situations cannot be changed or at least not at the moment. It is a ministry of support and encouragement when what had been broken or impaired is incapable of total restoration. When a situation is such that at least for the time being, change is not possible, a pastor or minister stands by or make sustenance available. The ministry of sustenance becomes dominant in two areas such as bereavement and divorce. In such situations, it is not possible at least for the moment to restore the previous actual situations.[393] The ministry of sustaining in the case of divorced women may be sustaining those with low ego strength or who are emotionally crippled to allow them to continue to function constructively. For divorced women sustaining ministry is particularly important to block the precipitous action, which might result in irreversible consequences. Sustaining is also crucial in the lives of divorced women because of the overwhelming nature of the experience. Pastoral caregivers can sustain people in crisis with care and consolation.

---

the kidney was lost yet in terms of functioning of the whole body wholeness has been restored. Thus, healing is understood as a process of restoring functional wholeness. Seward Hiltner, *Preface to Pastoral Theology* (Nashville: Abington Press, 1958), 89.

390 Paul Tillich, "Theology and Counseling," in *The Meaning of Health*, edited by Perry LeFevre (Chicago: Exploration Press, 1984), 121.

391 Hiltner, *Preface to Pastoral Theology*..., 111.

392 Purves, *Reconstructing Pastoral Theology: A Christological Foundation*..., xxiii.

393 Hiltner, *Preface to Pastoral Theology*..., 117.

Guiding

The third aspect is guiding. For Hiltner, the ministry of guiding is to "assist troubled persons in making difficult choices in thought or action that affect both the present and future state of soul."[394] This implies guiding troubled persons make truthful and confident choices. Divorced women are confused concerning issues of life meaning and concern and are in need of guidance. Guiding can be employed by pastoral caregivers in order to help divorced women make the right choice in their future course of action. Through proper guidance divorced women may find the potential within them and thrive their growth stunning situation. Guiding can be done through helping them to learn from their experience of failure and shame instead of being trapped in self-devaluing, contempt, and self-hatred and to help them develop a positive outlook.

Reconciling

The ministry of pastoral care involves reconciliation with both God and fellow humans. The ministry of reconciliation as defined by Clebsch and Jaekle is "helping alienated persons to establish or renew proper and fruitful relationships with God and neighbour."[395] It is a ministry of re-establishing both horizontal and vertical relationship. This pastoral care function is crucial for divorced women as they experience alienation and are in need of such reconciliation both with God as well as with fellow humans.

E. E. Acolatse mentions that Christians experience acute stress of divorce because of their belief in their calling to "a life of reconciliation and for whom marriage is viewed as the ultimate location of the reconciled and reconciling life."[396] Thus, the process of adjustment may take longer period of time because of the conflict between their religious belief and personal experience. Reconciliation as a pastoral care function to divorce women is to help reconcile one's belief and values with the singleness. As divorced women suffer from negative attitudes and perceptions towards their single status, the church can provide resources of support networks and assist them to establish new networks of support to enhance and adjust to their changed social status. Belonging to a social group may decrease their social isolation and gives them a sense of belonging, worth and dignity that is crucial for overall wellbeing of divorced women.

Nurturing

Nurturing presupposes that all human beings are developing and have not reached the full potential. Nurturing, according to Clinebell, seeks to promote growth of

394 Hiltner, *Preface to Pastoral Theology*..., 154.

395 Clebsch and Jaekle, *Pastoral Care in Historical Perspective*..., 56.

396 E. E. Acolatse, "Christian Divorce Counselling in West Africa: Seeking Wholeness through Reformed Theology and Jungian Dreamwork," in The Journal of Pastoral Theology, vol. 21/1 (2011): 1.

people and society.[397] Lartey contends, "Here the pastoral caregiver needs skills in both comforting and challenging people to encourage growth."[398] Through nurturing, divorced women can learn to love and take care of themselves by attending to their personal needs and taking care of one's health and developing interpersonal relationships that might facilitate self-esteem.

Divorced women also need spiritual nurturing as many of them reported to have turned away from their religious/spiritual life post-divorce. Religious beliefs and spirituality have been identified as one of the crucial elements on the overall wellbeing of an individual. This implies that the ministry of nurturing divorced women must include spiritual nurturing in order to help them find meaning and purpose in life. The development of spiritual potential takes place in the context of warm and caring human relationships where divorced women feel being accepted, cared for and experience an atmosphere of belongingness for spiritual growth and development.

Liberation

Liberating involves "raising awareness about the sources and causes of oppression and domination in society.[399] It entails a process of concentizing people about the origin and causes of their suffering and oppression and journeying with them in the process of seeking solutions and transformation. Liberating involves consciousness raising about structures that keep them from living their full potential. Watkins-Ali defines liberating ministry as "action, including political activism that works towards the elimination of oppression."[400] Miller-McLemore argues that, pastoral care, when viewed from a liberation perspective "is about breaking silences, urging prophetic action and liberating the oppressed."[401] Betty Friedan asserts that it is in a woman's defining herself by her own actions, according to her own deepest sense of knowing, that she can break through to authenticity and liberation.[402] Divorced women need to be affirmed and encouraged to liberate themselves from their growth-stunting situations. Divorced women should be liberated from oppressive traditional norms of patriarchy by dismantling the systems and structures of oppression and working towards realization of full humanness.

---

397 Clinebell, *Basic Types of Pastoral Counseling...*, 19.

398 Lartey, *In Living Color: An Intercultural Approach to Pastoral Care and Counseling...*, 67.

399 Lartey, *In Living Color: An Intercultural Approach to Pastoral Care and Counseling...*, 67.

400 Caroll Watkins-Ali, *Survival and Liberation: Pastoral Theology in African American Context* (St. Louis, MO: Chalice Press, 1999), 121.

401 Bonnie J. Miller-McLemore, *Christian Theology in Practice: Discovering a Discipline* (Grand Rapids: Eerdmans, 2012), 91.

402 Betty Friedan, *It Changed my Life: Writings on the Women's Movement* (Cambridge, Massachusetts: Harvard University Press, 1976), 77.

Empowering

The empowering model emphasizes on the fact that there is something good, of worth and value within all human beings. Hence, empowering pastoral care means 'drawing out and building up' of the hidden strength and resources within an individual.[403] For Lartey, empowering is,

> the process of revaluing self and personal characteristics together with finding and using available resources outside oneself, in such a way as to enable and motivate persons and groups to think and act in ways that will result in greater freedom and participation in the life of the societies of which they are a part.[404]

For divorced women, this will mean to unlearn their "learned helplessness" and take back the power they have given away. It may also mean addressing the oppressive economic, political, social and cultural issues of injustices and reclaiming the rights and privileges that have been denied to them by giving them access to information, awareness and financial and legal resources. According to Miller-McLemore, an empowering pastoral ministry further entails advocacy on behalf of and tenderness towards the vulnerable.[405] Liberating and empowering are crucial as it assists and allows divorced women to start valuing and knowing herself and make her own decisions.[406] It is in the empowering of a woman through her own redefinition of self and development of unique solutions that she can become more authentically herself.

Redirection

Redirection can be added as one important pastoral care functions in assisting divorced women. In order to establish growth towards wholeness, caregivers can encourage divorced women to develop their unique potentialities of being single including the opportunity to invest the time and energy in other forms of fulfilling, satisfying, useful and generative ways such as uncovering the hidden talents and hobbies and handling different situations.[407] One important objective in redirection is to help divorced women learn and grow from the experience and prepare them either for remarriage or creative singlehood.[408] Divorced women should be redirected on how to live life constructively by avoiding bitterness

---

403 Lartey, *In Living Color: An Intercultural Approach to Pastoral Care and Counseling...*, 58.

404 Lartey, *In Living Color: An Intercultural Approach to Pastoral Care and Counseling...*, 68.

405 Bonnie J. Miller-McLemore, "Shaping the Future of Religion and Psychology: Feminist Transformations in Pastoral Theology," in *Religion and Psychology: Mapping the Terrain in Contemporary Dialogues*, Future Prospects, edited by D. E. Jonte-Pace & W.B. Parsons (New Haven: Routedge, 2001), 194.

406 Lartey, *In Living Color: An Intercultural Approach to Pastoral Care and Counseling...*, 67, 68.

407 Clinebell, *Basic Types of Pastoral Care & Counseling ...*, 295.

408 Clinebell, *Basic Types of Pastoral Care & Counseling ...*, 297.

and pain which may help them learn to transform the painful experiences into an opportunity to learn and grow in their mental, emotional, spiritual and interpersonal lives. While painful, divorce can be a learning and growth experience where one can learn from the past and get to know oneself better and also develop new aspects of life previously unknown to them. As divorced women go through deep scars and struggle to come to terms with their new state of singlehood, restructuring and re-establishing of life post-divorce is to help them come to terms with the situation their lives have acquired.

In most of the literature, divorce is seen as problem centered involving issues such as depression, loneliness, low self-esteem, self-hatred etc., but that might not always be true. Such socially constructed idea underlining the socio-cultural stereotyping of divorced women reinforces the negative factors. In fact, such one-sided approach had been challenged. E. Mavis Hetherington who has done extensive studies on some families in the 1970s reports that "Divorce can and does ruin lives...but I also think much current writings on divorce—both popular and academic—has exaggerated its negative effects and ignored its sometimes considerable positive effects."[409] Although, there is clearly a need to identify and respond to the negative outcomes of divorce, there are also some indications that some individuals eventually adjust favourably to divorce and make positive personal change as a result of the experience. Given the evidence from the empirical data that some divorced women experience being independent and happy, being empowered and experiencing inner peace and satisfaction post-divorce, it is also crucial that counselors and caregivers focus on the deeper understanding of the factors that encourage positive growth apart from understanding the potential negative psychosocial aspects. Attention should be given to the positive side of being single and the values of these benefits sociologically and psychologically by maintaining healthy lifestyle, achieving personality integration and finding personal fulfilment rather than focusing only on pathology. Caregivers need to deconstruct the stereotype of divorced women as being bogged down with problems and start promoting approaches and attitudes that can help bring about a creative singlehood.

The experience of divorced women in Naga context requires going beyond the traditional understanding of care. Pastoral care of divorced women needs to include functions such as liberating, empowering and redirecting approaches. This calls for a move towards ministry beyond the traditional functions in order to help them achieve the optimal level of functioning. All these aspects of pastoral care are closely intertwined and lead to improve sense of psychosocial wellbeing.

---

409 E. Mavis Hetherington, *For Better or for Worse, Divorced Reconsidered* (New York: W.W. Norton, 2002), 77.

Functions of Pastoral Counselling

Growth Counselling and Therapy

Growth counselling perceives people as possessing a wealth of unlived life and unused assets. The aim of growth counselling is to facilitate and accelerate potentializing the ongoing process of growth work by which people actualize their emerging capacities. Implicit to this concept is the conviction that most people have significant unused resources and the latent ability to develop these assets and strengths throughout their lives.[410]

Growth process has been explored by many prominent psychologists and psychotherapists including Erich Fromm, Karen Horney, Carl Jung, Gordon Allport, Carl Rogers, Rollo May, Fritz Pearls, Erik Erickson and Abraham Maslow using such term as "individuation," "potentializing," "self-actualization," "becoming," "growth work" "self realization" etc. Maslow has explored in depth the dynamics of the process of self-actualization. He has identified the hierarchy of needs in human beings, the most fundamental being need for safety. In ascending order, the other basic needs of all person need of belonging, love, respect, and self-esteem. Transcending these basic needs is the "meta-need" to continue growing.[411]

The crude premise of pastoral care and counselling and all psychotherapies is to maximize human wholeness. Various methods and techniques employed in counselling and psychotherapy are means of enabling people to handle life crisis more growthfully. The techniques of psychotherapy are essential ways of helping people whose lives have been impaired and growth diminished by painful life experiences, to help them free themselves for continuing growth. The central task of pastoral counselors and therapists is to awaken realizable hopes for creative change and help persons to actualize their hopes. Growth counselling is a process of helping people unearth the unused assets so as to grow and achieve their highest potentials through counselling and therapy.

Clinebell has proposed three objectives in accomplishing ministry of growth in pastoral counselling with divorced women. First, helping them work through and resolve grief and painful experiences. He contends that divorcees need to complete their grief work of an earlier marriage before plunging into remarriage otherwise the new relationship will be impaired by unresolved conflicts from the earlier relationship. Second, helping divorcees learn from the experience that could prepare them for remarriage or to creative singlehood. In this learning-growth process, the counsellor helps divorcees identify and change whatever they have contributed to the dissolution of the marriage and help them learn new communication and conflict resolution skills. Third is to help reduce to a

410 Howard Clinebell, *Growth Counselling: Hope-Centered Methods of Actualizing Human Wholeness* (Nashville: Parthenon Press, 1982), 42.

411 Abraham Maslow, *Motivation and Personality* (New York: Harper & Row, 1970), 38.

minimum the emotional damage done to the children.[412] As divorced women experience psychosocial ramifications; growth counselling and therapy is necessary in the process of readjustments for smooth functioning.

Pastoral Psychotherapy

Pastoral psychotherapy also known as pastoral therapy is a more extended form of pastoral counselling that involves exploring complex emotional and relationship issues. People whose brokenness is pronounced, intense and who has reached an impasse because of their life situations often benefit from such reconstructive therapeutic methods. The therapeutic goal is to facilitate healing and growth that makes the very foundations of people's lives stronger, more satisfying and more productive. This therapeutic process usually takes longer period of time because it deals with the deeper conflicts and problems of the counselee including those problems and conflicts that the person is not aware of.[413] Professionals who have had rigorous academic and clinically supervised training should carry out pastoral therapy.

As is evident from the data that divorced women experience a number of symptoms as they try to reorganize their lives. Pastoral psychotherapy can be helpful in multiple ways such as individual therapy and group therapy. When implemented effectively, psychotherapy allows divorced women to move past the point of crisis. It can also help them to develop tools for success in overall adjustment post-divorce.[414]

In addition to the loss of spouse, divorced women also experience sadness and uncertainty associated with redefining their identity outside the role of wife or mother. In such situation, psychotherapists can offer support and aid to such women by exploring potential identities these women may occupy post-divorce. Such exploration may involve highlighting those roles the woman plays as a married person that may have been overshadowed by the role of wife such as employment or developing new hobbies. Encouragement by psychotherapists to consider the identity that the counselee would now like to assume and how to develop this new identity may also be beneficial in this situation.[415] Therapists also may assist in discovering a new facet of the individual's personality and help her avoid negative self-image for the things that had gone wrong and help cultivate a positive outlook.

412 Clinebell, *Basic Types of Pastoral Care and Counseling*…, 10.

413 Clinebell, *Basic Types of Pastoral Care and Counseling*..., 10, 11.

414 Winetta A. Baker, "Psychotherapy for Adults," in *Cultural Sociology of Divorce: An Encyclopaedia*, vol. 1. edited by Robert E. Emery (New Delhi: Sage Publications, 2013), 1008.

415 Baker, "Psychotherapy for Adults"..., 1008.

Individual Counselling

Individual counselling is one of the many ways professionals can assist persons going through rough patch. It is a one-on-one session between the counselor and the counselee. Individual counselling offers the most contained safe, caring and confidential environment providing an opportunity for therapeutic experience. It also offers many opportunities for extended and in-depth intrapsychic exploration. Persons who need to move at their own pace and are not comfortable disclosing their most painful experience to others can be helped through one-on-one counselling. In the case of divorced women, focus should be given to processing their feelings of sadness, stress, grief, and depression in order to turn the negative emotions to a positive one so that they can function better.

Group Counselling

Group counselling constitutes one of the most useful and effective resources for broadening and deepening a church's ministry of healing and growth.[416] There are many significant advantages of group counselling. First, as Jerome D. Frank contends, "Intimate sharing of feelings, ideas, and experiences in an atmosphere of mutual respect and understanding enhances self-respect, deepens self-understanding, and helps a person live with others. Such an experience can be helpful at any level of illness of health."[417] Second, it provides better stewardship of a counselor's time to help more people simultaneously then to spend the same amount of time helping just one. Third, group counselling also allows counselees to help themselves even as they help others. One unique element pointed out by Clinebell is the presence of mutually "giving" relationship where "The group climate of interdependency facilitates the growth that comes when one becomes an agent of healing in the lives of others, even when one's healing is being nurtured by them."[418] Fifth, group counselling can also encourage those persons who are not willing or shy away from individual counselling.

For divorced women group therapy can be especially effective in counteracting the feelings of isolation and rejection and move beyond loss and grief. Sharing the journey with other women, helps defuse the isolation and despair and increase a sense of belongingness. It allows them to think through different areas of their lives impacted by divorce as they share one another's stories of shattered dreams, disappointments, and grief. A divorced woman needs compassion of another woman who truly understands her struggles and pains. Group therapy is important to explore their commonalities, affirm each other's strength, and understand their concerns. Group therapy can be highly

416 Clinebell, *Basic Type of Pastoral Care and Counseling...*, 377.

417 Jerome D. Frank and Julie B. Frank, *Persuasion and Healing: A Comparative Study of Psychotherapy* (London: The Johns Hopkins University Press, 1993), 22.

418 Clinebell, *Basic Type of Pastoral Care and Counseling...*, 380.

effective in helping divorced women as it offers a support system. For some divorced women, members of the family and friends are unable to be supportive because they do not live in close proximity and are unavailable for other reasons or because divorced women do not wish to share their experiences with them. Group therapy may provide a safe space, a nonjudgmental environment to talk about their experiences with the hope of receiving support from those who understand them and meeting their emotional and social support and explore greater possibilities for their lives.

Women Friendly Pastoral Counselling

Even in the postmodern age, many women who seek counselling face difficulty because psychotherapists and counselors see women as weaker and dependent and define them based on their biological function and their relationship to men and label them "unfeminine" if they assert themselves. Hence, there is a need for therapists, professionals and counselors to focus on helping the counselees define in terms of her own needs and potential rather than in terms of the assumptions and expectations of the society or of the particular therapist about her needs.[419]

It is crucial that the therapists and counselors commit to gender equality and free oneself from culturally defined gender stereotypes in order to deliver therapy that enhances, supports and encourages women's development and growth. Counselors informed and guided by gender equality would make a huge difference in helping divorced women who are afflicted by constricting cultural values and practices and help them explore other ways of being and relating to enhance their wellbeing. Pastoral counselors need to be gender sensitive and challenge culturally defined stereotypes and affirm women's dignity and worth. Emma Justes rightly says that "[pastors and pastoral counselors] who find that they are unable to travel the route of enabling women to break free from cultural stereotypes that define their existence, should not be doing pastoral counseling with women."[420]

In a patriarchal structure like Naga context, it is imperative for pastoral caregivers to focus on the issue of patriarchy and its negative impacts on the lives of women as they are being denied of their rights, excluded and are mistreated in many ways. Women being treated inferior to men, tend to internalize their oppression that manifests not only in certain behaviour towards others but also within the individual. Self-blame, depression, unhealthy relationship choices, drug or alcohol abuse, hopelessness, helplessness and despair can all be manifestations of the internalization of mistreatment experienced in the larger society. Internalized oppression feeds negative beliefs and behaviours. Women friendly therapists can interrupt the internalized oppression by countering the oppressive structures and

419 Charlotte Holt Clinebell, *Counseling for Liberation* (Philadelphia: Fortress Press, 1973), 19.

420 Emma Justes, "Women," in *Clinical Handbook of Pastoral Counseling*, edited by Robert Wicks, Richard D. Parsons and Donald Capps (New York: Paulist Press, 1985), 298.

help them realize that their behaviour as unhealthy and destructive as it might be, is a resistance strategy to deal with oppression. It can also help them identify how they have tried to resist internalizing in both adaptive and self-destructive ways and to explore ways and means to replace the destructive coping mechanisms with healthy ones.[421]

In the book, *Through the Eyes of Women,* Brita L. Gill-Austern underscores six psychological, cultural and theological roots for the tendency of women to express love and care in self-sacrificial forms and explains why these qualities and behaviours are reinforced. Although all the six points are important and have implications, two are particularly crucial and relevant to the self-perception of single women and how the predominantly family oriented institution of the church views them. First, such behaviour is deeply rooted in women's experience that identity is essentially defined in connectivity and relation; and in a culture that substantially informs this sense of self by raising women to consider the needs of others, to take care of men and children at their expense.[422] Jean Baker Miller has rightly mentioned that women are raised with an idea that they should help others and that their survival depends on taking care of the wellbeing of others.[423] If a woman's self-identity is tied up in caring for men and children, and if social convention dictates that marriage is the most acceptable vehicle to fulfil that expectation what does it imply about the self-worth and self-esteem of single women who are divorced. Second, women are motivated toward self-sacrifice because they have grown up in culture that gives them a message that in order to remain connected and maintain relation, they must sacrifice themselves and their needs. This perception is compounded by the idea that their identities as women and Christians have been shaped by a theological tradition that view self-denial and self-sacrifice as the defining attribute of Christian love. The church subscribes to the view that in order to be a good Christian woman, she must sacrifice her needs and desires for the needs and welfare of her husband and her family. If there is no husband and children, how does one define these qualities? And how do divorced women exhibit these qualities publicly?[424]

In order to help women to discover and nurture her full potential and unique humanness, it is necessary that pastoral caregivers be able to deal with their attitudes and expectations regarding gender roles and differences and how much

421 Huge Vasquez and Sukie Magraw, "Building Relationships across Privilege: Becoming an Ally in the Therapeutic Relationships," in *Psychotherapy with Women: Exploring Diverse Contexts and Identities*, edited by Marsha Pravder Mirkin, Karen L. Suyemoto and Barbara F. Okun (New York: The Guilford Press, 2005), 76.

422 Brita L. Gill-Austern, "Love Understood as Self-Sacrifice and Self-Denial: What Does It Do to Women," in *Through the Eyes of Women*, edited by Jeanne Stevenson Moessner (Minneapolis: Fortress Press, 1996), 305-307.

423 Jean Baker Miller, *Towards a New Psychology of Women* (Boston: Beacon Press, 1986), 34.

424 Gill-Austern, "Love Understood as Self-Sacrifice and Self-Denial"..., 308.

they have been influenced by the cultural and social expectations and attitudes. By identifying these aspects, pastoral counselors must be very clear about how much these attitudes influence their approach to pastoral care giving especially with women. The goal of this is to diminish the limitations of constricting cultural values and practices on pastoral work particularly while dealing with divorced women.

Culturally Sensitive Pastoral Counselling

The traditional psychotherapy lens through which a counselee's issues are viewed derives from Western monoculture values and beliefs systems. In today's multicultural society, therapists must expand and go beyond the monoculture to view the person's situations in multiple ways thereby challenging the assumptions of traditional theories and approaches. If the social condition of divorced women is the root cause of their worthlessness, depression, shame and self-blame etc. and since most of the divorced women's problems arise from social condition rather than from individual deficiency, the therapists need to identify the effects of these life experiences on the counselees. Within the context of being a woman, there are culturally relevant variables that shape and influence the woman's view of herself and her world. Social and cultural context is crucial to understand vulnerability of women. Therapists can also evaluate their own reactions to their counselees that may be based on cultural beliefs and could influence the process of therapy.

Cultural pressures for women to be married, to turn to others for protection and to focus their own energies on taking care of the needs of others often lead women to hold attitudes that make it difficult for them to imagine a happy and creative single life. In addition, culturally normative behaviours make many divorced women economically vulnerable. Pastoral counselling that is rooted in the culture needs to consider seriously the destructive cultural perceptions and concepts that influence such attitude.

Crisis Counselling

There may be many events in life that one has no control over. Some events are part of natural cycle of growth such as death of a loved one. However, unexpected events including separation or divorce can create havoc in the life of an individual. Divorce presents acute crisis for many women as they face major changes in the family structure. Feelings of shock, anger, grief, shame, and deep hurt accompany a significant loss. Whether the trauma has occurred recently or many decades ago, the woman's sense of hurt, the bottled up emotions must be expressed and released for healing and growth to take place. Crisis counselling may help divorced women to move away from negative patterns of depression, anger, self-hatred that may have been learned due to the overwhelming crisis. Counselling should offer the possibility to learn from past experiences and to grow stronger, helping them to view oneself not as a victim but as a survivor. Through counselling, different areas such as personal growth, self-development, assertiveness and self-esteem can be explored as divorced women survivor unique journey towards wholeness and wellbeing.[425]

Referral

In situations where the caregiver does not know what course of action should be taken, it is imperative that he/she seeks professional assistance and advice instead of giving up on counselees. A wise referral is one of the most effective and significant services a pastor can render to persons in trouble. A minister can multiply his/her service to the troubled persons by availing helping resources of the community. In this regard, Clinebell asserts:

> Properly conceived, referral is a means of using a team effort to help a troubled person. It is a broadening and sharing, not a total transfer of responsibility. It employs a division-of-labour principle that is the basic of interprofessional cooperation. Only by drawing on the specialized helping skills of others can ministers have time and energy to fulfill their unique pastoral function as spiritual growth enablers for the entire congregation.[426]

Networking and referrals are indispensable in caring and counselling divorced women by referring them to different agencies and groups that works with such women. Such networking can enhance and broaden the boundaries of effective pastoral assistance.

Psychotherapeutic Models

One of the main objectives of psychotherapeutic approaches is to help people gain insight into the nature and development of the problem. Although, variously developed and deviated from the psychoanalytic tradition pioneered by Sigmund Freud and each theorist has particular understanding of human growth and development they all share the same overarching view that when persons know more constructively what the hidden dynamics of their lives are, they can be enabled to structure their lives in a more satisfactory and creative fashion.[427] Psychodynamic therapy focuses on the unconscious processes as they are manifested in the person's present behaviour. Hence, it focuses on counselee's self-awareness and understanding of the influence of the past on present behaviour. It enables them to examine unresolved conflicts and issues that arise from past dysfunctional relationships impairing their full functioning. The goals of Freudian psychoanalytic therapies are to bring the unconscious into the conscious, enabling the individuals to work through the past and understand the present behaviours.

425 Lucy Costigan, *Women and Healing* (New York: iUniversity Inc., 2005), 50.

426 Clinebell, *Basic Types of Pastoral Care and Counseling...*, 325.

427 Lartey, *In Living Color: An Intercultural Approach to Pastoral Care and Counseling...*, 83.

Only then, can individuals decrease their self-defeating behaviours and improve their mental health.[428] Psychotherapy aims at strengthening the individuals' mental and emotional resources so that they can function more effectively.

Psychosocial wellbeing of divorced women has received marginal attention in Indian context, resulting in the paucity of literature and documentation of experiences with respect to the use of psychotherapeutic interventions. Divorced women's psychosocial experiences need a close attention and continuous engagement through psychotherapeutic interventions. This section deals with four models of psychotherapy namely *Person Centered Therapy*, *Logotherapy*, and *Rational Emotive Behaviour Therapy* and *Feminist Therapy* interventions in order to deal effectively with divorced women. These therapeutic techniques can facilitate a deeper engagement of women within the process of counselling divorced women.

Person Centered Therapy

Person centered therapy was originally developed by Carl Ransom Rogers, an American psychologist during the 1950s and 1960s formerly known as client centered therapy, non-directive counselling or Rogerian counselling. This approach was developed from the humanistic psychology concepts that views humans as autonomous beings with the ability to resolve their difficulties, realize their potential and change their lives in positive ways.

It is a non-directive therapy and one of the basic tenets is the emphasis on the ability of counselee to determine the issues and solve their problems. Rogers strongly believes that human beings strive toward becoming full functioning persons, which he calls "self-actualization."[429] He contends that there is one motivational force called "actualizing tendency" that determine the development of human beings. Despite all hindrances, an individual will thrive and grow towards the best possible fulfilment of their potential because of the actualizing tendency. If the individual experiences the right conditions, this actualizing tendency would become a reality. Put it differently, the counselor's ability to provide conducive atmosphere to the counselee is central to the therapeutic process. In order to create growth producing and enhancing climate, Rogers has underlined three core conditions in counselor-counselee relationship. The first is genuineness or realness of the counselor meaning the counselor is himself/herself without putting on professional masks. The counselor is transparent and refuses to present an image of himself/herself as superior avoiding the I-Thou relationship. Such relationship encourages the counselee to express himself/herself and finds resources within himself/ herself. The second is empathetic understanding where the counselor understands the thoughts, feelings and beliefs from the counselee's perspective

428 Norman L. Keltner and Debbie Steele, *Psychiatric Nursing* (Missouri: Elsevier Inc., 2015), 25.

429 Carl Rogers, *On Becoming a Person: A Therapist's View of Psychotherapy* (Boston; Houghton-Mifflin, 1961), 34.

and values the counselee's views. The third is the counselor's ability to offer a total acceptance or an unconditional positive regard and creating a climate for change and growth. When the counselor exhibits acceptance and non-judgmental attitude, then the counselee feels safe to explore negative feelings and move into the core of his/her anxiety and depression. The counselee is also able to face himself/herself honestly without fear of rejection or condemnation. Acceptance of the counselee by the counselor creates a context in which the counselee also senses a feeling of self-acceptance.[430] Rogers affirms that these essential qualities of therapeutic relationship enhance growth.

Person centered variables such as empathy, warmth, unconditional positive regard, and genuineness are seen as clearly associated with positive change by many scholars. Rogers contends that no matter how deprived the early experience of a human person was, he/she has within him/her a potential and a drive to fulfil one's potential. The role of the counselor is to provide the requisite environment through relating with the counselee with open, warmth, understanding, and accepting ways within which such potential will be realized. Rogers posits that, "If I can provide a certain type of relationship, the other person will discover within himself the capacity to use that relationship for growth, and change and personal development will occur."[431] This relationship of genuineness, acceptance and non-judgmental attitude enables them to develop self-concept that allows them to be in touch with their deepest feelings and experiences. These therapeutic conditions help them move towards becoming "fully functioning persons." Most importantly, the counselees develop trust and confidence in their organismic valuing process that was formerly lacking,[432] especially in the case of divorced women who have been continuously battling with the adverse judgments of others.

Divorced women undoubtedly experience a vulnerable state of disorganization and disequilibrium as their world, the original dreams of their lives have been shaken to the core. Reorganizing life without a spouse and children can raise deep fears, panic, anxiety, and disturbance. Feeling of shame, guilt, and anger that is attached to this role often exacerbates women's experience and ability to recover. The approach that the therapists take or the relational experience between counselee and therapist can have a critical impact on the counselee's ability to feel safe, supported, and understood. Through person centered therapy, counselors may help facilitate divorced women to explore their painful emotions of fears, anxieties, guilt, shame, anger, and sadness. This therapeutic approach to counselling is crucial while dealing with divorced women as they need a safe, supportive, and empathic relationship. The counselor or therapist can aid the counselees in gaining awareness in their inner reactions so that the "organismic valuing process" may guide growth and lead to health-promoting choices. Person

430 Carl Rogers, *Client Centered Therapy* (Boston: Houghton Mifflin, 1951), 62.

431 Rogers, *On Becoming a Person: A Therapist's View of Psychotherapy* ..., 33.

432 Rogers, *On Becoming a Person: A Therapist's View of Psychotherapy* ..., 33.

centered therapy emphasizes on relationship that heals. It views counselees as the best authority of their experience, being capable of their own growth. Counselors can apply these principles in dealing with divorced women to enhance their wellbeing. Such a therapeutic approach is synergistic with the needs of divorced women as they experience crisis and the subsequent challenges of reorganizing their lives without a spouse. Divorced women need to be accepted and help them to accept themselves as they grapple with negative emotions. This unconditional positive regard is invaluable as they work their way through the pain and loss. Divorced women's experiences must be heard, valued, and understood in their context. Empathetic understanding should supersede all other considerations. It is within a real human encounter that counselling at its best provides the tools for change and transformation that divorced women seek.

The caring, empathy and non-judgmental attitude of the therapist allow the counselee to explore fearful and anxiety producing experiences. By exploring feelings that are deeply felt, the counselees can experience total honesty and self-awareness. As individuals deal with their anger and hostile feelings, they gradually encounter positive feelings about themselves and others. The therapist warm presence makes the counselee deal with issues that may have been upsetting, difficult, and hence repressed. The therapist genuineness, acceptance, and empathy help facilitate the counselee to positive self-exploration and also deal with the disturbing thoughts and feelings. Experiencing genuineness, acceptance, and empathy from the therapist leads to changes in how the individual relates to others. In other words, sharing their fears, anxiety, and shame in the presence of the therapist genuine caring, warmth and empathetic relationship helps counselees trust their own experience, feel a sense of richness in their lives, become psychologically more relaxed, and experience life more fully.[433] Rogers's therapeutic approach is powerful in establishing healing and growth relationship especially for persons who are crippled by guilt and self-rejection.

Person centered therapy is one of the most widely adopted approaches to helping people due to the fact that its basic premises are so fundamental to pastoral counselling. However, while employing person centered therapy, pastoral caregivers and counselors need to be cautious of its downsides. One of the drawbacks of person centered therapy is its philosophical presupposition that assumes human beings as sole authority or ultimate force of one's destiny which is contrary to Christian belief. Another disadvantage is its emphasis on personal wholeness that assumes primacy often at the expense of one's responsibilities to others. In Christian tradition, the true self is defined by both vertical and horizontal relationships – with God as well as with other fellow beings. There are also critics who say that person centered approach emphasizes on the organismic self away from external authorities. The basic premise of person centered therapy is that the organism is the locus of all experience and potentially including everything

433 Rogers, *On Becoming a Person: A Therapist View of Psychotherapy* ..., 11.

available to awareness that is going on within it at any given moment.[434] Critics argue that this therapeutic model emphasizes only on the internal factors and does not take the sociological elements. It emphasizes on actualization of the self without taking into account the individual's relationship with others, the interconnectedness of individuals and social systems. Rogers failed to recognize that personal problems are rooted in social context. He also failed to address the therapeutic necessity of empowering persons to work towards changing systemic oppression in the wider social context. T. L. Holdstock argues that Roger's view of the self-focused exclusively on the individual that he termed it as "individuocentric approach."[435] Rogers's view of self is essentially a westernized view of the self, which contrasts with the interdependent model of self, found in many non-western cultures. Another criticism is its emphasis on the acceptance, congruence, and positive regard so much so that it left no room for constructive confrontation that is essential for growth in many cases. Nevertheless, pastoral caregivers can effectively make use of the core conditions laid down by Rogers in counselling relationships in helping counselees experience feelings, attitudes and values that emerges from an understanding, empathetic and congruent relationship.

Logotherapy

An Austrian psychiatrist and holocaust survivor Viktor Emil Frankl developed Logotherapy also known as the "Third Viennese School of Psychotherapy" in 1938. The term Logotherapy comes from the Greek word "Logos" which means "meaning." Frankl's theory and therapy was developed out of his experience at the Nazi concentration camps during World War II. He has observed that people who had hopes tended to have better chances of survival than those who had lost hope. Logotherpy premised on the idea that human's primary motivation or main goal in life is "the striving to find meaning in one's life."[436] Frankl reiterates, "There is nothing in the world... that would so effectively help one to survive even the worst conditions as the knowledge that there is meaning in one's life."[437] Thus, the infamous Neitzsche quote, "he who has a why to live for can bear almost any how."[438] He argues that those who "lack the awareness of a meaning worth living for. They are haunted by the experience of their emptiness, a void within themselves."[439] It is this lack of meaning, an inner emptiness that Frankl terms "existential vacuum." Logotherapy emphasizes on the importance of experiencing

434 Rogers, *On Becoming a Person...*, 13.

435 T. L. Holdstock, "Can we afford not to revise the Person-Centered concept of Self," in *Beyond Carl Rogers*, edited by D. Brazier (London: Constable & Company, 1993), 45.

436 Viktor E. Frankl, *Man's Search for Meaning* (Boston: Beacon Press, 2006), 121.

437 Frankl, *Man's Search for Meaning...*, 103-104.

438 Frankl, *Man's Search for Meaning...*, 104.

439 Frankl, *Man's Search for Meaning...*, 106.

meaning of life in maintaining physical and psychological health and wellbeing, particularly in distressing situations.

Logotherapy is premised on three basic tenets: freedom of will, will to meaning and meaning of life. Freedom of will involves freedom to choose one's reaction to life circumstances resulting in freedom to rise above those circumstances. The locus of Logotherapy is that every person has "freedom of will."[440] Frankl defines human freedom not as freedom from conditions, but "freedom to take a stand on whatever conditions might confront him."[441] The will to meaning refers to the primary motivation of seeking meaning and living a meaningful life. Human beings are driven by the need to fulfil future meanings. For Frankl, the ultimate meaning is not to gain pleasure or power as posited by Freud and Alfred Adler, but to find meaning in life. Will to meaning is essential for survival and health. It enables people to endure unimaginable sufferings and to persist in pursuing their ideals. Frankl has envisaged that human beings are characterized by the "will to meaning" which is an inner drive to find meaning and significance in life. Failure to achieve meaning in life results in psychological distress.[442] The will to meaning implies that human beings are not only free, but are also free to achieve goals and purposes. When a person cannot realize his/her "Will to meaning", they experience meaninglessness and emptiness that leads to neurosis, aggression, addiction, depression, and even suicidal tendency and may increase psychosomatic and neurotic disorders. When the will to meaning is blocked or frustrated one tends to experience emptiness.[443] Everyone must find meaning in what he/she experiences. By implication, if one finds meaning in what he/she is experiencing then, the person has a "why" to live. This means that a person can transcend his/her difficult circumstances because his/her will to live is stronger than the circumstances the person is in. It is by finding meaning that one is able to heal and move forward with one's life. In this sense, human's existence is not striving for pleasure or power, but for fulfilment of meaning.

Logotherapy assists counselees in perceiving and removing those factors that hinder them in pursuing meaningful goals in life. Counselees are sensitized for the perception of meaning, and are guided and assisted in the realization of those meaning. Meaning of life, for Frankl, is to bring forth the best in themselves and in the world.[444] Thus, the goal of Logotherapy is to help persons find meaning in life whose lives lack meaning.

In Logotherapy, meaning is unique to each individual and may change over time. Nevertheless, Frankl identifies three sources where people commonly find

---

440 Frankl, *Man's Search for Meaning...*, 16.

441 Frankl, *Man's Search for Meaning...*, 16.

442 Frankl, *Man's Search for Meaning...*, 20.

443 Viktor Frankl, *The Will to Meaning: Foundations and Applications of Logotherapy* (New York: Penguin Group, 1969). 74.

444 Frankl, *The Will to Meaning: Foundations and Applications of Logotherapy...*, 75.

meaning such as work and achievement; love and relationships and the attitude one takes towards unavoidable suffering. The therapist assists the counselee to discover meaning for their lives in one or more of these areas. The goal is to develop what Frankl calls "tragic optimism" in the midst of pain, guilt and death.[445] Even in trying circumstance, it is still possible to find meaning. "It is precisely when facing such fate, when being confronted with a hopeless situation, that man is given a last opportunity to fulfill a meaning—to realize even the highest value, to fulfill even the deepest meaning—the meaning of suffering."[446]

Pastoral caregivers and therapists can help divorced women gain a new perspective of life and explore new opportunities to find meaning. Of the three avenues postulated by Frankl, attitudinal values hold true and important for divorced women. Attitudinal values are realized by adopting the right attitude and taking a stand towards unavoidable suffering or an unchangeable situation. The attitude of acceptance is essential in overcoming guilt and suffering.[447] For Frankl, acceptance is key to self-transcendence. He argues that it is not suffering per se but failing to see meaning in suffering that causes people to despair. By maintaining an optimistic, accepting attitude, a person can turn suffering into something meaningful.[448] Finding meaning in life allows humans to reach the state of self-transcendence that is the ultimate state of being for healthy personality.

Women experiencing divorce can be helped by changing their attitude, thinking, emotions and behaviour towards life to find meaning in their experience. Finding meaning through experiencing divorce can facilitate acceptance of and adjustment in life. The ability of maintaining a meaning directed attitude enhances individual's adaptability which enables them to come to terms with their situations. Finding meaning in crisis situations is connected to better coping. Thus, finding positive meaning in negative life events help individuals to overcome their tragedy and maintain a feeling of meaning in their lives. Meaning of life has been recognized as a basic dimension of wellbeing.

Divorced women are often confronted with a new threatening and stressful reality leading to psychosocial crisis in their lives due to the changes they experience in physical, mental, emotional, economic, social, and spiritual health. Many of them go through depression as one of the mental health symptoms as the situation demands an individual's adjustment to a new reality. While some individuals manage to adapt to their situation, others fail to accept this new reality. Logotherapy offers therapeutic techniques that would allow these women not only to address their experiences that adversely affect their wellbeing but also

445 Frankl, *The Will to Meaning: Foundations and Applications of Logotherapy*…, 84.

446 Viktor Frankl and James C. Crumbaugh, *Psychotherapy and Existentialism: Selected Papers on Logotherapy* by Viktor E. Frankl (Washington: Washington Square Press, 1967), 15.

447 Frankl and James C. Crumbaugh, *Psychotherapy and Existentialism: Selected Papers on Logotherapy* by Viktor E. Frankl ..., 24.

448 Frankl, *Man's Search for Meaning*..., 139.

to find a way to move beyond. Meaning can be found in their suffering. It is the job of the therapists to open their eyes to search for meaning and to guide them through the therapeutic process with the hope of arriving at optimal wellbeing. The role of the therapist is to challenge people to find their own meanings that are present in their concrete life situations.

Divorced women also exhibit psychopathological symptoms such as social isolation, alienation from self, others and the world, boredom and feeling of despair. Many of the divorced women stated that one of their most significant struggles is to find meaning and purpose in lives. Logotherapy can be used in helping divorced women find meaning in their suffering. Logotherapy being a meaning centered therapy can be employed by pastoral caregivers to deal with divorced women who are experiencing depression and sense of meaninglessness.

Logotherapy is used by many professionals in diverse settings in helping people with wide range of concerns. It is known for effective treatment of many mental health conditions and is uniquely suited for people undergoing traumatic experience because it was in a traumatic situation that the therapy was developed. If this therapy is successfully applied, it would help divorced women to find meaning in life who would otherwise suffer from meaningless. This therapeutic approach offers invaluable growth enabling resources based on the basic philosophy of nature and human growth. Nevertheless, Frankle's therapy like most traditional and contemporary therapies is apolitical as it does not deal with the therapeutic value that necessitates helping and empowering the oppressed groups by challenging oppressive social structures and systems. Although Frankl's position was deeply influenced by his own experience in the concentration camps and his life deeply affected by a social catastrophe, he failed to address the problem of communal action to seek justice in the struggle against militarism, racism, poverty, and imperialism. He made no references to violence, evil and injustices meted out by Hitler regime.

Logotherapy recognizes the individual's ability to view beyond tragedy and to find the opportunity to gain meaning from their experience, reaching his/her spiritual dimension that helps him/her to transcend all the negative effects in one's life. Pastoral caregivers and counselors have the responsibility to support and encourage divorced women to move forward in spite of difficulties and challenges. Meaning is also an important concept in understanding the predicaments and complexities of life as well as in developing faith and spirituality. More than any other psychotherapists, Logotherapy conceptualizes the characteristics of human beings as meaning-seeking creatures.

Rational Emotive Behaviour Therapy (REBT)

Albert Ellis, a clinical psychologist, originally propounded rational Emotive Behavioural Therapy in the 1950s. He developed an approach he believed would be effective and efficient in bringing about psychotherapeutic change. REBT is primarily a cognitive approach although it has significant behavioural and emotive aspects. It is a system of psychotherapy designed to help people minimize emotional disturbances and self-defeating behaviours and actualize themselves so that they live a more fulfilling life.

A-B-C model is the basic premise on which Ellis built his theory. According to this theory "A" (the activating event) does not cause "C" (consequence). Instead, "B" which is the person's belief about A largely causes C, the emotional reaction. When the activating event is a pleasant one, the resulting beliefs are likely to be harmless, but when the activating events are not pleasant, irrational beliefs may develop. These irrational beliefs (B) often cause difficult emotional and behavioural consequences. The major role of the therapist is, therefore, to dispel (D) these irrational beliefs (B) through a variety of therapeutic techniques. E stands for New Effect that take place as a result of disputing the irrational beliefs.[449] Thus, the core of REBT is to help people change their irrational beliefs that directly cause disturbed emotional consequences. There is a variety of interactions among A, B and C meaning the activating events, beliefs and consequences can each have components that are emotional, behavioural and cognitive. When cognition, emotion, and behaviour interact and influence one another, it results into a set of dysfunctional philosophical assumptions leading to emotional disturbance.[450]

REBT believes that virtually all human beings have several irrational beliefs that interfere with healthy thoughts, emotions, and behaviour and when these irrational beliefs are replaced with positive emotions, the dysfunctional behaviour significantly changes. Irrational beliefs lead to self-defeating emotional and behavioural consequences and are expressed as "should" "musts" and "oughts." Ellis argues that if people hold rigid views and beliefs about how they, others, and the world should or must be under all circumstances, they experience some form of disturbance. Whereas beliefs that are expressed not as demands but as preferences leads to more adaptive levels of emotion and behaviour.[451] REBT believes that humans are fallible and imperfect beings and endeavours to help counselees realize and accept their fallibility and construct more stratifying thoughts and beliefs. The focus of REBT is to help counselees understand the interconnection between their irrational beliefs and their present problem. The counselor exposes the irrational and self-destructive beliefs and challenges their value to the counselees. Therapist identifies this belief and disputes the counselee's

449 Albert Ellis, "The Biological Basis of Human Irrationality: A reply to McBurnet and LaPointe," in Journal of Individual Psychology 35/1 (1979d): 111-116.

450 Windy Dryden, "Rational Emotive Behavior Therapy," in *Encyclopaedia of Cognitive Behavior Therapy*, edited by Arthur Freeman (New York: Springer Science + Business Media, Inc., 2005), 321.

451 Albert Ellis, *Humanistic Psychotherapy: The Rational Emotive Approach* (New York: Crown & McGraw, 1973), 63.

reason for holding that belief.[452] Once exposed, the therapist and the counselee work towards identifying more appropriate and rational beliefs so that new feelings and hope will arise.

One of the major goals of REBT is "minimizing the counselee's self-defeating outlook and acquiring a more realistic, tolerant philosophy of life,"[453] in order to help them become more self-actualized and lead a happier life. Other important therapeutic goals include reducing a tendency for blaming oneself or others for what goes wrong in life and teaching different ways to effectively deal with future difficulties. Helping the counselees fulfil psychological health is another specific goal towards which REBT therapists strive to achieve. REBT not only helps individuals minimize or remove emotional disturbances, it is the teaching of philosophical change that prevents individuals from redisturbing/recurring of irrational thoughts.[454] The A-B-C philosophy can help counselees see when they are creating new symptoms or recreating new ones. REBT believes that people have the potential to change their self-defeating habits which requires actively working at modifying thoughts, behaviours and feelings. The following are some of the therapeutic techniques that can be applied while dealing with divorced women.

The study reveals that there are specific emotions that correspond to irrational beliefs of divorced women. They experience low self-esteem and do not regard themselves valuable. Many of them reported not having social life, experience shame associated with stigma as a result of their assumption that others also feel the same way about them. Hence, they withdrew themselves from situations because they do not value themselves and they expect rejection, criticism, or humiliation. While distancing from others may allow them to escape anticipated negative situations, it also isolates them from positive contributions others might make in their lives. Divorced women experience dysfunctional emotional and behavioural patterns including low self-esteem, self-hatred, shame, guilt, anger etc. and some of these experiences occur because of their irrational beliefs or unrealistic high expectations on themselves as well as on others. Such irrational expectations lead them to believe that they are worthless and feel rejected by others. Their irrational beliefs may be correlated with their depressive symptoms. Hence, pastoral caregivers can work towards helping them dispel their irrational thoughts and expectations and set realistic goals and assist them in minimizing emotional disturbances, decrease self-defeating behaviours and develop healthy relationships.

REBT has a unique approach to persons experiencing low self-esteem. It advocates unconditional self-acceptance meaning accepting oneself

452 Albert Ellis and Windy Dryden, *The Practice of Rational Emotive Behavior Therapy* (New York: Springer Publishing Company, 1984), 228.

453 Ellis and Windy Dryden, *The Practice of Rational Emotive Behavior Therapy*..., 229.

454 Ellis and Windy Dryden, *The Practice of Rational Emotive Behavior Therapy*..., 230.

unconditionally regardless of whether one behaves competently or correctly and whether others are likely to express approval or respect.[455] Ellis endorses the concept of "unconditional self-acceptance" as "one accepts oneself—one's existence, one's aliveness, without any requirement or conditions whatever."[456] REBT therapist encourages counselees to accept themselves as fallible human beings and therapists help them accept themselves as fallible beings who try their best yet inevitably make mistakes.[457]

REBT has been used successfully in helping people with clinical as well as non-clinical problems using a variety of techniques. It can be used to help people develop and act on a more functional philosophy of life. REBT can be employed in both individual and group settings. The basic aim of REBT is to help counselees achieve freedom to choose their emotions, behaviours, and lifestyle within the confines of their physical, social and economic situations. REBT neither sees all unpleasant emotions as dysfunctional nor all pleasant emotions as functional. It aims at realistic thoughts, emotions and behaviour that are in proportion to the events and circumstances an individual experience. The relationship between the therapist and the counselee is important which is understood as facilitating the therapeutic work, with the therapist empathy, unconditional acceptance, and encouragements. It is task-oriented and focuses on the problem solving in the present (here and now). The emphasis is on helping people change how they feel and behave in reaction to life events. Consequently, REBT helps people change themselves and their unwanted and unpleasant circumstances. Most importantly, REBT emphasizes on the profound and lasting change in the underlying belief system of the counselee rather than simply eliminating the presenting problems/ symptoms. The counselee is taught self-help techniques to enable them to cope in the long term.[458]

One advantage of employing REBT in dealing with divorced women is its non-judgmental perspective. This approach can be reassuring to divorced women who are accustomed to being judged for the life situation they have acquired. REBT is considered as cross-cultural therapy because of its effectiveness in dealing with people from different ages, races, culture and lifestyles. It emphasizes on the depth of solution to problems and profound as well as lasting change in the underlying belief system of the counselee. Through the use of REBT divorced women who are shame ridden can be helped to restore a sense of self-respect and self-esteem.

Even the most efficient psychotherapy has its own weaknesses and REBT is no exception although REBT is successful in validating its effectiveness in various

455 Albert Ellis, *Reason and Emotion in Psychotherapy* (New Jersey: Lyle Stuart, 1994), 9.

456 Albert Ellis, *Growth Through Reason: Verbatim Cases in Rational Emotive Therapy* (New York: Science and Behaviour Books, 1971), 21.

457 Ellis, *Reason and Emotion in Psychotherapy*..., 11.

458 Ellis, *Reason and Emotion in Psychotherapy*..., 12.

aspects. REBT therapists forcefully confront counselee's self-defeating thoughts, emotions and behaviours or irrational attitudes and assist counselees in cognitive restructuring of distorted ideas, thoughts, beliefs, and philosophies. Ultimately, they facilitate the counselee's self-direction cognitive and behavioural activity or rational self-management. The counselee is helped to develop awareness of his/her self-defeating thoughts, irrational thinking, or attitudes and finally commits himself/herself to the development of skills for rational self-management. REBT does not take into account the external factors that may contribute to the underlying issues. It fails to take into consideration the contradiction between a person's total responsibility and the limits of choice within his/her social environment. The therapy solely holds people responsible for the choices they make without recognizing the limits of their social environment. A person's social environment shapes his/her actions and influences for rational and irrational choices and decisions and one cannot trivialize or ignore the impact the social environment makes on an individual. Nevertheless, by employing REBT, pastoral caregivers can dispel the negative emotions and behaviours and help divorced women replace negative emotions and actions to positive ones.

Feminist Therapeutic Approach

Feminism is a complex notion that has vast differences in meaning and connotation for different groups of people. It is not a static concept but had evolved over the years shaped by various lenses. There have been many attempts to define what feminism is, yet the task is extremely complex because feminism is not just one unitary concept but rather a diverse and multifaceted grouping with sometimes conflicting ideas and actions. However, "Any attempt to provide a baseline definition of a common basis of all feminisms may start with the assertion that feminisms concern themselves with women's inferior position in society and with discrimination encountered by women because of their sex."[459] The bottom line is that women are human beings and they must be considered as full human beings.

Feminism can be grouped into three broad categories such as liberal, radical and socialist. Each has different starting assumptions and goals and implies different cultural politics. Theoretically, liberal feminist leans towards equality of both men and women and work towards achieving through legal means and social reform. Liberal feminist claims that women and men should not be treated differently under the law and that both should be given equal educational and work opportunities.[460] Their basic tenet is based on the premise that "sex and gender

459 Jane Freedman, *Feminism: Concepts in the Social Sciences* (Philadelphia: Open University Press, 2001), 1.

460 Judith Lorber, *The Variety of Feminisms and their Contribution on Gender Equality* (Oldenburg: University of Oldenburg, 1997), 9.

should not infringe on individual liberty or potential for self-development."[461] They advocate women's rights and opportunities by challenging inequalities between men and women in the society.

Radical feminists premised on the idea that "women are fundamentally different from men. They assert that women's true nature, potential, and creativity are suppressed by patriarchy, which exercises its authority through male control of female sexuality and women's reproductive powers."[462] The only alternative to challenge patriarchy for radical feminists is to create "new meanings, values, culture and lifestyle"[463] different from men which will be achieved by withdrawing from the existing patriarchal structures and practices and by redefining knowledge and rationality and setting new criteria to estimate the qualities that are traditionally attributed to female and by valuing "women's biological and psychic otherness to men."[464]

For socialist feminism although addressing the areas of education and culture is important it is not enough because social power resides beyond patriarchy and biological functions. Hence, focus should be given to other forms of power structures such as class and race that are interwoven with gender discrimination. In order to combat power relations, it has to be understood and made visible how and in whose interest it works. "To denaturalize sex and gender is to show how they are socially produced in ways that guarantee and reproduce particular social relations."[465] Gender norms may widely vary across different classes and ethnic groups, yet it is important to understand how norms are established and where and how they can be best challenged.[466]

Feminist therapy and counselling emerged from the civil rights and social change movement in the 1960s and 1970s in the US to understand better and meet the needs of women experiencing psychological distress. Awareness of women as an oppressed group surfaced out of the privileged class mostly White and educated women who sought to change the social, political and cultural beliefs about the role of women in a patriarchal and raciest society. This movement conceptualized mutual respect and equality between men and women in allocating power and resources.[467]

---

461 Chris Weedon, "Post-structuralist Feminist Practice," in *Theory/Pedagogy/Politics: Texts for Change*, edited by Donald E. Morton and Masud Zavarzadeh (Chicago: University of Illinois Press, 1991), 47.

462 Weedon, "Post-structuralist Feminist Practice,"..., 48.

463 Weedon, "Post-structuralist Feminist Practice,"..., 48.

464 Weedon, "Post-structuralist Feminist Practice,"..., 48.

465 Weedon, "Post-structuralist Feminist Practice,"..., 49.

466 Weedon, "Post-structuralist Feminist Practice,"..., 49.

467 Kathy M. Evans et al, "Feminism and Feminist Therapy," in Journal of Counseling & Development 83 (2005): 269.

Feminist therapists were critical with the way psychoanalysis and psychotherapy operates as it was androcentric and sought for alternative approaches to therapy. They challenged the traditional patriarchal approaches to intervention and treatment that defines women as inadequate and deviant, distort their experiences by assimilating to male norms, and ignore women's mental health concerns. Models of counselling and psychotherapy that target inappropriate or limited aspects of women's life with an aim to remove pathology are inadequate since it fails to touch the core aspects of women's lived experiences. They criticized the traditional therapists for being agents of society for encouraging women to adapt to the traditional gender roles.[468] Feminist therapists counter such one-sided approach as inefficient to address the multiple forces that affect women's wellbeing. Since its inception, feminist therapy has evolved in theory, therapeutic techniques and scope of application. The core focus of feminist therapy is to change the unhealthy external situation and the internalized effects owing to the external situation rather than helping counselees adapt to a dysfunctional environment. Feminist therapy emerged as a result of the newly acquired awareness through consciousness raising and self-help group developed as an alternative to traditional male bias therapy.

Unlike many theoretical orientations, there is no one single theory that underlies feminist therapy and no single person can be identified as the founder. In fact, there are many different therapies all grounded in the interconnection of the individual, gender and culture. Feminist therapists share the basic belief that women are valuable and that there is a need for social change if women are to experience wholeness. Feminist model of intervention mandates for public policy and social change. Innovative strategies and approaches need to be developed, if women are to experience wholeness and growth.

Feminist therapy premised on the concept of "personal is political," the assumption that there is an interconnection between personal problems and the political and social realm in which people live.[469] Put it differently, a person is viewed as a political entity meaning a person is not an isolated individual, but one who is rooted and impacted by the political and social environments. Thus, a primary source of a counselee's "pathology" is not intrapsychic or personal alone but rather, social and political."[470] Hence, identifying the societal sources of women's individual issues and making the women aware of the sources of the pathology is central to feminist therapy.

---

468 Judith Worell and Pamela Remer, *Feminist Perspectives in Therapy: Empowering Diverse Women*, Second edition (New Jersey: John Wiley & Sons, Inc., 2003), 62.

469 J. Dianne Garner and Carolyn Z. Enns, *Feminist Theories and Feminist Psychotherapies: Origins, Themes and Diversity*, Second edition (New York: The Haworth Press, 2004). 11.

470 Worell and Remer, *Feminist Perspective in Therapy...*, 68.

If divorced women are to grow and develop, feminists' issues must be incorporated in divorce therapy for women. The following are some of the feminist therapeutic approaches that can be employed in helping divorced women:

Cultural Analysis

Divorced women may be experiencing one or more aspects of institutional bias and discrimination, had internalized this worldview, is trapped in a subordinate and marginalized situation, and believes that they are essentially responsible for their own situation, even though they have few or no control over it. In spite of their adverse social conditions, they believe that they are solely accountable and they over accommodate the behavioural prescriptions of the dominant culture. Hence, awareness for understanding of the counselee is essential for effective counselling.[471] Moreover, the counselor's experiences might have shaped their personal biases, attitudes, values, and expectations. Thus, both counselee's and therapist's personal experiences influence the course of counselor-counselee relationships and interactions. In the counselling process, diagnosis and intervention with counselees is crucial to identify the influences of external pressures as well as attending to their internal processes. Many divorced women experience mental and emotional discomfort that interfere their effective functioning and personal wellbeing. Divorced women should be helped to look beyond her and consider the inequities in resources and power imbalance in the family and society as a contributing factor in their feeling of worthlessness and despair. Pastoral caregivers need to explore how the context –the cultural and gender-based socialization and self-expectations, their isolation from community, intimacy and emotional support have contributed to their present situation. Divorced women's negative reaction such as depression, anxiety and shame can be seen as logical response to being oppressed.

Gender Role Analysis

Gender role analysis is designed to increase counselees' awareness of how the societal gender role related expectations negatively affect their lives because of the way women and men are being socialized. Counselees are assisted to identify the lived experience of the direct and indirect gender-role messages such as verbal, nonverbal and modelled and to name both the positive as well as the negative consequences in their personal life and the society as a result of the gender role messages and how they have internalized these messages consciously or unconsciously. Having identified the internalized messages, counselees decide the internalized messages they want to change and implement the change and counter negative environmental reactions to their implemented change.[472] It

471 Susan Morrow and Donna M. Hawxhurst, "Feminist Therapy: Integrating Political Analysis in Counseling and Psychotherapy," in Women & Therapy 21/2 (1998): 40.

472 Worell and Remer, *Feminist Perspective in Therapy...*, 77, 78.

is apparent from the data that many of the problems divorced women face is because of living in society that devalues them, limit their access to resources and discriminate them economically, legally and socially. In a patriarchal structure like Naga society, men and women do not share equal status and power, women are the oppressed lot and in a subordinate power position. Women differ from men primarily because social forces encourage differential constructions of gender. This gender role stereotype limits the potential of women. Through gender role analysis, divorced women may get insights about the various social roles and how it affects their lives and work towards changing the unequal gender disparity.

Power Analysis

The purpose of power analysis in feminist therapy is twofold. First, to help counselees increase awareness of the existing power differential between the dominant and the subordinate groups in a society such as role, resources, legal, institutional etc. Second is to empower counselees to have influence on the external institutional power affecting their lives.[473] It is crucial for pastoral caregivers to address the power imbalance between males and females in the family and society.

As noted earlier, divorced women experience a dramatic shift in their lifestyle such as coping with single parenting or living alone, interrupted careers, coping with financial stress and loneliness compounded by exclusion and discrimination as a result of being a divorcee. All these life events present situational coping problems and issues. By employing power analysis, pastoral caregivers and counselors can help divorced women identify the multiple factors that contribute to stress and distress as well as their strength and resilience. Pastoral caregivers may also analyze concepts of power, privilege, and oppression in counselling divorced women as a means to increase their awareness so that they could critically analyze the various oppressive systems affecting their lives both directly and indirectly. The counselor can also explore messages that they received as a young woman related to gender role and expectations placed on them within their families and communities and how they influenced them as adults. In this way, divorced women can acquire a new way of looking at and responding to their life situation.

Assertiveness Training

Assertive skills are important in feminist therapy if women are to impact the environment effectively and to initiate social change.[474] Patricia Jakubowski has developed a four-component of assertiveness training such as teaching counselees to differentiate between assertive passive and aggressive behaviour; to develop a belief system that support their rights and to assert their rights and have them met; to reduce psychological blocks to their being assertive and to

473 Worell and Remer, *Feminist Perspective in Therapy...*, 78.

474 Worell and Remer, *Feminist Perspective in Therapy...*, 79.

develop assertiveness skills through behavioural rehearsal.[475] She feels that the real problem lies within the male dominated society that depicts normal feminine woman as a victim. "The victim is the woman who has successfully adopted a situation of social powerlessness... The victim is the woman who sees herself through male eyes and thus learns to devalue, limit, and even hate herself."[476] When working with members of oppressed groups, it is not enough to work only on mental, emotional/psychological issues when external realities are creating conflict and oppression. To provide an authentic service/help, it is important to develop awareness about the interlocking nature of oppression and the continued subjugation. This implies paying attention to and questioning the nature of power and the oppressive structures that perpetuate exercise of that power in the society. It also implies paying attention to the individual woman and her specific circumstances and the personal interpretation of those circumstances. In spite of the limitations imposed on them, several behavioural patterns reveal that divorced women work hard at creating/shaping lives for themselves and are resourceful and resilient.

Empowering Model

Empowerment is one of the goals of feminist intervention that enables individuals, families, and communities to exert influence over the personal, interpersonal and institutional factors that impact their health and wellbeing. It emphasizes on counselee's strength and resilience in coping with past, current, and future stress and trauma.[477] Worell and Remer have conceptualized empowerment in the context of therapy in two ways: First, counselees are empowered in dealing with their life situations through achieving skills and flexibility in problem solution and developing a full range of interpersonal and life skills. Second, empowerment encourages women to identify and challenge the external conditions of their lives that devalue and subordinate them as women or as members of minority groups and are denied equal opportunity and access to social, economic and institutional resources.[478] The focus of treatment in feminist therapy is on empowering the counselee to change the social, interpersonal as well as political environment that adversely impact their wellbeing instead of helping them to fit into an oppressive environment.[479] Since many of the problems women face are the by-products

475 Patricia. A. Jakubowski, "Assertion Training in Women," in *Psychotherapy for Women*, edited by E. I. Rawlings and D. K. Carter (Springfield IL: Charles C. Thomas, 1977), 153.

476 Patricia. A. Jakubowski, "Assertive Behaviour and Clinical Problems of Women; Self Assertion Training for Women," in *Psychotherapy for Women: Treatment toward Equality* (Springfield III: Charles C. Thomas Publisher, 1977), 172.

477 Worell and Remer, *Feminist Perspective in Therapy...*, 23.

478 Worell and Remer, *Feminist Perspective in Therapy...*, 25.

479 L. S. Brown and A. M. Brodsky, "The Future of Feminist Therapy," in Psychotherapy 29 (1992): 54.

of their secondary position in the family and society, feminist therapists focus on empowering women to make changes in their lives as well as the society. It focuses on their strength rather than on their weaknesses. Shifting the label of pathology from the individual to external factors can empower divorced women, as they understand that their sense of shame, self-hatred are a direct result of the contextual reality and a logical and reasonable response to their traumatic life experiences.

Consciousness Raising

Consciousness raising is important in order to engage the oppressed group in active pursuit of their own liberation. The first step of which is interrupting the process of acceptance as described by Paulo Freire, "As long as the oppressed remain unaware of the causes of their condition, they fatalistically 'accept' their exploitation."[480] To achieve liberation, the oppressed must not only be aware but must also "perceive the reality of oppression not as a closed world from which there is no exit, but as limiting situation which they can transform."[481] For Freire, "Conscientizacao refers to learning to perceive social, political, and economic contradictions, and to take actions the oppressive elements of reality."[482] The oppressed groups need to develop critical consciousness so as to examine, understand, and transform the world around them.[483] Through consciousness raising divorced women can be helped to develop critical consciousness and an increase awareness of oppression and the ways they have been impacted by it and help them to actively engage in opposing the previously accepted restrictions and limitations imposed to them by the systems. Consciousness raising can help divorced women to examine and critique the oppressive systems and structures that impact their lives and to recreate their identity and integrate this new identity into their everyday life and positive functioning.

Feminist therapy often adopts the format and goals of consciousness raising groups in counselling women that has particular advantage in group settings where interpersonal sharing is spread over many individuals rather than just one. Consequently, it offers a wider base of identifying the commonalities and divergences of their experiences. It also serves as a source of healing, "often taking turns of being the healed and the healer—a process that helps turn 'victims' into 'survivors.'"[484] This will further lead to individual empowerment. Besides,

480 P. Freire, *Pedagogy of the Oppressed* (New York: Continuum, 1970), 46.

481 Freire, *Pedagogy of the Oppressed...*, 31.

482 Freire, *Pedagogy of the Oppressed...*, 17.

483 He believes that all human beings irrespective of occupation, educational qualification, or socioeconomic status possess this ability and in doing, so not only helps the oppressed group to interrupt acceptance but also helps in the process of reclaiming their humanity. Freire, *Pedagogy of the Oppressed...*, 17.

484 Worell and Remer, *Feminist Perspective in Therapy...*, 79.

women, when work together as a group will bring about social change more effectively than working alone.

Reframing and Relabeling

Unlike the popular psychotherapeutic understanding of reframing which usually refers to a shift where the counselor changes the frame of reference for looking at the individual's behaviour, in feminist therapy "reframing shift is usually from interpersonal and individual to societal and political and is accompanied by identifying the contribution of the external environment to the individual's problem."[485] For instance, feminist therapists reframe a woman experiencing depression normally viewed by dominant psychotherapists as a result of dysfunctional thoughts, feelings, and behaviour patterns of the individual as women's natural response to being in a subordinate power position.[486] In relabeling, therapists help counselees to shift their focus from a negative to a positive one. They are taught to relabel previously evaluated weaknesses as strengths. A woman who had been told as being "too emotional" may relabel herself as having the ability to express her feelings and as empathetic to other's feelings.

Divorced women internalize blame as they see themselves failed in their responsibility to hold the family together which results in negative belief about oneself and may also contribute to the formation of negative beliefs about other people, relationships and the world. These beliefs lead to emotions of guilt, shame, low self-esteem, humiliation, fear, hopelessness, depression and isolation. Therapists and pastoral caregivers need to help divorced women reframe some of their self-blame messages and replace it with positive ones such as "I am a failure because I could not keep up the marriage relationship and I am responsible for the failure of the marriage" to social messages such as "I feel responsible for the failure of my marriage because I was taught that women are supposed to hold the relationships together." Similarly, divorced women's attribution of the problem they face in life need to be reframed in a manner that suggests the possible role of sexism and discrimination. They can also be encouraged to use their new perceptions to re-evaluate their situation and to view their thoughts, feelings and behaviours in a more positive and self-affirming manner.

Feminist therapy also emphasizes on identifying the counselees' strength while exploring their problems. It involves reframing, revaluing and reappreciating previously held negative traits and assists women in identifying the formerly devalued sets of behaviour that are traditionally socialized in women to reconceptualize weakness into strength, and negative deficit into positive advantage.[487] Women are taught to define themselves in terms of their own lived

485 Worell and Remer, *Feminist Perspective in Therapy...*, 80.

486 Worell and Remer, *Feminist Perspective in Therapy...*, 80.

487 As for instance, women are reinforced for being appropriately female and at the same time are devalued for being that way. Women are taught to be nurturing of their families and to put the

experiences rather than resorting to internalizing the androcentric double bind messages by denying themselves of their womanhood that Susan Sturdivant termed it as "woman-defined-woman."[488] Thus, the characteristics of women, which were devalued by traditional therapist by terming them as deviant and deficits, are revalued as strength in feminist therapy.

Maintaining Egalitarian Relationship

Feminist therapists promote egalitarian therapeutic relationships as far as practicable. They posit that the general social and sexual power imbalances affect the dynamics of the therapy relationships. Hence, they model egalitarian counselling relationship to reduce the social control aspects of therapy so as to redress therapists' misuse of power to get counselees adapt to an oppressive society. In egalitarian relationship, therapists have less power base to impose their views and values on counselees. Most importantly, feminist therapists believe that therapy should not recreate the power imbalances women and other subordinate groups experience in society.[489] It also means that the counselor-counselee relationship does not reproduce or replicate the power imbalances women experience in society, rather it promotes a model for egalitarian relationships in general.[490] Both the counselee and counselor are considered to be of equal worth in which the counselee is respected as his/her own best expert on his/her life experience. It facilitates counselee's trusting themselves, their inner wisdom, and intuition.[491] By advocating egalitarian counselee-counselor relationship and mutual respect, it creates a supportive and safe space in which counselees learn to trust themselves, challenge their self-blame attitude, and become empowered to accomplish both internal and external changes.[492]

Public Policy and Social Change

Feminist therapists mandate for public policy and social change that includes three levels of outreach component. First, therapists involve with agencies and local groups that work on behalf of women's issues. Second, dissemination of information about women takes place to relevant groups so that information can be integrated toward modifying prevailing attitudes, beliefs, and practices.

---

needs of the family members before their own needs, yet they are criticized and pathologized for providing the nurturance, caring and attachment as being enmeshed with their families and for being economically dependent on men. Worell and Remer, Feminist Perspective in Therapy..., 73.

488 Susan Sturdivant, *Therapy with Women: A Feminist Philosophy of Women* (New York: Springer Publishers, 1980), 92.

489 Worell and Remer, *Feminist Perspective in Therapy...*, 304.

490 Worell and Remer, *Feminist Perspective in Therapy...*, 71.

491 Worell and Remer, *Feminist Perspective in Therapy...*, 71.

492 Worell and Remer, *Feminist Perspective in Therapy...*, 72.

Third, influencing legislation, public policies that will eliminate gender based stereotypes, prevailing power differentials, and discriminatory practices.[493]

Feminist therapists challenged the male biases that have distorted normal human development for women and exposed the need for pastoral counselors to be sensitive to the different experiences and needs of women and deviate from male biases and perception. Feminist therapy integrates personal growth as well as socio-political change. Feminist therapy may be effectively employed by pastoral caregivers in restoring a sense of self-esteem, competence and make people aware about the role of societal oppression in their problems and empower the oppressed groups to join with others in order to bring about social change. The techniques that are employed in feminist therapy can be effectively employed to bring about therapeutic change and liberation. Feminist therapy is thus essential for the growth and wellbeing of all oppressed groups including divorced women.

Health and wellbeing cannot be achieved solely by women acquiring healthier behaviours and changing individual internalized societal messages unless changes take place in the wider front such as family, schools, religion, workplace, economics, laws and political structure, because they are the means by which sexism and other forms of oppression are perpetuated. Changes in social structure must take place and women must have access to social and personal power. Feminist therapy stands out because of its focus on the dynamics between the personal and the political.

Feminist therapy has made a significant contribution to psychotherapy by taking the lead for gender sensitive practice, increased public awareness of the impact of culture and oppression of different groups and its impact on mental health and the therapeutic process. Another major contribution of feminist therapy is questioning the traditional therapy theories that are largely anthropocentric. Nevertheless, feminist therapy has attracted some criticism. One criticism is that therapist may be too feminist and militant in their views thereby influencing counselees. Another criticism is that feminist therapists do not take a neutral stance during therapy. Critics maintain that feminism originated and was developed by middle-class, white women who were overly represented in the lesbian community and have excluded other races and culture in developing their theoretical approach. However, in the recent times, there has been an effort to include women from all cultures and ethnic groups and have become more inclusive.[494]

Liberative Model

There has been a massive attack and criticism on pastoral care and counselling because of its exclusive emphasis on individual's needs and problems. Pastoral

493 Worell and Remer, *Feminist Perspective in Therapy...*, 27.

494 Elsie Jones-Smith, *Theories of Counseling and Psychotherapy: An Integrative Approach* (California: SAGE Publications, Inc., 2012), 376.

theologians such as Archie Smith, Larry Kent Graham, Immanuel Lartey, Stephen Pattison, Nancy Ramsey and Pamela Couture are among those who have vehemently criticized the tendency to diagnose and treat the individual without taking into consideration the wider web of social, economic, political and cultural aspects. Pastoral care and counselling need to be oriented to personal healing as well as social change in order to have a lasting impact.

Psychotherapies and pastoral care and counselling approaches that focused upon the health and growth of individuals are often criticized for contributing to individualism and privatism. Much like the feminist therapy, pastoral care and counselling must go beyond private sphere and address issues in the public arena, as there is interconnectedness between the private and public spheres. Pastoral caregivers must be aware of how the broad cultural, social, political, and economic realities affect individuals and families. It is crucial to understand personal need or distress within the context of social analysis of oppression, discrimination, exploitation, and alienation. Caregivers need to be committed to system analysis and transformation and help individuals and families within the system. It has rightly been pointed out by Couture that the individualistic understanding of pastoral care and counselling has contributed to the spread of "the contagious disease of individualism."[495] Most often, pastoral care and counselling has been focusing only within the individual psyche or at best within the family systems as a consequence it touches only the symptoms rather than seeking the roots of the disorder in the extended system.[496] Michael Wilson drives home the point to sharp criticism when he says "You cannot help people fully unless you also do something about the situation which makes them what they are."[497] In any given society, issues of deprivation, marginalization in terms of economic and social power structure, access, and control have a direct bearing on the personal and emotional wellbeing of the people. This implies that the problems faced by persons are not always interpersonal or intrapsychic, but are situated within the structures and ideologies of a wider public context. Hence, liberative perspective in pastoral care and counselling will be instrumental in bringing about changes in the lives of an individual as well as the society at large.

Pastoral Care and Liberation Theology

In his book, *Pastoral Care and Liberation Theology*, Pattison has articulated the importance of incorporating a socio-political analysis into the theory and practice

495 Pamela Couture, "The Context of Congregations: Pastoral Care in an Individualistic Society," in Journal of Pastoral Theology 2/1 (1992): 2.

496 Bridget Clare McKeever, "Social Systems in Pastoral Care," in *Handbook of Basic Types of Pastoral Care & Counseling*, edited by Howard W. Stone and William M. Claments (Nashville: Abington Press, 1991), 79.

497 Michael Wilson, *A Coat of Many Colours: Pastoral Studies of the Christian Way of Life* (London: Epworth Press, 1988), 21.

of pastoral care of persons whose suffering derives largely from their oppressive social location. He presented his case by pointing out commonalities of liberation theology and pastoral care. First, both pastoral care and liberation theologies share a common concern for human flourishing and wellbeing. Second, they both focus on the actual practice of increasing human flourishing.[498] He is critical of the individualistic approach of pastoral care that fails to take into consideration the larger social realities of persons.[499] Pastoral care and counselling need to expand its horizon by dealing with systemic, structural and policy levels and challenge the lack of fairness and equity that results in human suffering. For him, "pastoral care should be open to the voices of the powerless on the margins, recognize its own implicit and explicit biases and adopt a preferential option toward the poor and the marginalized with a view to helping them attain their own liberation."[500]

The experience of divorced women points to the vital analysis and understanding of societal structure. Their experiences need to be understood in a larger socio-economic and religious setting. The ministry of pastoral care and counselling must go beyond the traditional understanding where the focus is mainly on the individual. Pastoral caregivers must recognize and own the extent to which the church is fused into oppressive structures. The identity of pastors and pastoral caregivers has been contaminated by oppressive values including the patriarchal values. This calls for a personal as well as collective effort in bringing about changes in the structures. As envisioned by many pastoral theologians, the ministry of pastoral care and counselling need to focus on liberating not only individuals and families but engage in transforming ideologies, systems and structures to promote psychosocial health and wellbeing and equality and justice.

Psychosystemic Approach

In his quest to fill the lacuna between care of persons and to respond to the larger social order, Larry Kent Graham has proposed a theoretical framework known as "psychosystemic" approach. It refers to "the reciprocal interplay between the psyche of individuals and the social, cultural, and natural orders...The character of persons and the worlds come into being by the mutual influences of each upon the others."[501] Besides liberation theology, he finds family system theory and process theory suggestive. Family system therapy emphasizes that individual symptoms are signs of serious dysfunction in the larger family system. Hence, Graham calls for rethinking pastoral care and counselling that requires a new constructive relationship between prophetic ministries blended with pastoral care.

498 Pattison, *Pastoral Care and Liberation Theology...*, 89.

499 He pointed out four important drawbacks of pastoral care from liberation theology perspective. See Pattison, *Pastoral Care and Liberation Theology...*, 5.

500 Pattison, *Pastoral Care and Liberation Theology...*, 67.

501 Larry Kent Graham, *Care of Persons, Care of Worlds: A Psychosystems Approach to Pastoral Care and Counseling* (Nashville: Abington Press, 1992), 13.

Graham seeks to turn caregivers' attention to the interconnectedness of all systems and forces that shape human life. For him, reality is organized into a complex whole in which everything is related to everything else, and the maintenance of homeostatic balance is both critical and very difficult.[502] To care for persons means, then, to care for and perhaps transform the worlds that the system surrounding persons have created. The defining ministry is not the personal enhancement of one individual, although that cannot be negated; rather it is to increase love, justice, and ecological partnership.[503] Graham asserts that it is not enough to respond pastorally to the people whose lives are loveless; the systems of injustice that perpetuate that lovelessness also need to be transformed. For him, "A major goal of the ministry of care is to move from contextual impairment to contextual integrity."[504] This work of systemic transformation ought to be a part of the ministry of care and counselling. Caregivers are called to be advocates for those in need of pastoral attention, care and justice. Graham addresses the issues of love, justice, ecological partnership in responding to suffering persons and destructive situations and advocates a model that move from psyche to system in the practice of care and counselling.

Relational Humanness

There are many pastoral theologians who advocated that relational humanness needs to be supplemented with relational justice. The sufferings and plight of many individuals is to a significant degree the result of the impact of dominance and oppression associated with unjust social system, structures, and policies. Pastoral ministry in such case requires social analysis, critique, advocacy, and action for change. A holistic ministry of care and counselling incorporates both relational humanness and relational justice. Archie Smith postulates:

> Oppression is both an external and internal reality, therefore the process of liberation must seek to transform the social and political order and to emancipate the inner life of human subjects from internalized sources of oppression. The reproduction of oppression is inevitable if emancipation of the inner life of the oppressed is not a part of the larger process of social change and transformation.[505]

In the same vein, McLemore is of the opinion that "Genuine care requires understanding the human document as necessarily embedded within

502 Graham, *Care of Persons, Care of Worlds...*, 40.

503 Graham, *Care of Persons, Care of Worlds...*, 44.

504 Graham, *Care of Persons, Care of Worlds...*, 211.

505 Archie Smith, *The Relational Self: Ethics & Therapy from a Black Church Perspective* (Abington: Nashville, TN, 1982), 15.

an interlocking the public web of constructed meaning."[506] Many pastoral theologians have endeavoured to stress the point that attention should be paid to the social, cultural and political aspects in pastoral care and counselling. Widening its horizon to include the analysis of public policies and socio-cultural structures and investigating their contribution to person's oppression and suffering is crucial in pastoral care and counselling. Such a perspective invites care providers to understand persons as participants in a web comprised of personal, internal, social, political and cultural structures that are intertwined and interdependent. It is crucial for pastoral practitioners to understand distress both as personal and as socially derived.[507] Couture rightly asserts that "As caregivers, we can become seers who...can interpret the relationship between the suffering of individuals and the structures and policies of our social ecological web."[508] Pastoral care and counselling in this vein emphasizes the diagnosis of oppressive structures and power imbalances and suggests advocacy and policy change as appropriate interventions.

The data reveals gender dynamics that have resulted in women's oppression and marginalization. Because of its historic concern for the wellbeing of all persons, pastoral care and counselling needs to address these fundamental areas of women's experiences and pastoral needs. Pastors and other professional caregivers need to advocate change in women's subordination in families and churches; promote change in the unjust practices in the socialization of boys and girls which impact gender dynamics in both the church and the society; redress the distortions of women and men's images in culture and religion; promote women's wellbeing in families, churches and society; advocate for programs responsive to women's experiences and needs in the church. Make a commitment to empower women and men so that they will participate in transforming oppressive gender relations and engage in the renewal of community between women and men, work toward transforming unequal power dynamics in marriages, families and churches; and encouraging women's participation and work toward eliminating oppressive cultural values and practices that adversely impact women's growth towards wholeness.[509]

---

506 Bonnie J. Miller McLemore, *Christian Theology in Practice: Discovering a Discipline* (Grand Rapids/Michigan: William B. Eerdmans Publishing Co., 2012), 81.

507 Barbara Mcclure, "Pastoral Care," in *The Wiley Blackwell Companion to Practical Theology*, edited by Bonnie J. Miller-McLemore (West Sussex: Blackwell Publishing Limited, 2012), 276.

508 Pamela Couture, "Rethinking Private and Public Patriarchy," in *Religion, Feminism, and the Family*, edited by Anne Carr and Mary Steward Van Leeuwen (Louisville: Westminster John Knox Press, 1996), 102.

509 Mpyana Fulgence Nyengele, *African Women's Theology, Gender Relations, and Family Systems Theory: Pastoral Theological Considerations and Guidelines for Care and Counseling* (New York: Peter Lang Publishing, Inc., 2004), 176.

Understanding the position of women in the society is imperative to address the issues divorced women face. In Naga society, being divorced is associated with damaging the family status and image in addition to one's own status. Such condition underscores the importance of understanding the relationship of social and cultural factors to diagnosis, treatment, and delivery of services to women and of developing culturally appropriate approaches. In order to understand the problems and dynamics involved in divorce, pastoral counselors and caregivers need to understand and realize that the internal interactions of family members and the presenting problems must be viewed as being more than an internal event or an intrafamilial or interfamilial problem, independent or devoid of the larger Naga cultural and social context. In fact, problems internal to the family may reflect problems in the larger culture and society. Hence, there is a need to address these both in familial and cultural levels. As Rachel T. Mustin rightly argues, "When we alter the internal functioning of families without concern for the social, economic, and political context, we are in complicity with the society to keep the family unchanged."[510] In some cases, it is women who oppress other women having internalized patriarchal expectations/notions of gender roles. Pastoral care and counselling aimed at the larger socio-cultural context would help both women and men unlearn attitudes and values that diminish each other in an effort to conform to gender-based cultural prescriptions. Values and structures that stand in the way of divorced women's full realization of their worth and dignity must be combated with more encompassing means that reach people on a larger scale.

Another crucial aspect that needs to be addressed by caregivers is the issue of "learned attitudes and values." There are times when women themselves participate in their own oppression by internalizing "learned helplessness" values and attitudes that diminish women's wellbeing. Thus, pastoral counselors and caregivers must work towards helping women who have internalized these sexiest values, practices, beliefs and patterns and create new models that inspire women to seek personal improvement and fulfilment in life. However, it involves two sides of the male-female relationship to make substantial and meaningful change. As feminist family therapist Harriet Lerner posits, the differentiation and clarification of the self would be impossible tasks for women unless both women and men collectively change and challenge the constricting and distorting roles, rules, and structures that block their ability to define self and shape culture.[511]

510 Rachel T. Hare-Mustin, "Problem of Gender in Family Therapy Theory," in *Family Process* 26/1 (1987): 68.

511 Harriet Lerner, "Is Family System Theory Really Systemic? A Feminist Communication," in *A Guide to Feminist Therapy*, edited by Lois Braverman (New York: Harrington Park Press, 1988). 53.

Hare-Mustin contends that the differentiation and clarification of the self "are utopian tasks for women until the structure of the family and society changes."[512]

Divorced women experience of alienation and deprivation are clearly structural issues. Women contribute to the economy of the household, yet it is not accounted, and their labour is always unpaid. Even in public spheres, women receive non-comparative wages and own very little property or none. Many divorced women face economic problems. This economic crisis may be attributed to several factors such as socio-structural and personal. The former may be attributed to women's secondary position in the economy and the latter to the women's educational level, whether she is employed or is expected to be a homemaker and whether she dropped out of the work force after marriage to take care of the family which is directly linked to the cultural expectations of women to be homemakers. All these works together to create women's economic status difficult after divorce. In most of the cases, divorced women were not employed and depend economically on their husbands but after divorce they have to fend for themselves because the money that her husband earns is considered "his money" dictated by social convention. For many women, the primary responsibility is domestic homemaking. Most women do not own a house. Hence, women have fewer opportunities and entitlements. These aspects need to be kept in mind when counselling divorced women. They are being deprived and are oppressed by the structural norms and standards. Even the best of pastoral care and counselling, family counselling and group counselling is liable to fail or at best offer a minimal restorative effect so long as the wider social, political, economic and cultural norms are left unaddressed. In this regard, Bridget Clare McKeeve has rightly asserted that pastoral counselors need to reconsider theology of liberation in order to refocus on the ultimate meanings and to reflect on ways taking a cue from systems theory and go beyond the family to the wider systemic web of the society.[513]

As mentioned, divorced women's experiences are shaped by their social location and are connected to various social structures that shaped their understanding and structure their beliefs, attitudes and values about others in the society. Therefore, counselors need to be sensible while working with divorced women who come from different socio-economic backgrounds. In the Naga context, cultural analysis of behaviour coupled with analysis of oppression is crucial in making counselling relevant to the women's reality. The counselor also needs to be aware of the various forms of oppressions that divorced women in particular have to face in their daily lives, their experiences of biases within the law enforcement agencies and the overwhelming fear of humiliation and shame within the context of the patriarchal culture. Unless the counselor expands his/

512 Hare-Mustin, "Problem of Gender in Family Therapy Theory"..., 20.

513 McKeever, "Social Systems in Pastoral Care"..., 75.

her worldview on these issues, intervention will remain superficial and will fail to achieve the goal.

The plight of divorced women is due to unequal power distribution, social status, economic, political and legal power between men and women. It is also the consequences of learned powerlessness and passivity that women were conditioned when they relate with men. Thus, liberative model of pastoral care and counselling is required to liberate women from the destructive self-images and help them unlearn their learned helplessness and to address the oppressive wider systemic and structural issues.

In many cases, divorced women are victims of structural injustice and many of the problems they face are direct results of circumstances and do not result primarily from their own choices and actions, but they endure most of the social injustices. A pastoral care, which deals only with the distressed individual but ignores or condones social forces, which cause the distress, can be regarded as a tacit acceptance of injustices. Thus, the prophetic and the pastoral must be viewed as two aspects of a single ministry of love, and caring must include a critique of the structures of both church and society.[514] Holistic approach to pastoral care and counselling can have a significant impact in the lives of people in general and divorced women in particular and thereby address a wider spectrum of the needs and problems of divorced women. Holistic approach to pastoral care and counselling requires ministry that includes all aspects that affect an individual person for wholeness and healing to take place. Since many of the experiences of divorced women are suggestive of their secondary position in the patriarchal structures, the ministry of pastoral care and counselling has a crucial role to play in bringing about change in their life situation.

G. Moane identifies four areas of psychological functioning impacted by oppression such as self and identity, emotions, interpersonal relationships and mental health, which is very much applicable to divorced women psychosocial experience.[515] People who are at the receiving end of the unjust and oppressive systems and structures are conned into developing thoughts, beliefs and behaviours and personality traits that subscribe or serve the purpose of the existing system of oppression. Put it differently, the subordinate groups are encouraged to internalize their experience of oppression. Mental, emotional/psychological, financial dependency, lack of agency, failure to rebel or question, feelings of insecurity, inferiority complex, learned hopelessness and helplessness and self-judgment and self-hate are some of the traits internalized by divorced women.

Divorced women concerns are indeed human concerns. Their concerns were unheard of; it is largely private, untold, and unknown. It is neither a particular

514 Alastair V. Campbell, "Nature of Pastoral Care"..., 189.

515 G. Moane, *Gender and Colonialism: A Psychological Analysis of Oppression and Liberation* (London: Macmillan, 1999), 22.

interest to the wider theological fraternity in India and Naga context in particular. Hence, Naga churches are being called to pay attention to this important issue and take necessary steps to correct and heal the wounds of many divorced women in the family, church, and society. Thus, it becomes imperative that the issues faced by divorced women be considered among many issues which pastoral theology and pastoral caregivers in particular find its vocation and its validity in Naga context. Pastoral theology should promote liberation from all kinds of oppression for all people irrespective of sex, class, race etc., must be attuned to the experience of the people, and must emerge primarily from the lived experiences of the people. Genuine care means addressing the issues and concerns that impact women adversely. The issues of divorce or singleness are never purely interpersonal or intrapsychic. Rather they must be understood within the structures and ideologies of a wider public context.[516] Hence, the issues surrounding divorce are not merely interpersonal and intrapsychic, but also have cultural, religious, and social implications.

The plight of Naga divorced women can be understood as the culmination of myriad social malaise including structural injustices resulting in the polarized inequality in the society. The experiences of divorced women demand a pastorally relevant contextual theology located in Naga context. A community care theology exploring resources from traditional community life may provide the answer. Traditionally, the Nagas upheld a very strong value of community and lived in harmony. Feeling of isolation was not felt by any individual in many situations and there was no place for individualistic tendencies. In most cases, Nagas maintained the same status without any distinction between the rich and the poor. Each individual was given equal treatment in the community. The poor and the needy were taken care of in the community. In fact, the values and ethos of the Nagas in the past vividly show a clear concept of communitarianism "a concept and life principle of tribal community in which a homogeneous people live together sharing their joy and sorrow in mutual love and care."[517] In this regard, K. Thanzauva opines that tribal community in the Northeast was characterized by unity where the community takes care of the sick, the poor and the widow. "A sense of security among the members goes on healing and binding the community together. The widow, the sick and the handicapped, all are taken care of by the community. As a community they build their houses together, labour together in their jhum, mourn together and celebrate together if there is anything to celebrate."[518] There was a strong sense of communal responsibility

516 Bonnie Miller-McLemore, "Pastoral Theology as Public Theology: Revolutions in the 'Fourth Area'," in *Pastoral Care and Counseling: Redefining the Paradigm*, edited by Nancy J. Ramsay (Nashville: Abingdon Press, 2004), 51.

517 K. Thanzauva, *Theology of Community: Tribal Theology in the Making* (Aizawl: Mizo Theological Conference, 1997), 106.

518 K. Thanzauva, *Theology of Community: Tribal Theology in the Making ...*, 113.

and obligations. Traditionally, for the Nagas, community was not just a casual relatedness to person, but it is more of action and praxis-oriented life expressed in their mutual love, respect, selflessness where justice and equality were the norms. For the Nagas, community precedes individuals. The wellbeing of the community comes first. For instance, the Ao-Nagas were guided by sobaliba and each of the Naga tribe has their own version of moral code known by their distinct tribal terms but similar in essence.[519] Some implications of Sobaliba according to Longchar, an advocate of tribal theology includes generosity, hospitality especially to the needy, the poor, the aged and strangers. Respect and honour for everyone, sharing of materials, being truthful, not seeking position, power or self-glory and defend and protect the community from danger and harm.[520] It was characterized by honesty, integrity, love, compassion, respect and selflessness. "Morality in Naga context was broadly described as learned communal values that were life-enhancing thus contributing to the common good."[521] However, the innate nobility, social values and ethos have become a thing of the past. Hence, there is a need for rediscovering and developing a theology of pastoral care based on the Naga communitarian life. A theology of pastoral care thus needs to rediscover the core values and concerns for the wellbeing, the essence of tribal communitarian life and care system to bring about transformation in the society.

The ministry of pastoral care and counselling has social implications because of the fact that Christians stand not only in relation to God but also to one another. Christian ministry demands not only binding the wounds of the victims but also calls to confront and transform oppressive structures and systems that cause suffering and deprivation because of its historic concern for the wholeness and wellbeing of all persons. The task of pastoral theology is to build a just and harmonious community free from discriminations and injustices, where the weaker sections of the society are taken care and the poor live with dignity leading towards realization of God's intended life for all humanity and where everyone lives in dignity and live life in all its fullness. The Naga traditional ethos based on the communitarian relationship can be a viable starting point for liberating divorced women from their struggles. Theology of pastoral care has a critical role in emphasizing care and respect for all humans and creation. Pastoral theology needs to exhibit this communitarian care for everyone. To love God is to care for the community, respect the worth of all human beings and seek the flourishing

519 Narola Ao McFayden, "Reclaiming Sobaliba: The Vital Role of Culturally Relevant Moral Education to Counter Increasing Patterns of Violence against Women," in *Religion and Education in the (Un)making of Violence* (Illinois: Religious Education Association, 2014): 1,2.

520 A. Wati Longchar, "Interaction Between Gospel and Culture Among the Nagas," in *Encounter Between Gospel and Culture*, edited by A. Wati Longchar (Jorhat: Tribal Studies Centre, 1999), 55.

521 McFayden, *Reclaiming Sobaliba: The Vital Role of Culturally Relevant Moral Education* ...: 2.

of all humans created in God's image. Respect the sanctity of life by making sure that everyone is respected and protected.

Pastoral ministries including care and counselling and psychotherapy can be used as a mechanism for social change. Counselling and psychotherapies together with pastorally relevant contextual theology can accomplish a great deal in transforming the social structures and promoting social justice. Pastoral counselors and practitioners are in unique position to transform oppressive structures and be agents of social justice by identifying the social cause of human suffering and work towards transforming it. In other words, pastoral care and counselling should be seen as ethic of care and justice. The ministry of pastoral care and counselling needs to assume prophetic ministry, if it has to be relevant in today's context.

The proposed Liberative Pastoral Care and Counselling Paradigm emphasizes the following core values, deriving its basic insights from psychotherapeutic models such as person centered therapy, logotherapy, rational emotive behaviour therapy, feminist therapy and liberation theology.

1. Liberative pastoral care and counselling paradigm considers women as persons but not as objects.
2. It transfers the ownership of meanings of women's lived stories and experiences from the counselor to the women.
3. It takes both reason and emotion seriously.
4. Liberative pastoral care and counselling follows feminist centered principles in dealing and understanding the issues face by divorced women.
5. It attempts to place the concerns of divorced women in a cultural context.
6. It challenges the existing oppressive power structures.
7. It affirms assertiveness of women.
8. It validates the experiences of women.
9. It challenges pastoral care and counselling to move from coping to empowering.
10. Liberative pastoral care and counselling paradigm challenges the existing power structure, affirming assertiveness and empowering through consciousness raising.
11. It proposes reaffirming and relabelling as powerful processes.
12. It moves towards maintaining egalitarian relationships.
13. Social change through advocacy for public policy is part of liberative pastoral care and counselling paradigm.
14. It advocates going beyond the intrapersonal and interpersonal level and start addressing issues in the larger socio-cultural structures and systems where individuals are embedded.

Conclusion

Divorced women's concerns require a strategic intervention and ministerial involvement of pastoral care and counselling to cater to their needs. Together with the classical pastoral care task of healing, sustaining, guiding, reconciling, and nurturing the research expanded to include prophetic efforts towards liberation, empowerment, and redirection in justice seeking and public advocacy as all these dimensions are interconnected. Failing to effectively deal with the interplay between the individual and his/her wider world through the ministry of pastoral care and counselling will not produce functional care and intervention. Hence, the desire outcome of the thesis is to see new understanding of human persons and a clearer vision of what is required for effective ministry of care and counselling. Besides, a sound theological and biblical understanding will enable pastoral caregivers to get a clearer picture in tackling the issue.

Given the realities of the psychosocial ramifications of divorced women, it is imperative that the ministry of pastoral care and counselling rediscover, re-engage, and reformulate its ministry in the light of the wider contextual engagement and to recover from some of the negative consequences of the one-sided individualistic approach. In order to have a meaningful and long lasting impact, the ministry of pastoral care and counselling needs to address the wider web of human society without negating the personal aspects. The experiences of divorced women call for a broader interpretation of the person-world relationship. Supports from family, friends and the church are crucial for people going through divorce as they try to adjust to the new life situation and in their healing journey. The different therapeutic approaches mentioned above can be powerful resources for growth towards wholeness for divorced women.

Taking a cue from feminist theory and therapy, the thesis proposes a liberative model of pastoral care and counselling. Feminist theory and therapy are explicit how personality theories and psychotherapies directly incorporated into the ministry of care and counselling feeds and maintain unjust power differentials between men and women. This androcentric personality theories and psychotherapies limit the fullest development of persons particularly women, thereby neglecting the social and ethical dimensions of the ministry of pastoral care and counselling. Persons who are shunned to participate in the religious, social, and economic systems through imposition of unjust cultural practices that hinders them to experience the fullness of life needs to be addressed in pastoral ministry. Divorced women are being confronted with injustice and exclusion. Therefore, there is a need to address this issue by the church and raise voice against the present social order to create a dignified life for divorced women. Reclaiming the prophetic position in pastoral care and counselling in ways that are integrating personal and social healing is crucial, if the ministry of the church is to transform injustice and oppressions and create the world a better place to live in.

The ministry of care and counselling needs to help people in their needs, to cope with their challenges and suffering and to strengthen them in their daily lives in their physical, mental, emotional/psychological, social, economic, and religious/spiritual contexts. The ministry of pastoral care and counselling thus needs to work towards challenging and transforming the social and structural systems that deny people to experience the fullness of life. Divorced women need to experience liberation from all areas of life then only they will experience the fullness of life envisaged based on Kingdom's value.

Concluding Remark

This section deals with the general conclusion of the topic under investigation. The first chapter introduced the research problem. The researcher selected some broad indicators such as physical, mental, psychological/emotional, social, economic, religious/spiritual to study psychosocial wellbeing of divorced women in Nagaland. It is important to understand that all these six areas of functioning are not independent of one another but are all part of the dynamic system and are therefore interrelated and interdependent. When one of these areas is affected, it affects the other areas and the ramifications and impact is felt in all the other areas. The various effects of divorce on the wellbeing of divorced women have been highlighted. Divorce leads to psychosocial problems touching all areas of life that leads to diminished wellbeing. This research brought to light that wellbeing of divorced women is often a neglected topic. Issues of psychosocial wellbeing of divorced women are often overlooked in research. In most studies the main foci are the causes of divorce and also the economic consequences post-divorce and little attention is paid on psychosocial wellbeing of divorced women. But, it is important to recognize the multifaceted ramification that divorced women go through.

Statistics show that divorce in on the rise in India and Nagaland is no exception. At the backdrop of that context the plight of divorced women in Naga context is highlighted. Nagaland being a patriarchal society, women in general and divorced women in particular suffer immensely owing to their sub-ordinate status. This calls for a response from Christian ministry especially in its ministry of care and counselling.

To adequately address the psychosocial issues face by divorced women the theoretical section focused on divorce and its ramifications on psychosocial wellbeing. The existence of various theories of divorce points to the fact that divorce is not caused by just one factor but involves many problems. Divorce has adverse impact on individuals, members of the family and the society as a whole. While divorce is a unique, personal and subjective experience there are commonalities within the process of most divorce particularly for women. The critical discussion of the various theories provides the necessary background for understanding the subject under investigation. It provides a strong foundation to research divorce as each of the theory drive home important and unique insights although not without limitations when used exclusively.

The second chapter presented divine wholeness for all in the context of divorced women's wellbeing. The purpose of this discussion is that the holistic understanding of wellbeing is derived from divine wholeness and reflects God's desire for all creation. When injustice and oppression prevail, God takes the side of the oppressed. God is concerned about the vulnerable section of the society. The plight of divorced women needs to be addressed that requires a specific response. The theological basis of divorce was discussed based on the theology of the image of God and theology of redemption. The church must develop a redemptive outlook toward divorced persons. Despite their failure in their marital life, the church is called to be a community that meets all people where they are, even in their sin, with the message of the grace of God. Theological analysis and understanding on the issue of divorce needs to be incorporated in the pastoral treatment of divorced women.

Chapter three presented the data followed by the analysis of the major findings of the data in chapter four. It emerged from the empirical study that the experience of divorce has negative impact on women's psychosocial wellbeing. Analysis of the data indicated a significant difference on the scores of psychosocial wellbeing between the experimental and control groups. Women in the experimental group scored lower in all the six dimensions under investigation. Lower scores indicate lower levels of wellbeing. Divorced women reported more depressive symptoms. Particularly important in this respect are a reduced availability of social support and a deteriorated financial situation. Divorce women also reported reduce in physical wellbeing, display more negative health behaviour, more depressive symptoms, expressed less feeling of happiness, and experience shame, guilt and anxiety suggesting mental and emotional/psychological disturbances and diminished spiritual/religious wellbeing as a result of being a divorcee. These findings were compared with other research findings to validate and strengthen the research.

The above findings present important implications for the ministry of pastoral care and counselling. Based on the major findings the final chapter presented a liberative pastoral care and counselling paradigm. Together with the existing models of pastoral care and counselling and psychotherapies such as Carl Rogers's *Person Centered Therapy*, Viktor Frankl's *Logotherapy*, Albert Ellis *Rational Emotive Behaviour Therapy* and *Feminist therapies*, the research proposed a liberative paradigm. Such a model is important if the ministry of pastoral care and counselling is to be effective in dealing with issues face by divorced women. It is imperative for the ministry of pastoral care and counselling to employ liberative model of care and counselling since many of the problems in Naga society has its roots in the patriarchal structure of the society. Women are relegated to secondary position in the family as well as in the church and society. Divorced women depressive symptoms reflect a reaction of their feelings of powerlessness and helplessness. Unless the larger issues confronting divorced women are tackled, the ministry of pastoral care and counselling will remain irrelevant. The ministry of pastoral care and counselling need to address issues beyond the intrapersonal and interpersonal level and start addressing issues in the larger socio-cultural structures and systems where individuals are embedded. Christian theology and the ministry of pastoral care and counselling will be incomplete without attention been given to the experiences of divorced women. Addressing the complex ways in which multiple causative elements blend together to generate crucial and unpleasant situations and despair for divorced women must be dealt with adequately if divorced women are to be helped. The thesis argues that structural change such as systemic oppression both in domestic as well as societal front must be addressed through the ministry of pastoral care and counselling.

The six dimensions such as physical, mental, emotional/psychological, economic, social and spiritual growth is the key to the total growth of persons towards wholeness and wellbeing. Pastoral caregivers need to have the skills to effectively deal with all these domains as growth enablers. The church can be a major agency for advocating change through care and counselling ministry. Divorced women experiences of alienation and distress should not only be attributed to their own weaknesses or shortcomings rather their experiences need to be seen from the larger socio-economic, cultural and political context. The ministry of pastoral care and counselling need to address divorced women's pathology not only in their personal but should address the external environmental stressors as a major source of pathology and focus on the social and political change. One major aspect of care and counselling divorced women need to focus on the familial, social and political environment that has adverse impact on their wellbeing rather than helping the counselee to adjust to an oppressive environment. The focus needs to be on social change.

Divorced women need to be integrated into the society and the church and their problems and concerns need to be addressed by the church instead of being stigmatized and desocialized. Divorced women's needs and concerns should be addressed theologically and validate their experience in order to be more holistic in the approach of Christian ministry. Instead of focusing on how these women accept what social convention or the society dictates the greater question is how Christian ministry especially in its care and counselling can address the issues faced by divorced women and work on changing the society and to be more inclusive. The church should increasingly give importance to social engagement and should consider such action as working towards healing and wholeness of all people including divorced women. Many of the problems divorced women are facing have to do with their experiences of oppression and as such the church has a role to play in liberating them in areas where they are being oppressed and discriminated be it familial and societal. Taking a cue from feminist therapy the church should strive towards social and political change. Christian ministry engaged in care and counselling needs to make strides in the direction of holistic ministry integrating social change in its theory and practice. Although, many of the issues that emerge apply to women in general, there are still needs that remain unique to divorced women. With care and counselling intervention, divorced women who are experiencing internalized oppression may learn to embrace their own selves and develop their full potentials and live with dignity and authenticity. They may also be helped to work towards their own liberation.

Bibliography

Books

Allen, Katherine R. and Angela C. Henderson. *Family Theories: Foundations and Applications*. Sussex: John Wiley & Sons Ltd., 2017.

Ambert, Anne-Marie. *Divorce: Facts, Causes & Consequences*. 3rd Edition. Ontario: York University, 2009.

Anderson-Rajkumar, Evangeline. "New Eyes, New Reading, New Woman: Feminist Hermeneutics." In *Feminist Hermeneutics*. Edited by Lalrinawmi Ralte and Evangeline Anderson-Rajkumar. Delhi: IWTI/ISPCK, 2002.

Angolkar, Dinesh. "Family in the Post-Modern Era." In *Marriage Tradition: Changes, Challenges Ahead*. Edited by Bendangmenla Longkumer. Delhi: ISPCK, 2018.

Argyle M. and B. Beit-Hallahmi. *The Social Psychology of Religion*. London: Routledge & Kegan Paul, 1975.

Aulette, Judy Root. *Changing Families. Belmont:* Wadsworth Publications, 1994.

Baker, Adrienne. *The Jewish Women in Contemporary Society: Transitions and Traditions.* New York: New York University Press, 1993.

Baker, Maureen. *Families, Labour and Love: Family Diversity in a Changing World.* Vancouver: UBC Press, 2001.

Bandura, Albert. *Social Leaning Theory.* New York: General Learning Press, 1971.

Beck, Aaron. *Cognitive Therapy and the Emotional Disorder.* New York: Meridian, 1976.

Beller, Andrea H. and John W. Graham. "Variations in the Economic Well-Being of Divorced and Their Children: The Role of Child Support Income." In *Horizontal Equity, Uncertainty, and Economic Well-Being*. Edited by Martin David and Timothy Smeeding. Illinois: University of Chicago Press, 1985.

Bohannon, Paul. *Divorce and After: An Analysis of the Emotional and Social Problems of Divorce.* New York: Anchor, 1970.

Bonheoffer, Dietrich. *A Testament to Freedom: The Essential Writings of Dietrich Bonheoffer.* San Francisco: Harper Collins, 1995.

Boss, Pauline E., Chalandra M. Bryant and Jay A. Mancini, *Family Stress Management: A Contextual Approach.* Singapore: SAGE Publications, 2017.

Bowden, Vicky R. and Cindy Smith Greenberg. *Children and their Families: The Continuum of Care.* Philadelphia: Lippincott Williams & Wilkins, 2010.

Bowen, Murray. *Family Therapy in Clinical Practice.* New York: Rowan & Littlefield Publishers, Inc., 1978.

Bowlby, John. Loss, *Sadness and Depression.* New York: Basic Book Inc., Publishers, 1980.

________. *A Secure Base: Parent-child Attachment and Healthy Human Development.* London: Routledge, 1988.

Brandon, Nathaniel. *The Power of Self-esteem.* Deerfield Beach, FL: Health Communications 1992.

Broota, Krishan D. *Experimental Design in Behavioral Research.* New Delhi: New Age International (P) Ltd., 1989.

Brown, F. S. R., Driver and C. A. Briggs. *A Hebrew and English Lexicon of the Old Testament.* Oxford: Clarendon Press, 1972.

Brown, Ken. *Introducing Sociology for AS Level.* Second edition. Cambridge: Polity Press, 2006.

Brueggemann, Walter. *A Social Reading of the Old Testament: Prophetic Approaches to Israel's Communal Life.* Minneapolis: Fortress Press, 1994.

Burgess, E. W. and H. J. Locke. *The Family.* New York: American Book Co., 1950.

Campbell, A. *The Sense of Well-being in America: Recent Patterns and Trends.* New York: McGraw Hill, 1981.

Caperon, John. *A Vital Ministry: Chaplaincy in Schools in the Post-Christian Era.* London: SCM Press, 2015.

Carducci, Bernardo J. *The Psychology of Personality: Viewpoints, Research, and Applications.* West Sussex: John Wiley & Sons, 2007.

Cherlin, Andrew J. *The Marriage-go-round.* New York: Knopf Doubleday Publishing Group, 2009.

Chiriboga, David A. and Linda S. Catron. *Divorce: Crisis, Challenge or Relief.* New York: New York University Press, 1991.

Choudhary, J. N. *Divorce in Indian Society.* Jaipur: Printwell Publishers, 1998.

Clarke-Steward, Alison and Cornelia Brentano. *Divorce: Causes and Consequences.* London: Yale University Press, 2006.

Clebsch, William A. and Charles R. Jaekle. *Pastoral Care in Historical Perspective.* New York: Jason Aronson Inc., 1964.

Clinebell, Charlotte Holt. *Counseling for Liberation*. Philadelphia: Fortress Press, 1973.

Clienbell, Howard J. *Basic Types of Pastoral Counseling.* Nashville: Abingdon Press, 1984.

________. *Basic Types of Pastoral Care & Counseling: Resources for the Ministry of Healing and Growth.* Revised by Bridget Clare McKeever. 3rd edition. Nashville: Abingdon Press, 2011.

________. *Growth Counseling.* Nashville: Abingdon Press, 1979.

________. *Growth Counselling: Hope-Centered Methods of Actualizing Human Wholeness.* Nashville: Parthenon Press, 1982.

________. *Well Being: A Personal Plan for Exploring and Enriching the Seven Dimensions of Life.* San Francisco: Harper San Francisco, 1992.

Cook, Carol J. "The Practice of Marriage and Family Counseling and Liberal Protestant Christianity." In *The Role of Religion in Marriage and Family Counseling.* Edited by Jill Duba Onedera. New York: Routledge, Taylor & Francis Group, 2008.

Costigan, Lucy. *Women and Healing.* New York: University, 2006.

Couture, Pamela. "Rethinking Private and Public Patriarchy." In *Religion, Feminism, and the Family.* Edited by Anne Carr and Mary Steward Van Leeuwen. Louisville: Westminster John Knox Press, 1996.

Davidson, Michele R. *A Nurse Guide to Women's Mental Health.* New York: Springer Publishing Company, 2012.

Dell, Mary Lynn. "Will My Time Ever Come." In *In Her Own Time.* Edited by Jeanne Stevenson-Moessner. Minneapolis: Fortress Press, 2000.

Derrett, J. and M. Duncun. *The Death of Marriage Law.* New Delhi: Vikas Publishing House, 1971.

Doherty, William J. and David A. Baptiste. "Theories Emerging from Family Therapy." In *Sourcebook of Family Theory and Methods: A Contextual Approach.* Edited by Pauline Boss et al. New York: Springer Science + Business Media, 2009.

Dominian, Jack. "Factors which Contribute to Marital Difficulties." In *Celebrating Christian Marriage.* Edited by Adrian Thatcher. Edinburgh: T&T Clark Ltd., 2001.

Ellis, Albert and Windy Dryden. *The Practice of Rational Emotive Behavior Therapy.* New York: Springer Publishing Company, 1984.

Ellis, Albert. *Reason and Emotion in Psychotherapy.* New Jersey: Lyle Stuart, 1994.

________. *Growth Through Reason: Verbatim Cases in Rational Emotive Therapy.* New York: Science and Behaviour Books, 1971.

________. *Humanistic Psychotherapy: The Rational Emotive Approach.* New York: Crown & McGraw, 1973.

Emerson, James G. Jr., *Divorce: The Church and Remarriage.* Philadelphia: Fortress Press, 1977.

Eysenck, Michael W. *Psychology: An International Perspective.* Psychology Press: New York, 2004.

Fagan, Patrick F. and Aaron Churchill. *The Effects of Divorce on Children.* Washington D.C: Research Synthesis, 2012.

Fernandes, Walter and Geeta Bharali. "Customary Laws-Formal Law Interface: Impact on Tribal Culture." In *Christianity and Change in North East India.* Edited by T. B. Subba et al. New Delhi: Concept Publishing Company, 2009.

Fernandez, Walter, Melville Pereira and Vizalenu Khatso. *Tribal Customary Laws in Northeast India: Gender and Class Implications.* Guwahati: North East Social Science Research Center, 2008.

Fine, Mark A, Lawrence H. Ganong and David H. Demo. "A Risk and Resilience Perspective." In *Families and Change: Coping with Stressful Events and Transitions.* Edited by Sharon J. Price, Christine A. Price and Patrick C. McKenry. Fourth edition. California: Sage Publications, 2010.

Fiorenza, Elisabeth Schussler. *Jesus: Miriam's Child, Sophia's Prophet.* New York: Continuum, 1994.

Flower, Barri R. *Male Crime and Deviance: Exploring Its Causes, Dynamics and Nature.* Illinois: Charles C. Thomas Publisher, Ltd., 2003.

Fonseca, *Mabel. Counselling for Marital Happiness.* Bombay: Manaktalas, 1966.

Frank, Jerome D. and Julie B. Frank. *Persuasion and Healing: A Comparative Study of Psychotherapy.* London: The Johns Hopkins University Press, 1993.

Frankl, Viktor and James C. Crumbaugh. *Psychotherapy and Existentialism: Selected papers on Logotherapy by Viktor E. Frankl.* Washington: Washington Square Press, 1967.

Frankl, Viktor E. *Man's Search for Meaning.* Boston: Beacon Press, 2006.

________. *The Will to Meaning: Foundations and Applications of Logotherapy.* New York: Penguin Group, 1969.

Freedman, Jane. *Feminism: Concepts in the Social Sciences.* Philadelphia: Open University Press, 2001.

Freire, P. *Pedagogy of the Oppressed.* New York: Continuum, 1970.

Frensch, Florian. *The Social Side of Mergers and Acquisition: Cooperation Relationships after Mergers and Acquisitions.* Berlin: Springer Science+Business Media, 2007.

Freud, Sigmund. *New Introductory Lectures on Psycho-Analysis and Other Works.* Translated by James Strachey. Vol. xxii. London: The Hogarth Press, 1981.

Friedan, Betty. *It Changed My Life: Writings on the Women's Movement.* Cambridge, Massachusetts: Harvard University Press, 1976.

Gaffal, Margit. *Psychosocial and Legal Perspectives of Marital Breakdown: With Special Emphasis on Spain.* London: Springer Science+Business Media, 2010.

Gangrade, K. D. *Social Legislation in India.* Vol. 1. New Delhi: Concept Publishing Company (p) Ltd. 2011.

Garner, J. Dianne and Carolyn Z. *Enns. Feminist Theories and Feminist Psychotherapies: Origins, Themes and Diversity.* Second edition. New York: The Haworth Press, 2004.

George, Joseph. "Marriage & Family Counselling." In *A Study Book on Counselling.* Edited by George Varghese. Tiruvilla: Christian Sahithy Samithy, 2012.

Gill-Austern, Brita L. "Love Understood as Self-Sacrifice and Self-Denial: What Does It Do to Women?" In *Through the Eyes of Women.* Edited by Jeanne Stevenson Moessner. Minneapolis: Fortress Press, 1996 .

Goldberg, Carl. *Understanding Shame.* New Jersey: Jason Aronson, 1991.

Goode, William J. *The Family.* New Delhi: Prentice-Hall of India Private Limited, 1982.

_________. *World Changes in Divorce Patterns.* New Haven: Yale University Press, 1993.

Graham, Larry Kent. *Care of Persons, Care of Worlds: A Psychosystems Approach to Pastoral Care and Counseling.* Nashville: Abingdon Press, 1992.

Green, M. Christian. "'There but for the Grace': The Ethics of Bystanders to Divorce." In *Propositions.* Edited by W. Bradford Wilcod. New York: Institute of American Values, 2012.

Gutierrez, Gustavo. *A Theology of Liberation: History, Politics and Salvation.* Lima: CEP, 1971.

Guttentag, Marcie and Paul F. Secord. *Too Many Women?: The Sex Ratio Question.* California: Sage Publication, 1983.

Guttman, Joseph. *Divorce in Psychosocial Perspective: Theory and Research.* New York: Psychology Press, Taylor and Francis Group, 1993.

Handbook of Statistical Indicators on Indian Women. New Delhi: *Ministry of Women and Child Development* (Government of India). 2007.

Harkonen, Juho. *Divorce: Trends, Patterns, Causes, Consequences.* Stockholm: Wiley-Blackwell, 2013.

Harries, Judith Rice. *The Nurture Assumption: Why Children Turn Out the Way They Do.* New York: Free Press, 1998.

Hatfield, Elaine, Megan Carpenter and Richard L. Rapson. "Emotional Contagion as a Precursor to Collective Emotions." In *Collective Emotions: Perspectives from Psychology, Philosophy and Sociology.* Edited by Christian von Scheve and Mikko Salmela. Oxford: Oxford University Press, 2014.

Hawkins, Alan J. and Tamara A. Fackrell J. D. *Should I keep Trying to Work it Out: A Guidebook for Individuals and Couples at the Crossroad of Divorce.* Utah: Np, 2009.

Hetherington, E. Mavis. *For Better or for Worse, Divorce Reconsidered.* New York: W. W. Norton, 2002.

Hiltner, Seward and Lowell G. Colston. *The Context of Pastoral Counseling.* Nashville: Abingdon Press, 1961.

Hiltner, Seward. *Pastoral Counselling: How Every Pastor Can Help People Help Themselves.* Nashville: Abingdon Press, 1949.

________. *Preface to Pastoral Theology.* Nashville: Abingdon Press, 1958.

________. *Religion and Health.* New York: The Macmillan Company, 1947.

________. *The Christian Shepherd: Some Aspects of Pastoral Care.* Nashville: Abingdon Press, 1959.

Hobfoll, Steven E. Stress, *Social Support, And Women.* New York: Routledge, 2013.

Holdstock, T. L. "Can we Afford not to Revise the Person-Centered Concept of Self." In *Beyond Carl Rogers.* Edited by D. Brazier. London: Constable & Company, 1993.

Holladay, William Lee. Ed. *A Concise Hebrew and Aramaic Lexicon of the Old Testament.* Grand Rapids: William B. Eerdmans Publishing Company, 1971.

Hurlock, Elizabeth B. *Developmental Psychology: A Life-Span Approach.* New Delhi: Tata McGraw-Hill Education Private Limited, 1981.

Jahoda, Marie. *Current Concepts of Positive Mental Health.* New York: Arno Press, 1980.

Jakubowski, Patricia. "Assertive Behaviour and Clinical Problems of Women; Self Assertion Training for Women." In *Psychotherapy for Women: Treatment toward Equality.* Springfield: Charles C. Thomas Publisher, 1977.

________. "Assertion Training in Women." In *Psychotherapy for Women.* Edited by E. I. Rawlings and D. K. Carter. Springfield: Charles C. Thomas, 1977.

Jenks, Richard J. Divorce, *Annulments, and the Catholic Church: Healing or Hurtful.* New York: The Haworth Press, 2002.

Jones-Smith, Elsie. *Theories of Counseling and Psychotherapy: An Integrative Approach.* California: SAGE Publications, Inc., 2012.

Justes, Emma. "Women." In *Clinical Handbook of Pastoral Counseling.* Edited by Robert Wicks, Richard D. Parsons and Donald Capps. New York: Paulist Press, 1985.

James, Richard K. and Burl E. Gilliland. *Crisis Intervention Strategies.* 7th Edition. Belmont: Brooks/Cole, Cengage Learning, 2013.

Kauffman, Jeffrey. "Restoration of the Assumptive World as an Act of Injustice." In *Handbook of Restorative Justice: A Global Perspective*. Edited by Dennis Sullivan and Larry Tifft. London: Routledge 2006.

Kaufman, Gershen. *Shame: The Power of Caring*. Rochester: Shenkman Books, 1985.

________. *The Psychology of Shame*. London: Routledge Publishers, 1993.

Keltner, Norman L. and Debbie Steele. *Psychiatric Nursing*. Missouri: Elsevier Inc., 2015.

Keyes, C. L. M and J. L. Magyar-Moe. "The Measurement and Utility of Adult Subjective Well-being in Positive Psychological Assessment." In *A Handbook of Models and Measures*. Edited by S. J. Lopez and C. R. Synder. Washington DC: American Psychological Association, 2003.

Klever, Phil. "Marital Fusion and Differentiation." In *Clinical Applications of Bowen Family Systems Theory*. Edited by Peter Titelman. New York: Routledge, 2013.

Koons, C. and M. Anthony. *Single Adult Passages: Unchartered Stories*. Grand Rapids: Baker Publishers, 1991.

Kostenberger, Andreas J. and David Jones. *God, Marriage, and Family: Rebuilding the Biblical Foundation*. Illinois: Crossway, 2010.

Kumar, Rajesh. *A Universal's Guide to Constitution of India*. New Delhi: Universal Law Publishing Co., 2011.

Lamb, Michale E. and Richard M. Lerner. *Handbook of Child Psychology and Developmental Science*. Vol. 3. New Jersey: John Wiley & Sons, Inc., 2015.

Larson, David B, James P. Sawyers and Susan S. Larson. *The Costly Consequences of Divorce: Assessing the Clinical, Economic, and Public Health Impact on Marital Disruption in the United States*. Maryland: National Institute for Healthcare Research, NY.

Lartey, Emmanuel Y. *In Living Color: An Intercultural Approach to Pastoral Care and Counseling*. Second edition. London: Jessica Kingsley Publishers, 2003.

Lee, Jeffrey D. "Toward a Theology of Wellness." In *All Shall Be Well: An Approach to Wellness*. Edited by William S. Craddock Jr. New York: Church Publishing, 2009.

Leete, R. *Population Trends*. London: HMSO, 1976.

Lerner, Harriet. "Is Family System Theory Really Systemic? A Feminist Communication." In *A Guide to Feminist Therapy*. Edited by Lois Braverma. New York: Harrington Park Press, 1988.

Leslie, Robert C. *Jesus and Logotherapy: The Ministry of Jesus As Interpreted through the Psychotherapy of Viktor Frankl*. Nashville: Abingdon Press, 1965.

Longchar, Wati. *Transforming Cultures and Praxis: Engaging Peoples in the Margins*. Kolkata: PTCA, 2017.

________. "Interaction Between Gospel and Culture Among the Nagas." In *Encounter Between Gospel and Culture.* Ed., A. Wati Longchar. Jorhat: Tribal Studies Centre, 1999.

Longkumer, N. Limatula. "Christianity and Naga Women." In *Transforming Theology from Empowering Women: A Theological and Hermeneutical Reflection in the Context of North East India.* Edited by R. L. Hnuni. Jorhat: Women's Studies Eastern theological College, 1999.

Lorber, Judith. *The Variety of Feminisms and their Contribution on Gender Equality.* Oldenburg: University of Oldenburg, 1997.

Maass, Vera Sonja. *Lifestyle Changes: A Clinician's Guide to Common Events, Challenges, and Options.* New York: Routledge Taylor & Francis Group, 2008.

Mahoney, Annette, Elizabeth J. Krumrei and Kenneth Pargament. "Broken Vows: Divorce as a Spiritual Trauma and Its Implications for Growth and Decline." In *Trauma, Recovery, and Growth: Positive Psychological Perspectives on Posttraumatic Stress.* Edited by Stephen Joseph and P. Alex Linley. New Jersey: John Wiley & Sons, Inc. 2012.

Mann, M. "War and Social Theory: Into Battle with Classes, Nations and States." In *The Sociology of War and Peace.* Edited by M. Shaw and C. Creighton. London: MacMillan, 1987.

Maslow, Abraham. *Motivation and Personality.* New York: Harper & Row, 1970.

McClure, Barbara. "Pastoral Care." In *The Wiley Blackwell Companion to Practical Theology.* Edited by Bonnie J. Miller-McLemore. West Sussex: Blackwell Publishing Limited, 2012.

McCubbin, Hamilton I. and Joan M. Patterson. "The Family Stress Process: The Double ABCX Model of Adjustment and Adaptation." In *Social Stress and the Family: Advance and Developments in Family Stress Theory and Research.* Edited by Hamilton I. McCubbin, Marvin B. Sussman and Jaon M. Petterson. New York: Routledge, 2013.

McKeever, Bridget Clare. "Social Systems in Pastoral Care." In *Handbook of Basic Types of Pastoral Care & Counseling.* Edited by Howard W. Stone and William M. Clements. Nashville: Abingdon Press, 1991.

McLemore, Bonnie J. Miller. *Christian Theology in Practice: Discovering a Discipline.* Grand Rapids/Michigan: William B. Eerdmans Publishing Co., 2012.

Mehta, Rama. *Divorced Hindu Women.* Delhi: Vikas Publishing House Pvt. Ltd., 1975.

Mensah, Kortet and Mark Fine. "Divorce and Children." In *Family Influences on Childhood Behaviour and Development: Evidence Based Prevention and Treatment Approaches.* Edited by Thomas P. Gullotta and Gary M. Blau. New York: Routledge, Taylor and Francis Group, 2010.

Miller, Jean Baker. *Towards a New Psychology of Women.* Boston: Beacon Press, 1986.

Miller-McLemore, Bonnie. "Pastoral Theology as Public Theology: Revolutions in the 'Fourth Area'." In *Pastoral Care and Counseling: Redefining the Paradigm.* Edited by Nancy J. Ramsay Nashville: Abingdon Press, 2004.

________. "Shaping the Future of Religion and Psychology: Feminist Transformations in Pastoral Theology." In *Religion and Psychology: Mapping the Terrain in Contemporary Dialogues, Future Prospects.* Edited by D. E. Jonte-Pace & W. B. Parsons. New Haven: Routedge, 2001.

________. *Christian Theology in Practice: Discovering a Discipline.* Grand Rapids: Eerdmans, 2012.

Moane, G. *Gender and Colonialism: A Psychological Analysis of Oppression and Liberation.* London: Macmillan, 1999.

Mooney, Linda A., David Knox and Carline Schacht. *Understanding Social Problems.* Ninth edition. Stamford: Cengage Learning, 2015.

Munhall, Patricia L. and Virginia Mackhen Fitzsimons. *The Emergence of Family into the 21st Century.* Boston: Jones and Bartlett Publishers, 2001.

Murry, Ezamo. *An Introduction to Pastoral Care and Counseling.* ISPCK: New Delhi, 2016.

Nagpal, Rub and Helmud Sell. *Assessment of Subjective Well-Being: The Subjective Well-Being Inventory (SUBI).* New Delhi: World Health Organization Regional Office for South-East Asia, 1992.

________. *Subjective Wellbeing Inventory.* New Delhi: World Health Organization, 1985.

Neuger, C.C. "Women's Depression: Lives at Risk." In *Women in Travail and Transition: A New Pastoral Care.* Edited by M. Glaz & J. S. Moessner. Minneapolis: Fortress Press, 1991.

Nicholas, Randall. *Ending Marriage, Keeping Faith: A new Guide through the Spiritual Journey of Divorce.* Oregon: Wipf and Stock Publishers, 2002.

Niemeyer, Robert A. and Heidi Levitt. "Coping and Coherence: A Narrative Perspective." In *Coping with Stress: Effective People and Processes.* Edited by C. R. Snyder. Oxford: Oxford University Press, 2001.

Nye, F. I. "Choice, Exchange and the Family." In *Contemporary Theories about the Family.* Vol. 2. Edited by W.R. Burr, R. Hill, F.I. Nye and I.L. Reiss. New York: Free Press, 1979.

Nyengele, Mpyana Fulgence. *African Women's Theology, Gender Relations, and Family Systems Theory: Pastoral Theological Considerations and Guidelines for Care and Counseling.* New York: Peter Lang Publishing, Inc., 2004.

O'Day, Gail. *The Word Disclosed: John's Story and Narrative Preaching.* St. Louis: CBP, 1987.

Oden, Thomas C. *Kerygma and Counseling*. Philadelphia: The Westminster Press, 1966.

________. *Pastoral Ministry: Essentials of Ministry*. San Francisco: Harper & Row Publishers, 1983.

Pargament, Kenneth I. and G. G. Ano. "Empirical Evidences in the Psychology of Religion and Coping." In *Religious Influence on Health and Well-Being in the Elderly.* Edited by K.W. Schaie, N. Krause and A. Booth. New York: Springer, 2004.

Parmenter, Bruce. *Christians Caught in Divorced Trap: Helping Families Recover from Divorce.* Missouri: College Press Publishing Company, 1995.

Parsons, Talcott E. *The Social System.* London: The Free Press of Glencoe, 1951.

Pattison, Stephen. *Pastoral Care and Liberation Theology*. Cambridge: Cambridge University Press, 1994.

________. *Shame, Theory, Therapy Theology.* Cambridge: Cambridge University Press, 2000.

Patton, John. *Pastoral Care in Context: An Introduction to Pastoral Care.* Louisville: John Knox Press, 1993.

Personal Wellbeing Index-Adult (PWI-A): The International Wellbeing Manual. 5th Edition. Melbourne: Australian Centre on Quality of Life, Deakin University, 2013.

Pippert, Timothy D. *Road Dogs and Loners: Family Relationship Among Homeless Men*. New York: Lexington Books, 2007.

Pothen, S. *Divorce: Its Causes and Consequences in Hindu Society.* New Delhi: Vikas Publishing House Pvt. Ltd., 1986.

Pui-lan, Kwok. *Introducing Asian Feminist Theology.* Cleveland: Pilgrim Press, 2000.

Raschke, Helen J. "Divorce." In *Handbook of Marriage and the Family.* Edited by Suzanne K. Steimetz and Marvin B. Sussman. New York: Plenum Press, 1987.

Richardson, Ronald W. *Couples in Conflict: A Family System Approach to Marriage Counseling.* Minneapolis: Fortress Press, 2010.

Rogers, Carl. *Client Centered Therapy.* Boston: Houghton Mifflin, 1961.

________. *On Becoming a Person: A Therapist's View of Psychotherapy.* Boston: Houghton Mifflin Company, 1961.

Rogers, Carl, *Wendy Stainton and Rex Stainton Rogers. The Psychology of Gender and Sexuality: An Introduction.* Berkshire: Open University Press, 2004.

Ruether, Rosemary R. *Introducing Redemption in Christian Feminism.* Sheffield: Sheffield Academic Press, 1998.

Ruether, Rosemary Radford. *Sexism and God-Talk*. Boston: Beacon Press, 1983.

Russell, Letty M. *Becoming Human*. Philadelphia: Westminster John Knox Press, 1982.

Russell, Letty M. *Human Liberation in a Feminist Perspective.* Philadelphia: The Westminster Press, 1974.

Sabates, Angela M. *Social Psychology in Christian Perspective: Exploring the Human Condition.* Madison: Intervarsity Press, 2012.

Scanzoni, John. *Contemporary Families and Relationships: Reinventing Responsibility.* New York: McGraw Hill Inc, 1995.

Schlauch, Chris R. *Faithful Companioning: How Pastoral Counseling Heals.* Minneapolis: Fortress Press, 1995.

Schottroff, Luise. "The Samaritan Woman and the Notion of Sexuality in the Fourth Gospel." In *What is John.* Edited by Fernando Segovia. Atlanta: Scholars Press, 1998.

Schultz, Duane P. and Sydney Ellen Schultz. *Theories of Personality.* Boston: Cengage Learning, 2013.

Segrin, Chris and Jeanne Flora. *Family Communication*. Second edition. New York: Routledge Taylor and Francis, 2011.

Sharf, Richard S. *Theories of Psychotherapy and Counselling.* Pacific Grove: Thompson Learning Inc., 2004.

Simmel, George. *The Philosophy of Money.* London: Routledge, 1978.

Simon, R. W. "Mental Health and Emotions." In *Handbook on the Sociology of Emotions: Volume 2.* Edited by Jan E. Stets, Jonathan H. Turner. Heidelberg: Springer Science +Business Media, 2012.

Smith, Archie. *The Relational Self: Ethics & Therapy from a Black Church Perspective.* Abingdon: Nashville, TN, 1982.

Snodgrass, Jill L. "Pastoral Counseling: A Discipline of Unity amid Diversity." In *Understanding Pastoral Counseling.* Edited by E.A. Maynard and Jill L. Snodgrass. New York: Springer Publishing Company, 2015.

Sprenkle, Douglas H. and Pilar Gonzalez-Doupe. "Divorce Therapy." In *Family Therapy Sourcebook.* Second edition. Edited by Fred P. Piercy, Douglas H. Sprenkle and Joseph L. Wetchler. New York: The Guilford Press, 1996.

Starbuck, Gene H. and Karen Soucier Lundy. *Families in Context: Sociological Perspective.* New York: Routledge, 2016.

Straus, Martha B. "Divorced Mothers." In *The Different Faces of Motherhood.* Edited by Beverly Birns and Dale Hay. New York: Springer Science+Business Media, 1988.

Strong, Bryan, Christine DeVault and Theodore F. Cohen. *The Marriage and Family Experience: Intimate Relationship in a Changing Society.* Belmont: Thomson Wadsworth, 2008.

________. *The Marriage and Family Experience: Intimate Relationships in a Changing Society.* Belmont: Thomson Wadsworth, 2011.

Strunk, Orlo Jr. "A Prolegomenon to a History of Pastoral Counseling." In *Clinical Handbook of Pastoral Counseling.* Vol. 1. Edited by Robert J. Wicks, Richard D. Parsons and Donald Capps. New York: Paulist Press, 1985.

Sturdivant, Susan. *Therapy with Women: A Feminist Philosophy of Women.* New York: Springer Publishers, 1980.

Thanzauva, K. *Theology of Community: Tribal Theology in the Making.* Aizawl: Mizo Theological Conference, 1997.

Thornton, Edward E. *Theology and Pastoral Counseling.* Philadelphia: Fortress Press, 1964.

Tillich, Paul. "Theology and Counseling." In *The Meaning of Health.* Edited by Perry LeFevre. Chicago: Exploration Press, 1984.

Trafford, Abigail. *Crazy Time: Surviving Divorce.* New York: Harper and Row Publishers, 1974.

Trible, Phyllis. *God and the Rhetoric of Sexuality: Overtures to Biblical Theology.* Augsburg: Fortress Press, 1978.

Umberson, Debra, Mieke Beth Thomeer and Kristi Williams. "Family Status and Mental Health: Recent Advances and Future Directions." In *Handbook of the Sociology of Mental Health.* Edited by Carol S. Aneshensel, Jo C. Phelan and Alex Bierman. New York: Springer Science+Business Media, 2013.

Vardhan, Ranjan. "Single-Parent Families and Public Policy." In *Marriage and Family in India.* Edited by Jasmeet Sandhu. Jaipur: Rawat Publications, 2016.

Vasquez, Huge and Sukie Magraw. "Building Relationships across Privilege: Becoming an Ally in the Therapeutic Relationships." In *Psychotherapy with Women: Exploring Diverse Contexts and Identities.* Edited by Marsha Pravder Mirkin, Karen L. Suyemoto and Barbara F. Okun. New York: The Guilford Press, 2005.

Vathi, Zana. "The Interface between Return Migration and Psychosocial Wellbeing." In *Return Migration and Psychosocial Wellbeing: Discourses, Policy-Making and Outcomes for Migrants and Their Families.* Edited by ZanaVathi and Russel King. London: Routledge, 2017.

Waite, Linda J. and Maggie Gallagher. *The Case for Marriage: Why Married People are Happier, Healthier and Better Off Financially.* New York: Random House Inc., 2000.

Watkins-Ali, Caroll. *Survival and Liberation: Pastoral Theology in African American Context.* St. Louis, MO: Chalice Press, 1999.

Weedon, Chris. "Post-structuralist Feminist Practice." In *Theory/Pedagogy/Politics: Texts for Change.* Edited by Donald E. Morton and Masud Zavarzadeh. Chicago: University of Illinois Press, 1991.

Weiss, Robert S. *Marital Separation.* New York: Basic Books, Inc., Publishers, 1975.

Weitzman, Lenore J. *The Divorce Revolution—The Unexpected Social and Economic Consequences for Women and Children in America.* New York: The Free Press, 1985.

Welsh, F. *Spiritual Resources in Family Therapy.* New York: The Guilford Press, 2008.

Westermann, Claus. "Peace [Shalom] in the Old Testament." In *The Meaning of Peace.* Edited by Perry B. Yoder and Willard M. Swartley. Elkhart: Institute of Mennonite Studies, 2001.

White, James M., David M. Klein and Todd F. Martin. *Family Theories: An Introduction.* Los Angeles: SAGE Publications, Inc., 2015.

Wilkinson, John. *Health and Healing: Studies in New Testament Principles and Practice.* Edinburgh: The Handsel Press Ltd., 1980.

Williams, Tammy R. "Is There a Doctor in the House." In *Practicing Theology: Beliefs and Practices in Christian Life.* Edited by Miroslav Volf and Dorothy C. Bass. Grand Rapids: B. Eerdamans Publishing Co., 2002.

Wilson, Michael. *A Coat of Many Colours: Pastoral Studies of the Christian Way of Life.* London: Epworth Press, 1988.

Worell, Judith and Pamela Remer. *Feminist Perspectives in Therapy: Empowering Diverse Women.* Second edition. New Jersey: John Wiley & Sons, Inc., 2003.

Wright, C. *The Sociological Imagination.* Revised edition. New York: Oxford University Press, 1999.

Wurmser, Leon. *The Mask of Shame.* New Jersey: Jason Aronson, 1995.

Dictionary and Encyclopedia

Baker, Winetta A. "Psychotherapy for Adults." In *Cultural Sociology of Divorce: An Encyclopaedia* Vol.1. Edited by Robert E. Emery. (New Delhi: Sage Publications, 2013): 395-397.

Campbell, Alastair V. "Nature of Pastoral Care." In *A Dictionary of Pastoral Care.* Edited by Alastair V. Campbell. London: SPCK, 1987, 188-190.

Dryden, Windy. "Rational Emotive Behavior Therapy." In *Encyclopaedia of Cognitive Behavior Therapy.* Edited by Arthur Freeman. (New York, Springer Science + Business Media, Inc., 2005): 321-324.

Harrison, R.K. "Healing, Health." In *Interpreters Dictionary of the Bible.* Edited by Katharine Doob Sakenfeld. Vol. 2. Nashville: Abingdon Press, 2008, 541-548.

Kayser, Keran and Jessica K. J. Johnson. "Divorce." In *The Encyclopaedia of Social Work*: 4 Volume Sets. Edited by Terry Mizrahi and Larry Davis (Oxford: Oxford University Press, 2008): 76-87.

Koteskey, P. L. "Divorce." In *Baker Encyclopaedia of Psychology*. Edited by David G. Benner (Michigan: Baker Book House, 1985): 318-323.

Smith, Sandra M. and Kyle C. Horst. "Domestic Violence." In *Cultural Sociology of Divorce: An Encyclopaedia* Vol.1. Edited by Robert E. Emery. (California: Sage Publications, 2013): 397-400.

Taber, C. R. "Divorce." In *The Interpreter's Dictionary of the Bible Supplementary Volume.* Edited by Keith Crim. Nashville: Abingdon Press, 1976, 215-245.

Commentary

Haenchen, E. *John 1: A Commentary on the Gospel of John.* Translated by Robert W. Funk. Philadelphia: Fortress Press, 1984.

Journals and Articles

Acolatse, E. E. "Christian Divorce Counselling in West Africa: Seeking Wholeness through Reformed Theology and Jungian Dreamwork." In The Journal of Pastoral Theology 21/1 (2011): 1-18.

Ainsworth, Mary and S. M. Bells. "Attachment, Exploration and Separation: Individual differences in Strange-Situation Behavior of One-year-olds." In Child Development 41 (1970): 49-67.

________. "Attachment Beyond Infancy." In American Psychologist 44 (1989): 709-716.

Amato Paul R. "Divorce in Social and Historical Context: Scientific Views." In Journal of Marriage and the Family 66/4 (November, 2004): 959-965.

________. "Research on Divorce: Continuing Trends and New Developments." In Journal of Marriage & Family 72/3 (June, 2010): 650-666.

________. "Life-Span Adjustment of children to their Parent's Divorce." In Children and Divorce 4/1 (1994): 143-164.

________. "The Consequences of Divorce on Adults and Children." In Journal of Marriage and Family 62/4 (November, 2000): 1269-1287.

________. "The Impact of Family Formation Change on the Cognitive, Social and Emotional Well-Being of the Next Generation." In The Future of Children 15/2 (Fall, 2015): 75-96.

Amato, Paul R. and Alan Booth. "The Legacy of Parents' Marital Discord: Consequences for Children's Marital Quality." In Journal of Personality and Social Psychology 81/4 (2001): 627-638.

Amato, Paul R. and Bruce Keith. "Parental Divorce and the Well-Being of Children: A Meta-Analysis." In Psychological Bulletin 110/1 (1991): 26-46.

Amato, Paul R. and Bryndl Hohmann-Marriot. "A Comparison of High-and Low-Distress Marriages that End in Divorce." In Journal of Marriage and Family 69/3 (2007): 621-638.

Amato, Paul R. and Jacob Cheadle. "The Long Reach of Divorce: Divorce and Child Well-being Across Three Generations." In Journal of Marriage and Family 67/1 (2005): 191-206.

Amato, Paul R. and Spencer James. "Divorce in Europe and the United States: Commonalities and Differences across Nations." In Family Science 1/1 (January, 2010): 2-13.

Andress, H. J. and M. Brockel. "Income and Life Satisfaction after Marital Disruption in Germany." In Journal of Marriage and Family 69 (2007): 500-512.

________. "The Economic Consequences of Divorce in Germany: What has Changed since the turn of the Millennium? Comparative Population Studies." In Comparative Population Studies 40/3 (2015): 1-37.

Bartholomew, Kim and Leonard M. Horowitz. "Attachment Styles Among Young Adults: A Test of Four Category Model." In Journal of Personality and Social Psychology 61/2 (1991): 226-244.

Baumeister Roy F. and Mark R. Leary. "The Need to Belong: Desire for Interpersonal Attachments as a Fundamental Human Motivation." In Psychological Bulletin 117/3 (1995): 497-529.

Becker, Gary S., Elizabeth M. Landes and David E. Bloom. "An Economic Analysis of Marital Instability." In Journal of Political Economy 85 (1977): 1141-1187.

Beckett, Megan and Marc N. Elliot. "Does the Association Between Marital Status and Health Vary by Sex, Race, and Ethnicity?" In Labor and Population Program, Working Paper Series 02-08 (September, 2002): 1-31.

Bjorck, J. P. "Faith, Coping and Illusory Control: Psychological Constructs with Theological Ramifications." In Journal of Psychology and Christianity 26/3, (2007): 195-206.

Blekesaune, Morten. "Partnership Transition and Mental Distress: Investigating Temporal Order." In Journal of Marriage and Family 70/4 (2008): 879-890.

Bloom, B., S. Asher and S. White. "Marital Disruption as a Stressor." In Psychological Bulletin 85/4 (July 1978): 867-894.

Boertien, Dietrik and Juho Harkonen. "Less Education More Divorce: Explaining the Inverse Relationship Between Women's Education and Divorce." In Demographic Research 38/41 (2018): 1241-1276.

Boruchovitch, Evely and Brigitte R. Mednick. "The Meaning of Health and Illness: Some Consideration for Health Psychology." In Psico-USF 7/2 (July-December, 2002): 175-183.

Boss, Pauline E. "Normative Family Stress: Family Boundary Changes Across the Life Span." In Family Relations 29 (1980): 445-450.

Brown, L. S. and A. M. Brodsky. "The Future of Feminist Therapy." In Psychotherapy 29 (1992): 51-57.

Butterworth, P. and B. Rodgers. "Mental Health Problems and Marital Disruptions: It is the Combination of Husband and Wives' Mental Health Problems That Predicts Later Divorce?" In Social Psychiatric Epidemiology 43 (2007): 758-763.

Caputo, Jennifer and Robin W. Simon. "Physical Limitation and Emotional Wellbeing: Gender and Marital Status Variations." In Journal of Health and Social Behaviour 54/2 (2013): 241-257.

Chapman, Amy. "Suffering Our Way to Salvation: Ivone Gebara, Elisabeth Schussler Fiorenza, and the Adequacy of the Cross as a Symbol for Women." In Lumen et Vita (June 2011): 1-18.

Chirico, Francesco. "Spiritual Wellbeing in the 21st Century: It's Time to Review the Current WHO's Definition?" In Journal of Health and Social Science 1/1 (2016): 11-16.

Couture, Pamela. "The Context of Congregations: Pastoral Care in an Individualistic Society." In Journal of Pastoral Theology 2/1 (1992): 1-13.

Davis, L., W. R. Avison and D. D. McAlpine. "Significant Life Experiences and Depression among Single and Married Mothers." In Journal of Marriage and the Family 59 (1997): 294-308.

De, Vaus David, Matthew Gray, Liia Qu and David Stanton. "The Economic Consequences of Divorce in Australia." In International Journal of Law, Policy and the Family 28/1 (2014): 1-22.

Dhal, Sangita. "Mapping Women's Economic Empowerment: Imperative for Inclusive Growth and Gender Justice." In Women's Link 20/4 (October-December, 2003): 21-28.

Dhar, Neera, S. K. Chaturvedi and Deoki Nandan. "Spiritual Health, The Fourth Dimension: A Public Health Perspective." In WHO South East Asia Journal of Public Health 2 (January-March, 2013): 3-5.

Diener, E. and R. E. Lucus. "Personality and Subjective Well-being." In Annual Review of Psychology 54 (1991): 403-425.

Dolan, Mary A. and Charles D. Hoffman. "The Different Effects of Marital and Custodial Status on Perceptions of Mothers and Fathers." In Journal of Divorce & Remarriage 29/3 (2008): 55-64.

Dommaraju, Pramchand. "Divorce and Separation in India." In Population and Development Review 42/2 (June, 2016): 195-223.

Ellis, Albert. "The Biological Basis of Human Irrationality: A reply to McBurnet and LaPointe." In Journal of Individual Psychology 35/1 (1979d): 111-116.

Evans, Kathy M., Elizabeth A. Kincade, Aretha F. Marbley and Susan R. Seem. "Feminism and Feminist Therapy." In Journal of Counseling & Development 83 (2005): 269-277.

Fergusson, D. M., L. J. Harwood and A. L. Beautrais. "The Measurement of Family Material Well-being." In Journal of Marriage and the Family 43/3 (1981): 143-150.

Fiala, W. E., J. P. Bjorck and R. L. Gorsuch. "The Religious Support Scale: Construction, Validation and Cross-Validation." In American Journal of Community Psychology 30 (2002): 761-186.

Fisher, John. "The Four Domains Model: Connecting Spirituality, Health and Wellbeing." In Religions 2 (2011): 17-28.

Gadalla, Tahany M. "Impact of Marital Dissolution on Men's and Women's Incomes: A Longitudinal Study." In Journal of Divorce and Remarriage 50 (2008): 55-65.

Gahler, Michael. "Life After Divorce: Economic, Social and Psychological Well-Being Among Swedish Adults and Children Following Family Dissolution." In Swedish Institute for Social Research Reports 2 (1998): 1-28.

Gimenez, M. "The Feminization of Poverty: Myth or Reality?" In Insurgent Sociologist 14/3 (1987): 5-30.

Glick, P. C. and A. J. Norton. "Divorce and Age at Marriage." In Journal of Marriage and Family 33/6 (1971): 307-327.

Goldman, Noreen. "Marriage Selection and Mortality Patterns: Inferences and Fallacies." In Demography 30/2 (1993): 189-208.

Gomez, Rapson and John W. Fisher. "Domains of Spiritual Well-Being and Development and Validation of the Spiritual Well-Being Questionnaire." In Personality and Individual Differences 35 (2003): 1975-1991.

Grad, Frank P. "Constitution of the World Health Organization." In Bulletin of the World Health Organization (2008): 123-135.

Greeff A. P. and I. N. Ritman. "Individual Characteristics Associated with Resilience in Single-Parent Families." In Psychological Reports 96/1 (2005): 3-42.

Hare-Mustin, Rachel T. "Problem of Gender in Family Therapy Theory." In Family Process 26/1 (1987): 15-27.

Hart, Karen E. and William Allen Kritsonis. "Critical Analysis of an Original Writing on Social Learning Theory: Imitation of Film-Mediated Aggressive Models by: Albert Bandura, Dorothy Ross and Sheila A. Ross." In National Forum of Applied Educational Research Journal 20/3 (2006): 1-7.

Hawkins, Daniel H. and Alan Booth. "Unhappily Ever After: Effects of Long-Term, Low-Quality Marriages on Well-Being." In Social Forces 84/1 (2005): 451-471.

Heer, David M. and Amyra Grossbard-Shechtman. "The Impact of the Female Marriage Squeeze and the Contraceptive Revolution on Sex ratio and the Women's Liberation Movement in the United States, 1960 to 1975." In Journal of Marriage and Family 43/1 (February, 1981): 49-65.

Helliwell, J. F. and R. D. Putman. "The Social Context of Wellbeing." In International Journal of Wellbeing 1/2 (2004): 1435-1446.

Hetherington, E. Mavis and John Kelly. "For Better or for Worse: Divorced Reconsidered." In The Journal of Family Communication 4/1 (2002): 57-60.

Hill, Reuben. "Genetic Features of Families under Stress." In Social Casework 49/2 (1948): 139-150.

Ingersoll, R. Elliott. "Refining Dimensions of Spiritual Wellness: A Cross-Traditional Approach." In Counseling and Values 42 (1998): 156-165.

Jamir, Toshimenla. "Gender Land relations in Nagaland: Dilemma of balancing tradition and Modernity." In International Journal of Gender and Women Studies 2/1 (March, 2014): 120-134.

Joshi, Shophna, Shilpa Kumari and Madhu Jain. "Religious Belief and Its Relation to Psychological Well-being." In Journal of the Indian Academy of Applied Psychology 34/2 (July 2008): 345-354.

Kahneman, Daniel and Ashton Acton. "Issues in General Science and Scientific Theory and Method: 2011 Edition." In Proceedings of the National Academy of Sciences 107/38 (September, 2010): 1-5.

Keyes, Corey L. M. "The Mental Health Continuum: From Languishing to Flourishing in Life." In Journal of Health and Social Behaviour 43 (June, 2002): 207-222.

Keyes, Corey Lee M. "Social Well-Being." In Social Psychology Quarterly 61/2 (1998): 121-140.

Koball, Heather L., Emily Moiduddinn, Jamila Henderson, Brian Goesling and Melanie Besculides. "What Do We Know About the Link Between Marriage and Health?" In Journal of Family Issues 31/8 (2010): 1019-1040.

Krumrei, Elizabeth, Carissa Coit, Sarah Martin, Wendy Fogo and Annette Mahoney. "Post-Divorce Adjustment and Social Relationships: A Meta-Analytic Review." In Journal of Divorce and Remarriage 46, 3/4 (2007): 145-166.

Kulu, Hill. "Premarital Cohabitation and Divorce: Support for the "Trial Marriage" Theory?" In Demographic Research 23 (November, 2010): 879-904.

Kumari, Arunima. "Increasing Rate of Divorce: A Social Stigma." In International Journal of Social Science and Humanities Research 1 (January-March, 2016): 235-240.

Lamberigts, M. "Competing Christologies: Julian and Augustine on Jesus Christ." In Augustinian Studies 36/1 (2005): 159-194.

Larson, James S. "The Measurement of Social Well-being." In Social Indicators Research 28/3 (1993): 285-296.

Lavee, Yaov., Hamilton I. McCubbin and Joan M. Patterson. "The Double ABCX Model of Family Stress and Adaptation: An Empirical Test by Analysis of Structural Equations with Latent Variables." In Journal of Marriage and Family 47/4 (November, 1985): 811-825.

Lehrer, Evelyn L. and Yeon Jeong Son. "Women's Age at First Marriage and Marital Instability in the United States: Differences by Race and Ethnicity." In Demographic Research 37/9 (August, 2017): 229-250.

Lienemann-Perrin, Christine. "The Biblical Foundation for Feminist and Participatory Theology of Mission." In International Review of Mission 95 (January, 2004): 17-34.

Lillard, Lee A. and Linda J. Waite. "Till Death Do Us Apart: Marital Disruption and Mortality." In The American Journal of Sociology 100/5 (March, 1995): 1131-1156.

Maddox, Randy L. "Toward an Inclusive Theology: The Systematic Implications of the Feminist Critique." In Christian Scholar's Review 16 (1986): 7-23.

Manning, P. J., W. D Smock, S. Gupta. "The Effect of Marriage and Divorce on women's Economic Well-being." In American Sociological Review 64/6 (1999): 794-812.

Maslow, Abraham. "The Theory of Human Motivation." In Psychological Review 50/4 (July 1943): 370-396.

Mastekaasa, Arne. "Psychological Wellbeing and Marital Dissolution: Selection Effects." In Journal of Family Issues 12 (1994): 208-229.

Mestekaasa, Arne. "Marriage and Psychological Well-being: Some Evidence on Selection into Marriage." In Journal of Marriage and the Family 54/4 (November, 1992): 901-911.

Moghadam, Valentine M. "The "Feminization of Poverty" and Women's Human Rights." In Social and Human Sciences 2/2 (July, 2005): 5-18.

Morrow, Susan and Donna M. Hawxhurst. "Feminist Therapy: Integrating Political Analysis in Counseling and Psychotherapy." In Women & Therapy 21 (1998): 37-50.

Mullet, Elizabeth and Arnold L. Stolberg. "Divorce and its Impact on the Intimate Relationships of Young Adult." In Journal of Divorce and Remarriage 38-1/2 (2002): 40-54.

Nakonezyn, Paul A. and Wayne H. Denton. "Marital Relationships: A Social Exchange Theory Perspective." In The American Journal of Family Therapy 36 (2008): 402-412.

Nelavala, Surekha. "Jesus Asks a Samaritan Woman for a Drink: A Dalit Feminist Reading of John 4." In Lection Difficilior 8/1 (2007): 1-25.

Nolan-Hoeksema, Susan and Benito Jackson. "Mediators of the Gender Differences in Rumination." In Psychology of Women Quarterly 25/1 (2001): 37-47.

Pandey, Manoj K. "Association Between Marital Status and Health: Examining the Role of Age and Gender." In ASARC Working Paper (2009/10): 1-23.

Rathi, Pooja and J. P. Pachauri. "Problems Faced by Divorced Women in their Pre and Post-divorce Period: A Sociological Study with Reference to district Meeru." In Journal of Pharmacognsy and Phytochamistry 7/1 (2018): 207-212.

Riggio, H. "Parental Marital Conflict and Divorce, Parent-child Relationships, Social Support, and Relationship Anxiety in Young Adulthood." In Personal Relationship 11 (2004): 99-114.

Roselima, Kamei Pamei. "Customary Law and Women in North East India." In International Research Journal of Social Sciences 3 (September, 2014): 59-62.

Russell, Letty M. "Hot-house Ecclesiology: A Feminist Interpretation of the Church." In Ecumenical Review 53/1 (2001): 48-56.

Ryff, Carol D. and Corey Lee M. Keyes. "The Structure of Psychological Well-Being Revisited." In Journal of Personality and Social Psychology 69/4 (1995): 719-727.

Schoen, Robert, Stacy J Rogers and Paul Amato. "Wives' Employment and Spouses' Marital Happiness: Assessing the Direction of Influence Using Longitudinal Couple Data." In Journal of Family Issues 27/4 (April, 2006): 506-528.

Schoenborn, Charlotte A. "Marital Status and Health: United States, 1999-2002." In Advance Data from Vital and Health Statistics 351 (Dec 15, 2004): 3-33.

Shapiro, A. and Corey Lee M. Keyes. "Marital Status and Social Well-Being: Are the Married Always Better Off?" In Social Indicator Research 8/8 (2008): 329-346.

Shapiro, A. M. "Explaining Psychological Distress in a Sample of Remarried and Divorced Persons." In Journal of Family Issues 17 (1996): 186-203.

Sharma, Bharti. "Mental and Emotional Impact of Divorce on Women." In Journal of the Indian Academy of Applied Psychology 37/1 (January, 2011): 125-131.

Sim, Ronnie. "The Samaritan Woman in John 4." In Journal of Translation 2/1 (2015): 1-34.

Simon, Robin W. "Revisiting the Relationship among Gender, Marital Status and Mental Health." In American Journal of Sociology 107/4 (January, 2002): 1065-1096.

Smock, P. J., W. D. Manning and S. Gupta. "The Effect of Marriage and Divorce on Women's Economic Wellbeing." In American Sociological Review 64 (1999): 974-812.

South, Scott J. and Katherine Trend. "Sex Ratios and Women's Roles: A Cross-National Analysis." In American Journal of Sociology 93 (1988): 1096-1115.

Strohschenin, L., P. McDonough, D. Monettec and Q. Shoab. "Marital Transitions and Mental health: Are There Gender Differences in the Short-Term Effects of Marital Status Change?" In Social Science and Medicine 61/11 (2005): 2293-2303.

Terrein, Samuel. "Towards a Biblical Theology of Womanhood." In Religion in Life (Autumn, 1973): 320-335.

Trend, Katherine and Scott J. South. "Structural Determinants of the Divorce Rates: A Cross-Societal Analysis." In Journal of Marriage and the Family 51/2 (1989): 391-404.

Wang, H. and Paul R. Amato. "Predictors of Divorce Adjustment: Stressors, Resources, and Definitions." In Journal of Marriage and Family 62/3 (2000): 655-668.

Wheaton, Blair. "Life Transitions, Role Histories and Mental Health." In American Sociological Review 55/2 (April 1990): 209-223.

Wilfong, Marsha M. "Genesis 2:1-24." In Interpretation 42/1 (1988): 58-63.

William, Kristi and Alexandra Dunne-Bryant. "Divorce and Adult Psychological Well-Being: Clarifying the Role of Gender and Child Age." In Journal of Marriage and Family 68/5 (December, 2006): 1178-1196.

Williams, David R. et al. "Religion and Psychological Distress in a Community Sample." In Social Science and Medicines 32/11 (1991): 1201-1318.

Yerby, Janet. "Family Systems Theory Reconsidered: Integrating Social Construction Theory and Dialectical Process." In Communication Theory 5/4 (November, 1995): 339-365.

Yesseldyk, Renate, Kimberly Matheson and Hymie Anisman. "Religiosity and Identity: Toward an Understanding of Religion From a Social Identity Perspective." In Personal and Social Psychology Review 12/1 (January, 2010): 60-71.

Young, Alison J. "In Likeness and Unity: Debunking the Creation Order Fallacy." In Priscilla Papers 23/2 (2009): 12-15.

Unpublished Materials

Weaver, T. Craig. "A Niebuhrian View of Divorce." Master's Thesis, Wake Forest University, 1982.

Woo, Hyeyoung. "Parental Status and Psychological Wellbeing Among Midlife Adult Women Using the Life Course Perspective." Doctor of Philosophy Dissertation, The University of Texas, Austin, 2008.

White, Vera A. "Race, Sex, Social Class: The Influence of Stress Responsiveness on Well-Being Among American Families." Doctorate of Philosophy Dissertation, Kansas State University, 2007.

Hickman, Daniel. "The Social Context of Divorce and Its Impact on Adolescent Psychological Well-being." An Honors Thesis, Cornell University, 2007.

Moe, Krista, "Factors Influencing Women's Psychological Well-Being Within a Positive Functioning Framework." A Doctoral Dissertation, University of Kentucky, 2012.

Murphy, Maura Jean. "Contingent Faculty: What Impacts Their Organizational Commitment?" Doctor of Education Dissertation, North Carolina State University, 2009.

Webliography

http://www.hindustantimes.com/sexandrelationships/why-number-of-young-indian-couples-getting-divorced-has-risen-sharply/article1-1303204.aspx (Accessed on 04/01/2020).

http://www.hindustantimes.com/sexandrelationships/why-number-of-young-indian-couples-getting-divorced-has-risen-sharply/article1-1303204.aspx (Accessed on 01 September 2015).

http://censusindia.gov.in/2011-Common/srs.html (Accessed on 19 September 2015).

Amrit Dhillon, "In India's Nagaland, men are on strike until women return to the kitchen," in Stuff http://www.stuff.co.nz/world/asia/89574768/In-Indias-Nagaland-men-are-on-strike-until-women-return-to-the kitchen (Accessed on 29 November 2017).

Quoted in Prasanta Mazumdar, "Standing Her Ground in Patriarchal Naga Society," in DNA. http://www.dnaindia.com/india/report-standing-her-ground-in-patriarchal-naga-society-1808598 (Accessed on 6 December 2017).

Soutik Biwas, "What Divorce and Separation Tells us About Modern India." BBC, https://www.bbc.com/news/world-asia-india-37481054 (Accessed on 04/01/2020)

Newspaper

Baburaj, Shilpa. "Chips Down for Marriage in Namma Silicon Valley." The Times of India (Bengaluru), 28 September 2015.

The Shillong Times (Bangalore), 10 March 2015. (Accessed on 24 July, 2015).

Reports

World Health Organization. Summary Report on Promoting Mental Health, Concepts, Emerging Evidence, Practice. Geneva: World Health Organization, 2011.

McFayden, Narola Ao. "Reclaiming Sobaliba: The Vital Role of Culturally Relevant Moral Education to Counter Increasing Patterns of Violence against Women." In Religion and Education in the (Un)making of Violence. Illinois: Religious Education Association Annual Meeting November 7-9, 2014.